5-INGREDIENT
AIR FRYER
RECIPES

200 Delicious & Easy Meal Ideas
Including Gluten-Free & Vegan

Camilla V. Saulsbury

Robert
ROSE

For complete cataloguing information, see page 288.

Disclaimer
The recipes in this book have been carefully tested by our kitchen and our tasters. To the best of our knowledge, they are safe and nutritious for ordinary use and users. For those people with food or other allergies, or who have special food requirements or health issues, please read the suggested contents of each recipe carefully and determine whether or not they may create a problem for you. All recipes are used at the risk of the consumer. Consumers should always consult their air fryer manufacturer's manual for recommended procedures and cooking times.

We cannot be responsible for any hazards, loss or damage that may occur as a result of any recipe use.

For those with special needs, allergies, requirements or health problems, in the event of any doubt, please contact your medical adviser prior to the use of any recipe.

Design and production: Alicia McCarthy & Daniella Zanchetta/PageWave Graphics Inc.
Layout: Alicia McCarthy/PageWave Graphics Inc.
Editor: Sue Sumeraj
Copy editor: Kelly Jones
Recipe editor: Jennifer MacKenzie
Proofreader: Sue Sumeraj
Indexer: Marnie Lamb
Photographer: Matt Johannsson, Reflector Inc.
Food stylist: Michael Elliott
Prop stylist: Charlene Erricson
Illustration: Diamond pattern © Diane Labombarbe / DigitalVision Vectors / Gettyimages.ca

Cover image: Hearts of Palm "Crab" Cakes (page 136)

Published by Robert Rose Inc.
120 Eglinton Avenue East, Suite 800, Toronto, Ontario, Canada M4P 1E2
Tel: (416) 322-6552 Fax: (416) 322-6936
www.robertrose.ca

Printed and bound in Canada

1 2 3 4 5 6 7 8 9 MI 25 24 23 22 21 20 19 18 17

CONTENTS

Introduction

Life is filled with countless little pleasures, and crispy, crunchy fried food is one of them.

Thanks to the invention of the home air fryer, which relies on hot air rather than hot oil to "fry" foods, you need not wait for weekend splurges or special occasions to savor this simple delight. Armed with your air fryer, you can have your fried foods and eat them too, all with a tiny fraction of the fat and calories. Plus, you avoid the messy cleanup left in the wake of traditional oil-fried foods.

But why stop there? What if the recipes for your favorite fried foods (and so many more) could be made with:

- a short list of readily available, familiar ingredients
- minimal preparation, and
- little time?

If it sounds too good to be true, think again, because such recipes are quite literally in your hands.

All of the recipes in this collection require no more than five ingredients (excluding salt, pepper, water and cooking spray) and — apart from a small few — can be made in 15 to 20 minutes with minimal preparation.

Each recipe is unique, designed exclusively for the air fryer and downright delectable. I think you will find the results are every bit as irresistible as higher-fat options — perhaps even more so. Moreover, each is delicious proof that a recipe needn't rely on expensive, hard-to-find ingredients and complicated steps to be excellent. Whether you are a novice or a well-seasoned air-fry cook, you will find recipe after recipe that delivers impressive results, time and again.

May this collection inspire you to head to the kitchen to let the air-frying fun begin. The recipes will carry you through every type of occasion, from an impromptu party with friends to quick meals before and after work, as well as through every season of the year. I'll be wondering which will become your favorites as I crunch into a crispy air-fried treat of my own.

— *Camilla*

Air-Frying 101

In contrast to frying in hot oil, air fryers use a combination of radiant and convection heat. Radiant heat in air fryers, like the heat in almost all standard ovens, refers to the infrared radiation emitted by both the heating element and the hot oven walls. When this radiation makes contact with the food in the oven, its energy agitates the food's molecules into a frenzy, which raises the temperature of the food.

But it is the convection aspect of air fryers that yields results akin to oil frying. Air fryers, like all convection ovens, have a fan that continuously circulates air through the oven. The moving air speeds up the rate of heat transference that naturally occurs when air of two different temperatures converges. Air fryers have especially rapid fans (many of which use patented technology).

This high-speed heat transference is one reason for the superior results you get from air-frying. The rush of heat speeds up the chemical reactions that occur as food cooks. The accelerated air fryer fan moves water away from the food surface more quickly, thereby greatly increasing surface crisping and rendering finished effects close to those of oil-frying.

In addition to creating deep-fried crispiness, the quick, even dry heat of an air fryer promotes uniform, efficient cooking of all kinds, including roasting, indoor grilling and baking. It is also an efficient tool for reheating leftovers: simply preheat the air fryer to 300°F (150°C), place the food in the air fryer basket (without overcrowding it) and heat for 10 to 15 minutes or until heated to the desired temperature.

A Safe, Practical Option

Air-frying has additional advantages beyond the considerable reduction of fat and calories. Topping the list is safety: frying in hot oil is intrinsically dangerous. Serious burns can result from splatters or spills, and the risk of fire is likewise a major concern. Air-frying "fries" with air instead of oil, eliminating the risk of oil spills, splatters and fires. Air-frying also eliminates the lingering smell associated with conventional hot-oil frying, as well as the messy cleanup of the fryer and surrounding surfaces.

Getting Started

Choosing an Air Fryer

All of the recipes in this collection were tested using an air fryer with an inner cooking chamber, removable cooking basket and adjustable thermostat. Air fryer options are broad, but almost all have the same essential design, with some variations in basket size, wattage and accessories.

WATTAGE

Air fryers typically require between 800 and 1400 watts. Before buying an air fryer, it's a good idea to check if your kitchen outlet can support this kind of wattage.

SIZE AND BASKET CAPACITY

Air fryers are relatively compact and easy to fit on a kitchen counter; simply choose what works for your space and your aesthetics.

Most air fryers have baskets with a capacity between $1\frac{1}{2}$ and $2\frac{1}{2}$ pounds (750 g and 1.25 kg). The recipes in this collection were all tested in air fryers that fell within this range. Larger air fryers are available, which is convenient for making larger batches of food. Cooking times are not affected by basket capacity, so choose the size that best suits your needs.

SETTINGS

Air fryers typically have a temperature range in the neighborhood of 150°F (75°C) to 200°F (100°C) for the lowest setting to a maximum setting of 390°F (200°C). Temperature controls are more variable. For example, some models have analog dials with preset temperature intervals, while some of the newest models have digital programmable settings.

Additional settings may include timers as well as preset options for different frozen or fresh foods (such as fries, bacon, fish and breaded chicken strips). Choose which bells and whistles best suit your needs and preferences.

A Removable Basket

When selecting an air fryer, check to make sure the basket is easily removable, since it will be inserted and removed many times. Removing the basket should be as simple as pressing the release button and lifting or sliding it out of the cooking chamber.

OTHER FEATURES TO CONSIDER

- **Safety features:** Some air fryer models include additional safety features, such as a removable pan with a cool-touch handle, nonslip feet, overheat protection, temperature light, ready signal and automatic switch-off.
- **Dishwasher safety:** Dishwasher-safe baskets make cleanup simple and convenient. Dishwasher-safe parts are fast becoming the standard in home air fryers, but with more and more models on the market, it is worth double-checking.
- **Nonstick surfaces:** Nonstick surfaces are particularly beneficial when it comes to cleaning air fryer parts, even though only a small amount of oil is used. Like dishwasher safety, nonstick basket surfaces are the norm in many air fryer models, but you may still want to check before purchase.
- **Additional accessories:** Some air fryers come with optional removable accessories, such as a removable rack that sits inside the basket and can be used to lift meats, fish and other foods off the bottom of the basket.

Preheating

It takes only 3 to 5 minutes to preheat most air fryers. Check your air fryer's manual to determine the preheating time for your particular model.

Air Fryer Cooking Tips

Successful cooking is easy with an air fryer. The following troubleshooting tips will guarantee it.

- **Avoid overcrowding.** Overcrowding foods in the basket prevents them from cooking and browning evenly, and will result in less crispy foods.
- **Shake the basket.** Occasional shaking of the basket can facilitate evenly browned, crispy food — but do so only when the recipe directs you to. To shake the ingredients, pull the basket out of the appliance by the handle and shake it (be sure to wear oven mitts when you do this). Do not press the basket release button during shaking.
- **Spray with nonstick cooking spray.** Spraying foods with a light coating of nonstick cooking spray helps them achieve a light, crispy, crunchy texture. Do not skip it if the recipe calls for it! (But likewise, do not spray unless the recipe tells you to.)
- **Check early.** Check the food for doneness at the earliest cooking time given in the recipe.

- **Use the correct bakeware.** As mentioned earlier, the air fryer can be used for baking and roasting in addition to air-frying. Glass, metal, ceramic and silicone bakeware can all be used in the air fryer, so long as it is the correct size. Bakeware should be no larger than 6 inches (15 cm) inches across to allow some space on either side of the pan. It should also be no higher than 2.95 inches (7.5 cm) high. Doubled foil or paper muffin cup liners, or single silicone muffin cup liners, can be used to air-fry muffins and breads.

Air Fryer Safety Tips

Air fryers are far safer than frying with hot oil, but they should still be used with care and caution. What follows are general tips for using your air fryer safely.

- **Mind the heat.** Air fryers become very hot, especially when heated to maximum temperature. Use oven pads or mitts when touching the appliance and when opening and closing the basket.
- **Mind the steam.** Hot air and steam will release from the air fryer throughout the cooking cycle. If your face is in close proximity to the appliance during the cooking cycle or when you are opening the basket, you risk being scalded by the release of accumulated steam.
- **Heed the hot basket.** The basket will be especially hot once the cooking cycle is complete. Avoid placing it on countertops or dishcloths, as it may cause damage.
- **Avoid overflow.** It is important to avoid any contact between food and the heating element. Before closing the basket to cook food, double-check that no ingredients have spilled out of the basket into the air fryer chamber.
- **Keep it clear.** Do not place anything on top of the air fryer or over the air inlets during the cooking cycle. Also, move the air fryer at least 6 inches (15 cm) from the wall before use.
- **Stick around.** Do not leave the air fryer unattended when it is in use. Unplug the air fryer when cooking is complete.
- **Do not use if damaged.** It may sound obvious, but never use the air fryer if there is any noticeable damage to the cord, plug, basket or any other parts.
- **Dry your hands.** Make sure your hands are not wet when using the air fryer, to avoid slippery handling of the basket.

Cleaning Your Air Fryer

Air fryer cleanup is a breeze, especially when compared to the greasy mess of conventional hot-oil fryers. Nevertheless, it is important to clean the air fryer after each use to prevent buildup of grease or stuck-on food particles.

CLEANING THE BASKET

1. Let the air fryer cool to room temperature.
2. If the air fryer basket is dishwasher-safe, wash it in a normal dish-washing cycle. Otherwise, remove the air fryer basket, place it in a plugged sink or a large bowl and fill with hot water and a drop or two of liquid dishwashing soap. Let soak for 10 to 15 minutes. Use a nonabrasive sponge or dishwashing cloth to gently clean the walls and bottom of the basket. Invert the basket and gently clean the bottom.

CLEANING THE INSIDE AND OUTSIDE OF THE APPLIANCE

1. Let the air fryer cool to room temperature.
2. Use a nonabrasive sponge or dishwashing cloth and hot water to clean the outside and the inner chamber of the air fryer.

CLEANING THE HEATING ELEMENT

1. Let the air fryer cool to room temperature.
2. Gently clean off any grease or food residue with a soft to medium bristle brush and hot water. It is important not to use a hard or steel bristle brush, as it can damage the coating on the heating element.
3. Dry the heating element with paper towels.

Suggested Tools and Equipment

Air-frying requires very little equipment to achieve success. The following items will ensure that you can make every recipe in this collection.

- 6-inch (15 cm) round metal cake pan
- $\frac{3}{4}$ cup (175 mL) ramekins
- Foil or paper muffin cup or cupcake liners
- Foil
- Tongs (preferably silicone-tipped, to prevent scratching if the basket has a nonstick coating)
- Pancake turner/spatula
- Slotted spoon
- Wire cooling rack

The Air Fryer Pantry

The recipes in this collection largely rely on fresh vegetables, fruits, lean meats, poultry, eggs and seafood, plus a short list of ingredients you likely already have in your pantry. Here are some of the most commonly used pantry ingredients to keep at the ready for a variety of air-frying recipes.

Eggs, Dairy and Nondairy Milks

EGGS
All of the recipes in this book were tested with large eggs. Select clean, fresh eggs that have been handled properly and refrigerated. Do not use dirty, cracked or leaking eggs, or eggs that have a bad odor or unnatural color when cracked open; they may have become contaminated with harmful bacteria, such as salmonella.

DAIRY MILK
All of the recipes in this collection calling for milk were tested with lower-fat (2%) milk. However, milk of any fat level can be used in its place, as can any of the nondairy milk options listed below.

NONDAIRY MILKS
Nondairy milks are essential for vegans, as well as those who are lactose intolerant or are allergic to dairy. The variety and availability of nondairy milks is vast; soy milk, rice milk, hemp milk and almond milk are readily available options in most well-stocked grocery stores. Opt for plain nondairy milk when substituting for milk in any of the recipes in this collection.

BUTTERMILK
Tangy buttermilk is a traditional ingredient in a wide range of fried foods, and it works wonders with air-fried foods, too. Commercially prepared varieties are made by culturing 1% milk with bacteria. When added to batters and baked goods, it yields a tender result and a slightly buttery flavor.

Buttermilk Substitute
If you do not have buttermilk, it's easy to make a substitute. Mix 1 tbsp (15 mL) lemon juice or white vinegar into 1 cup (250 mL) milk. Let stand for at least 15 minutes before using, to allow the milk to curdle. Any extra can be stored in the refrigerator for the same amount of time as the milk from which it was made.

YOGURT

All of the recipes in this collection call for either plain yogurt or plain Greek yogurt. Greek yogurt is a thick, creamy yogurt similar in texture to sour cream.

Flours and Grains

ALL-PURPOSE FLOUR

Made from a blend of high-gluten hard wheat and low-gluten soft wheat, all-purpose flour is fine-textured flour milled from the inner part of the wheat kernel and contains neither the germ nor the bran. All-purpose flour comes either bleached or unbleached; they can be used interchangeably.

GLUTEN-FREE ALL-PURPOSE FLOUR

Gluten-free all-purpose flour is readily available in most supermarkets, either in the health foods section or in the baking aisle. No single gluten-free flour performs exactly like wheat flour, so gluten-free all-purpose flours are a blend, most often of rice flours, other flours (such as millet or chickpea flour) and some form of starch, such as tapioca or potato starch. Gluten-free all-purpose flour works well as a substitute for all-purpose wheat flour for dredging before air-frying.

CORNMEAL

Cornmeal is simply ground dried corn kernels. There are two methods of grinding. The first is the modern method, in which milling is done by huge steel rollers, which remove the husk and germ almost entirely; this creates the most common variety of cornmeal found in supermarkets. The second is the stone-ground method, in which some of the hull and germ of the corn is retained; this type of cornmeal is available at health food stores and in the health food sections of most supermarkets. The two varieties can be used interchangeably.

ROLLED OATS

Two types of rolled oats are called for in these recipes. Large-flake (old-fashioned) rolled oats are oat groats (hulled and cleaned whole oats) that have been steamed and flattened with huge rollers. Quick-cooking rolled oats are groats that have been cut into several pieces before being steamed and rolled into thinner flakes. For the best results, it is important to use the type of rolled oats specified in the recipe.

Breading

PANKO (JAPANESE BREAD CRUMBS)

Panko bread crumbs are made from white loaves of bread that have had the crusts removed. The crumbs are larger than regular bread crumbs and have a light texture that becomes especially crunchy with air-frying. Look for panko in the Asian or international foods section of well-stocked supermarkets.

DRY BREAD CRUMBS

Dry bread crumbs are available in the baking section of the supermarket. They have a fine texture (finer than panko) that is ideal for coating a wide range of foods. Both plain bread crumbs and bread crumbs with Italian seasoning are used in this collection.

Gluten-free dry bread crumbs are increasingly available at well-stocked supermarkets. Look for them in the same location as other bread crumbs.

CORN FLAKES CEREAL

Crumbled corn flakes cereal — crispy toasted flakes of corn — can be used as a substitute for panko or dry bread crumbs as suggested in many of the recipes in this collection. It will take 3 cups (750 mL) whole corn flakes to yield 1 cup (250 mL) corn flake crumbs.

GLUTEN-FREE CRACKERS

Crushed gluten-free crackers can be used as a substitute for panko or dried bread crumbs as suggested in many of the recipes in this collection. For best results, use light, crispy crackers made from gluten-free grains rather than crackers made from nuts, seeds or legumes. It will take about $2^1/_2$ cups (625 mL) coarsely crushed crackers to yield 1 cup (250 mL) cracker crumbs.

Gluten-Free Corn Flakes

If using corn flakes cereal specifically as a gluten-free alternative to bread crumbs, be sure to choose a brand that is specifically labeled "gluten-free." Although corn is naturally gluten-free, many brands of corn flakes include glutinous ingredients, such as malt syrup (which is made from barley and contains gluten).

INSTANT POTATO FLAKES

Instant potato flakes are made from dehydrated russet potatoes that are then processed into flakes. Typically used to make mashed potatoes, they can be used as a light, crispy and naturally gluten-free coating for chicken, fish and other air-fried foods.

Sweeteners

GRANULATED SUGAR

Granulated sugar (also called white sugar) is refined cane or beet sugar, and is the most common sweetener used in this book. Once opened, store granulated sugar in an airtight container in a cool, dry place.

BROWN SUGAR

Brown sugar is granulated sugar with some molasses added to it. The molasses gives the sugar a soft texture. Light brown sugar (also known as golden yellow sugar) has less molasses and a more delicate flavor than dark brown sugar. Once opened, store brown sugar in an airtight container or a resealable plastic food bag, to prevent clumping.

CONFECTIONERS' (ICING) SUGAR

Confectioners' (icing) sugar (also called powdered sugar) is granulated sugar that has been ground to a fine powder. Cornstarch is added to prevent the sugar from clumping together. It is used in recipes where regular sugar would be too grainy.

HONEY

Honey is plant nectar that has been gathered and concentrated by honeybees. Any variety of liquid honey may be used in the recipes in this collection.

MAPLE SYRUP

Maple syrup is a thick liquid sweetener made by boiling the sap from maple trees. It has a strong, pure maple flavor. Maple-flavored pancake syrup is corn syrup with coloring and artificial maple flavoring added, and can be used as a substitute for pure maple syrup.

Storing Honey and Maple Syrup

Unopened containers of honey and maple syrup may be stored at room temperature. After opening, store honey and maple syrup in the refrigerator to protect against mold. Honey and maple syrup will both keep indefinitely when stored properly.

Fats and Oils

Fats and oils are used sparingly in air-frying, largely because they simply aren't needed. Where they are used, make sure to choose good-quality fats to ensure optimum flavor.

BUTTER

Fresh butter has a mild cream flavor and a pale yellow color. Using a small amount adds tremendous flavor to both sweet and savory recipes in this collection.

Butter quickly picks up off-flavors during storage and when exposed to oxygen, so once the carton or wrap is opened, place it in a sealable plastic food bag or other airtight container. Store it away from foods with strong odors, such as onions or garlic.

Freezing Butter

If you use butter only occasionally, I recommend storing it in the freezer. Wrap entire sticks, or use a method I developed in my student days: cut the butter into 1 tbsp (15 mL) pats and place them on a baking sheet lined with plastic. Place in the freezer for 30 to 60 minutes, until frozen, then transfer the frozen pats to an airtight container. Butter can be frozen for up to 6 months. Remove pats of butter as needed and thaw in the refrigerator or at room temperature.

VEGETABLE OIL

Vegetable oil is a generic term used to describe any neutral plant-based oil that is liquid at room temperature. You can use a vegetable oil blend, canola oil, light olive oil, grapeseed oil, safflower oil, sunflower oil, peanut oil or corn oil.

OLIVE OIL

Olive oil is a monounsaturated oil that is prized for a wide range of cooking preparations. I recommend using plain olive oil (simply labeled "olive oil"), which contains a combination of refined olive oil and virgin or extra virgin oil. The subtle nuances of extra virgin olive oil are not very noticeable after cooking in the air fryer.

TOASTED (DARK) SESAME OIL

Toasted sesame oil, also known as dark sesame oil, has a dark brown color and a rich, nutty flavor. It is used sparingly, mostly in Asian recipes, to add a tremendous amount of flavor.

NONSTICK COOKING SPRAY

Nonstick cooking spray is used extensively in this collection to coat foods in an even yet minimal layer of fat to promote a golden-brown, crispy exterior. While any type of cooking spray may be used, I recommend using an organic spray for two reasons: first, these sprays are typically made with higher-quality oils (in many cases expeller-pressed or cold-pressed oils) than most conventional brands; second, they are more likely to use compressed gas to expel the propellant, so no hydrocarbons are released into the environment. Read the label and choose wisely.

Leavening Agents

BAKING POWDER

Baking powder is a chemical leavening agent made from a blend of alkali (sodium bicarbonate, known commonly as baking soda) and acid (most commonly calcium acid phosphate, sodium aluminum sulfate or cream of tartar), plus some form of starch to absorb any moisture so a reaction does not take place until a liquid is added.

BAKING SODA

Baking soda is a chemical leavener consisting of bicarbonate of soda. It is alkaline in nature and, when combined with an acidic ingredient, such as buttermilk, yogurt, citrus juice or honey, it creates carbon dioxide bubbles, giving baked goods a dramatic rise.

Flavorings

When fat is kept to a minimum in sweet and savory recipes such as these, it is especially important to amplify other flavors. Here are my top recommendations for ingredients that will accentuate a range of air-frying recipes.

SALT

Unless otherwise specified, the recipes in this collection were tested using common table salt. An equal amount of fine sea salt can be used in its place.

BLACK PEPPER

Black pepper is made by grinding black peppercorns, which have been picked when the berry is not quite ripe and then dried until it shrivels and the skin turns dark brown to black. Black pepper has a strong, slightly hot flavor, with a hint of sweetness. Both freshly cracked and freshly ground black pepper are used in this collection.

SPICES AND DRIED HERBS

Spices, spice blends and dried herbs can elevate healthy air-fried foods to delectable heights with minimal effort. They should be stored in light- and air-proof containers, away from direct sunlight and heat, to preserve their flavors.

With ground spices and dried herbs, freshness is everything. To determine whether a ground spice or dried herb is fresh, open the container and sniff. A strong fragrance means it is still acceptable for use.

Note that ground spices, not whole, are used throughout this collection. Here are my favorite ground spices and dried herbs:

Ground Spices and Spice Blends

- Allspice
- Chili powder
- Cinnamon
- Cumin
- Curry powder
- Garlic powder
- Ginger
- Hot pepper flakes
- Jerk seasoning (salt-free)
- Paprika
- Pumpkin pie spice
- Smoked paprika (both hot and sweet)

Dried Herbs and Herb Blends

- Basil
- Italian seasoning
- Oregano
- Rosemary
- Rubbed sage
- Thyme

CITRUS ZEST

"Zest" is the name for the colored outer layer of citrus peel. The oils in zest are intense in flavor. Use a zester, a Microplane-style grater or the small holes of a box grater to grate zest. Avoid grating the white layer (pith) just below the zest; it is very bitter.

HOT PEPPER SAUCE

Hot pepper sauce is a spicy condiment made from chile peppers and other common ingredients, such as vinegar and spices. It is available in countless heat levels and flavors, so pick the multipurpose sauce that best suits your taste.

SRIRACHA

Sriracha is a multipurpose hot sauce made from red chile peppers, garlic, vinegar, salt and sugar. It is hot and tangy, with a slight sweetness that distinguishes it from other hot sauces. Sriracha is often served as a condiment in Thai, Vietnamese and Chinese restaurants, but it can be used in a wide range of cuisines and preparations.

THAI CURRY PASTE

Available in small jars, Thai curry paste is a blend of Thai chiles, garlic, lemongrass, galangal, ginger and wild lime leaves. It is a fast and delicious way to add Southeast Asian flavor to a broad spectrum of recipes in a single step. Panang and yellow curry pastes tend to be the mildest. Red curry paste is medium hot; green curry paste is typically the hottest.

SOY SAUCE

Soy sauce is a dark, salty sauce made from fermented soybeans, water, salt and sometimes added wheat or barley. If you're avoiding gluten, look for soy sauce specifically labeled as gluten-free.

HOISIN SAUCE

Hoisin sauce is a thick, reddish-brown sauce made with a blend of fermented soybeans, vinegar, garlic, sugar and spices. A combination of sweet and umami, it is used in a wide range of Chinese and other Asian dishes.

VANILLA EXTRACT

Vanilla extract adds a sweet, fragrant flavor to dishes, especially baked goods. It is produced by combining an extraction from dried vanilla beans with an alcohol-and-water mixture. It is then aged for several months.

MAYONNAISE

Mayonnaise is a thick and creamy dressing or sauce made from emulsified oil, eggs, seasonings and lemon juice or vinegar. Regular or reduced-fat mayonnaise (ranging from 25% to 50% less fat than regular) can be used in the recipes in this collection (unless otherwise specified).

Vegan mayonnaise is called for in many vegan recipes in this collection, but it can be used for any recipe calling for mayonnaise. Vegan mayonnaise is made from emulsified oil, seasonings, lemon juice or vinegar and other ingredients (ranging from tofu to chickpeas to algae) as replacements for eggs.

MUSTARD

Mustard adds depth of flavor to a wide range of dishes. I recommend Dijon mustard, honey mustard, spicy brown mustard or whole-grain mustard for their versatility.

MARINARA SAUCE

Jarred marinara sauce — a highly seasoned Italian tomato sauce made with onions, garlic, basil and oregano — is typically used on pasta, but it is also a great pantry staple for creating air-fryer meals and snacks in short order. For the best tomato flavor and the most versatility, choose a variety with minimal ingredients and low sodium.

THICK AND CHUNKY TOMATO SALSA

Like marinara sauce, ready-made thick and chunky salsa — rich with tomatoes, peppers, onions and spices but low in calories — packs tremendous flavor into recipes in an instant. For the best flavor and nutrition, select a brand that is low in sodium and has a short list of easily identifiable ingredients.

VINEGARS

Vinegars are multipurpose flavor powerhouses used to intensify sauces and dips and to brighten the flavor of a variety of air-fried dishes. Store vinegars in a dark place, away from heat and light.

Inexpensive and versatile, apple cider vinegar is an excellent multipurpose choice. It is made from the juice of crushed apples. After the juice is collected, it is allowed to age in wooden barrels. Red or white wine vinegars — produced by fermenting wine in wooden barrels — are also good multitasking options.

BLACK BEAN AND GARLIC SAUCE

Black bean and garlic sauce is a savory condiment made from fermented black soybeans, garlic and rice vinegar. It is available at Asian grocery stores or in the Asian foods section of well-stocked supermarkets, alongside soy sauce.

Vegan Ingredients

VEGAN MARGARINE

Vegan margarine is a dairy-free substitute for butter. It is important to use 100% vegetable oil varieties in stick form. Vegan margarine spreads — in tub or stick form — contain a significant amount of water, which will alter the results of the recipe.

NUTRITIONAL YEAST

Nutritional yeast (sometimes referred to as "nooch") is a nutritious, convenient ingredient that can be used as an alternative to Parmesan cheese and other cheeses in nondairy and vegan recipes.

Related to brewer's yeast, nutritional yeast is a nonactive, cultured strain of yeast (specifically, *Saccharomyces cerevisiae*). It is usually grown on molasses, deactivated with heat and dried into flake or powdered (granulated) form. It has approximately 3 grams of high-quality protein per 20-calorie serving and contains all nine essential amino acids. It is also a good source of B vitamins, notably B_{12}, as well as riboflavin, thiamine, niacin and folic acid.

The recipes in this collection call for nutritional yeast flakes. They are available in health food stores and the health food section of well-stocked supermarkets.

TOFU

All of the recipes in this collection were tested with refrigerated extra-firm tofu. While shelf-stable tofu is convenient, the flavor and texture are markedly inferior.

Tofu, or bean curd, is made from soybeans that have been cooked, made into milk and then coagulated. The soy milk curdles when heated, and the curds are skimmed off and pressed into blocks. Tofu can be found in extra-firm, firm and soft varieties in the refrigerated section of the supermarket. Be sure to use the variety specified in the recipe for optimal results.

TEMPEH

Tempeh (pronounced *TEM-pay*) is a traditional Indonesian food. It is made from fully cooked soybeans that have been fermented with a mold called *rhizopus* and formed into cakes. Some varieties have whole grains added to the mix, creating a particularly meaty, satisfying texture. Tempeh, like tofu, takes on the flavor of whatever it is marinated with, and also needs to be stored in the refrigerator.

Measuring Ingredients

Accurate measurements are important for air fryer recipes, to achieve the right balance of flavors. So take both time and care as you measure.

Measuring Dry Ingredients

When measuring a dry ingredient, such as flour, sugar, spices or salt, spoon it into the appropriate-size dry measuring cup or measuring spoon, heaping it up over the top. Slide a straight-edged utensil, such as a knife, across the top to level off the extra. Be careful not to shake or tap the cup or spoon to settle the ingredient, or you will have more than you need.

Measuring Moist Ingredients

Moist ingredients, such as brown sugar, coconut and dried fruit, must be firmly packed in a measuring cup or spoon to be measured accurately. Use a dry measuring cup for these ingredients. Fill the measuring cup to slightly overflowing, then pack down the ingredient firmly with the back of a spoon. Add more of the ingredient and pack down again until the cup is full and even with the top of the measure.

Measuring Liquid Ingredients

Use a clear plastic or glass measuring cup or container with lines up the sides to measure liquid ingredients. Set the container on the counter and pour the liquid to the appropriate mark. Lower your head to read the measurement at eye level.

Breakfasts

British Breakfast Fry-Up

A typical British fry-up — an assortment of breakfast meats, vegetables, eggs and toast, all cooked in bacon grease — is far too rich, caloric and time-consuming for anything other than rare occasions. By contrast, this version is protein-rich, hearty without being heavy, and a cinch to make (and clean up)!

TIPS

You can use $1/2$ cup (125 mL) drained canned diced tomatoes in place of the cherry tomatoes.

Air fryers become very hot, especially when heated to maximum temperature. Use oven pads or mitts when touching the appliance and when opening and closing the basket.

- Preheat air fryer to 390°F (200°C)
- 6-inch (15 cm) round metal cake pan

2	small breakfast sausages	2
1	thick-cut bacon slice, halved crosswise	1
5	small cherry or grape tomatoes	5
1	large egg	1
	Salt and freshly cracked black pepper	
1	slice sturdy white or whole wheat bread	1

1. Arrange sausages and bacon halves in pan. Place pan in air fryer basket and air-fry for 3 minutes.

2. Open basket and scatter tomatoes over meats. Air-fry for 2 minutes.

3. Open basket and, using a spoon or small spatula, make a space between the meats and tomatoes. Carefully crack egg into the space and season with salt and pepper. Air-fry for 3 to 5 minutes or until bacon is crisp, egg whites are set and yolk is cooked to desired doneness.

4. Remove pan from air fryer and place bread in air fryer basket. Air-fry bread for 30 to 60 seconds or until toasted. Transfer pan contents to a plate and serve with toast.

Hash Brown Breakfast Bake

Simple and convenient, this hash brown bake will be the highlight of many chilly weekday mornings.

TIP

Air fryers become very hot, especially when heated to maximum temperature. Use oven pads or mitts when touching the appliance and when opening and closing the basket.

- Preheat air fryer to 390°F (200°C)
- 6-inch (15 cm) round metal cake pan, sprayed with nonstick cooking spray

1⅓ cups	frozen shredded hash brown potatoes, thawed	325 mL
	Nonstick cooking spray	
2	large eggs	2
⅛ tsp	salt	0.5 mL
Pinch	freshly ground black pepper	Pinch
2 tbsp	finely chopped green onions	30 mL
¼ cup	shredded Cheddar or Monterey Jack cheese	60 mL

1. Arrange hash browns in an even layer in prepared pan and spray with cooking spray. Place pan in air fryer basket. Air-fry for 8 minutes.

2. Meanwhile, in a medium bowl, whisk together eggs, salt and pepper. Stir in green onions and cheese.

3. Open basket and pour egg mixture over hash browns. Air-fry for 3 to 5 minutes or until eggs are just set. Using a spatula, transfer to a plate and cut in half.

Variations

Add ¼ cup (60 mL) crumbled cooked bacon or ready-to-use bacon pieces along with the green onions in step 2.

Add 2 cooked breakfast sausages, chopped or crumbled, along with the green onions in step 2.

Florentine Omelet

Chopped tomato and spinach add pleasing hits of bright flavor in this almost effortless omelet.

TIPS

Look for bags of loose-leaf frozen spinach, rather than boxes or compressed cubes, as it is easier to remove smaller quantities at a time.

Air fryers become very hot, especially when heated to maximum temperature. Use oven pads or mitts when touching the appliance and when opening and closing the basket.

- Preheat air fryer to 390°F (200°C)
- 6-inch (15 cm) round metal cake pan, sprayed with nonstick cooking spray

3	large eggs	3
1 tsp	dried Italian seasoning	5 mL
$\frac{1}{8}$ tsp	salt	0.5 mL
$\frac{1}{8}$ tsp	freshly ground black pepper	0.5 mL
$1\frac{1}{2}$ cups	frozen chopped spinach, thawed and squeezed dry	375 mL
$\frac{1}{2}$ cup	shredded Italian cheese blend, divided	125 mL
$\frac{1}{4}$ cup	chopped tomato	60 mL

1. In a medium bowl, whisk together eggs, Italian seasoning, salt and pepper. Stir in spinach and $\frac{1}{3}$ cup (75 mL) cheese. Pour into prepared pan.
2. Place pan in air fryer basket. Air-fry for 3 to 5 minutes or until eggs are just set. Open basket and sprinkle with tomato and remaining cheese. Air-fry for 1 minute. Using a spatula, transfer omelet to a plate and cut in half.

Variations

Florentine Egg White Omelet: Replace the eggs with 6 large egg whites or $\frac{3}{4}$ cup (175 mL) egg whites (pasteurized liquid whites from a carton or fresh-cracked).

Greek Spinach and Feta Omelet: Replace the dried Italian seasoning with an equal amount of dried dillweed or $\frac{1}{2}$ tsp (2 mL) dried oregano. Replace the Italian cheese blend with an equal amount of crumbled feta cheese.

Bagel and Lox Strata

This healthy, protein-packed breakfast strata embraces the flavors of classic bagels loaded with the very best toppings.

Variation

Bagel and Ham Strata: Replace the lox with an equal amount of chopped cooked ham.

- 6-inch (15 cm) round metal cake pan, sprayed with nonstick cooking spray
- Blender or food processor

1	large onion-flavored or plain bagel, cut into small pieces (about 1¼ cups/ 300 mL total)	1
¼ cup	chopped lox or smoked salmon	60 mL
3 tsp	minced fresh chives, divided	15 mL
2	large eggs	2
⅓ cup	cottage cheese	75 mL
⅛ tsp	salt	0.5 mL
⅛ tsp	freshly cracked black pepper	0.5 mL

1. In prepared pan, toss together bagel pieces, lox and 2 tsp (10 mL) chives, then spread in an even layer.

2. In blender, process eggs, cottage cheese, salt and pepper until blended and smooth. Pour evenly over bagel mixture in pan. Place a piece of parchment or waxed paper over pan and press down to help bagel pieces absorb liquid. Let stand for 15 minutes.

3. Meanwhile, preheat air fryer to 330°F (165°C).

4. Remove parchment and place pan in air fryer basket. Air-fry for 13 to 16 minutes or until bubbling and golden brown. Transfer pan to a wire rack and let cool for 10 minutes before serving. Sprinkle with the remaining chives.

Breakfast Egg Rolls

Eggs, hash browns and ham go well together on more than a diner breakfast plate. Here, with a little help from egg roll wrappers, the trio combines to make the ultimate handheld breakfast on the go.

TIP

While assembling the egg rolls, keep the stack of wrappers moist by covering them with a damp towel.

3	large eggs	3
1 tbsp	water	15 mL
$\frac{1}{4}$ tsp	salt	1 mL
$\frac{1}{8}$ tsp	freshly cracked black pepper	0.5 mL
	Nonstick cooking spray	
2 cups	frozen shredded hash brown potatoes, thawed	500 mL
$\frac{1}{3}$ cup	chopped cooked ham	75 mL
8	refrigerated or thawed frozen 6$\frac{1}{2}$-inch (16 cm) square egg roll wrappers	8
1 cup	shredded cheese (such as Cheddar, Monterey Jack or Gruyère)	250 mL

1. In a medium bowl, whisk together eggs, water, salt and pepper.

2. Spray a medium skillet with cooking spray and heat over medium-high heat. Add hash browns and cook, stirring, for 3 to 5 minutes or until slightly browned. Reduce heat to medium and add egg mixture and ham. Cook, stirring, for 3 to 5 minutes or until just set but not dry. Remove from heat and let cool for 10 minutes.

3. Preheat air fryer to 390°F (200°C).

TIPS

Air fryers become very hot, especially when heated to maximum temperature. Use oven pads or mitts when touching the appliance and when opening and closing the basket.

The egg rolls can be assembled up to 1 day in advance. Place in an airtight container and refrigerate until ready to use. Increase the cooking time by 1 to 2 minutes for chilled egg rolls.

4. Place 1 wrapper on work surface, with an edge facing you. Spoon $\frac{1}{4}$ cup (60 mL) egg mixture onto bottom third; sprinkle with 2 tbsp (30 mL) cheese. Fold the sides in toward the center and roll tightly away from you, enclosing filling. Repeat with the remaining wrappers, filling and cheese.

5. Place 4 egg rolls, seam side down, in air fryer basket, spacing them evenly. Spray generously with cooking spray. Air-fry for 5 to 7 minutes or until golden brown. Serve immediately. Repeat with the remaining egg rolls.

Variations

An equal amount of crumbled or chopped cooked breakfast sausage, or $\frac{1}{4}$ cup (60 mL) crumbled cooked bacon, can be used in place of the ham.

Vegetarian Breakfast Egg Rolls: Omit the ham.

French Country Egg Rolls: Omit the ham. Add 1 tsp (5 mL) dried herbes de Provence or dried Italian seasoning to the eggs in step 1 and replace the shredded cheese with an equal amount of crumbled goat cheese.

Bacon and Egg Hand Pies

MAKES 8 HAND PIES

Prepare to rise and shine: this play on the classic morning duo of eggs and bacon forgoes an accompaniment of toast for a tender, biscuit casing.

TIPS

Taste the bacon before seasoning the eggs in step 1; if it tastes particularly salty, reduce the amount of added salt or omit it entirely.

If using your fingertips to press out the biscuit dough in step 2, moisten them slightly with water to prevent sticking.

• Preheat air fryer to 360°F (180°C)

4	large eggs	4
3 tbsp	milk	45 mL
¼ tsp	salt	1 mL
Pinch	freshly ground black pepper	Pinch
¼ cup	crumbled cooked bacon	60 mL
1 cup	shredded Cheddar cheese	250 mL
1	can (17.3 oz/490 g) refrigerated large dinner biscuits	1
	Nonstick cooking spray	

1. In a medium bowl, whisk together eggs, milk, salt and pepper. Stir in bacon.

2. In a medium nonstick skillet set over medium heat, cook egg mixture, stirring, for 3 to 5 minutes or until just set but not dry.

3. Remove dough from packaging and separate into biscuits. Using your fingertips or a rolling pin, press or roll each biscuit into a 5-inch (12.5 cm) circle.

4. Place 3 tbsp (45 mL) egg mixture slightly off-center on each dough circle; sprinkle each with 2 tbsp (30 mL) cheese. Fold biscuits over filling and press edges together with a fork to seal. Prick the top of each hand pie three times with a fork. Spray pies with cooking spray.

TIPS

The pies are best eaten soon after they are made.

Spraying the pies with a light coating of nonstick cooking spray helps them achieve a light, crispy, crunchy texture.

5. Place half the pies in air fryer basket, spacing them 2 inches (5 cm) apart (refrigerate the remaining pies). Air-fry for 10 to 14 minutes or until puffed and golden brown. Transfer to a wire rack and let cool for at least 10 minutes before serving. Repeat with the remaining hand pies. Serve warm or at room temperature.

Variations

Spinach Feta Breakfast Hand Pies: Use $\frac{1}{2}$ cup (125 mL) well-drained thawed frozen spinach (squeezed of excess liquid) in place of the bacon. Replace the Cheddar with $\frac{1}{2}$ cup (125 mL) crumbled feta cheese (add 1 tbsp/15 mL feta to each hand pie in step 4).

Tex-Mex Breakfast Hand Pies: Omit the bacon. Add $\frac{1}{2}$ tsp (2 mL) ground cumin along with the salt in step 1 and stir in 3 tbsp (45 mL) thick and chunky salsa at the end of step 1. Use shredded pepper Jack cheese in place of the Cheddar cheese.

Use $\frac{1}{2}$ cup (125 mL) chopped cooked ham or breakfast sausage in place of the bacon.

Ham and Egg Biscuit Cups

It's easy to forgo fast-food breakfast sandwiches when you have this easy recipe as an alternative. The biscuits, egg, ham and cheese cook up in all-in-one, on-the-go muffin form in almost no time at all.

TIP

The biscuit cups are best eaten soon after they are made.

- Preheat air fryer to 360°F (180°C)
- 10 standard-size foil or paper muffin cup liners

2	large eggs	2
Pinch	salt	Pinch
Pinch	freshly ground black pepper	Pinch
⅔ cup	chopped cooked ham	150 mL
1	small can (6 oz/175 g) refrigerated large dinner biscuits	1
⅓ cup	shredded Cheddar cheese	75 mL

1. Place one muffin cup liner inside another. Repeat to create 5 doubled liners.
2. In a small bowl, whisk eggs, salt and pepper until blended. Stir in ham.
3. Remove dough from packaging and separate into biscuits. Using your fingertips, flatten each biscuit slightly. Press biscuits into doubled liners, leaving a well in center of each.
4. Spoon ham and egg mixture into wells, dividing equally. Sprinkle evenly with cheese.
5. Place filled liners in air fryer basket, spacing them evenly. Air-fry for 14 to 18 minutes or until puffed and golden brown. Serve immediately.

Variations

An equal amount of cooked crumbled breakfast sausage or ⅓ cup (75 mL) cooked crumbled bacon can be used in place of the ham.

Other varieties of shredded cheese (such as Swiss, Monterey Jack or pepper Jack) can be used in place of the Cheddar.

Sausage and Maple Roll-Ups

Portable pastries, stuffed with breakfast sausages and sweetened with pure maple syrup? Please and thank you! Plan to have more than one.

TIPS

For convenience, look for fully cooked frozen breakfast sausages. Simply thaw before using.

These roll-ups are best eaten very soon after they are air-fried.

• Preheat air fryer to 360°F (180°C)

3 tbsp	packed light brown sugar	45 mL
4 tbsp	pure maple syrup, divided	60 mL
1	can (8 oz/250 g) refrigerated crescent dinner rolls	1
8	cooked breakfast sausages	8
	Nonstick cooking spray	

1. In a small bowl, stir together brown sugar and 3 tbsp (45 mL) maple syrup.
2. Remove dough from packaging and unroll onto a large cutting board. Separate dough into crescents.
3. Spread 2 tsp (10 mL) sugar mixture at the wide end of each crescent; top with sausage and roll up. Brush with the remaining maple syrup.
4. Place half the roll-ups in air fryer basket, spacing them 2 inches (5 cm) apart (refrigerate the remaining roll-ups). Air-fry for 8 to 12 minutes or until puffed and golden brown. Transfer roll-ups to a wire rack. Repeat with the remaining roll-ups. Serve warm.

Extra-Crispy Coated French Toast

MAKES 2 SERVINGS

French toast is familiar breakfast and brunch fare, but it need not be predictable. Cut the bread in half, add a crispy corn-flakes-cereal-and-butter coating, and you have a fresh, fun morning option that is primed for dunking in syrup.

Variations

Cinnamon raisin bread slices can be used in place of the white bread.

An equal amount of panko or plain corn flakes cereal can be used in place of the frosted cereal.

1	large egg	1
¼ tsp	salt	1 mL
⅔ cup	milk	150 mL
2	slices sturdy white bread, halved on the diagonal	2
1½ cups	frosted corn flakes cereal, crushed	375 mL
1½ tbsp	butter, melted	22 mL
	Nonstick cooking spray	
	Pure maple syrup (optional), warmed	

1. In a shallow dish, whisk together egg and salt. Whisk in milk until blended.

2. Arrange bread pieces in a single layer in egg mixture, gently pressing down on bread to help it absorb liquid. Turn bread pieces over and gently press down again. Let stand for 15 minutes.

3. Meanwhile, in another shallow dish, combine crushed cereal and butter.

4. Preheat air fryer to 360°F (180°C).

5. Working with 1 bread piece at a time, remove from egg mixture and dredge in cereal mixture, gently pressing to adhere. As they are dredged, place bread pieces in air fryer basket, leaving space in between. Discard any excess egg and cereal mixtures. Spray with cooking spray.

6. Air-fry for 6 to 9 minutes or until golden brown. Serve with maple syrup, if desired.

Grab-and-Go Pancake Muffins

Pancakes with butter and maple syrup on the go? Yes! Simply make them into muffins with the help of your air fryer, favorite pancake mix and a few muffin cup liners. Although perfect plain, they are *plus-perfect* with any number of stir-ins, such as berries, crumbled bacon, chocolate chips or nuts.

TIPS

An equal amount of maple-flavored pancake syrup can be used in place of the pure maple syrup.

Choose a pancake mix that calls for the addition of eggs and milk, rather than a "complete" pancake mix that calls for only the addition of water or milk.

- Preheat air fryer to 360°F (180°C)
- 8 standard-size foil or paper muffin cup liners

1	large egg	1
1/4 cup	milk	60 mL
1/4 cup	pure maple syrup	60 mL
1 1/2 tbsp	melted butter or vegetable oil	22 mL
1 cup	pancake mix (see tip)	250 mL

1. Place one muffin cup liner inside another. Repeat to create 4 doubled liners.

2. In a medium bowl, whisk together egg, milk, maple syrup and butter. Stir in pancake mix until blended and no lumps remain.

3. Divide batter equally among doubled liners.

4. Place filled liners in air fryer basket, spacing them evenly. Air-fry for 14 to 18 minutes or until tops are golden and a tester inserted in the center of a muffin comes out clean. Transfer to a wire rack and let cool completely.

Variations

Berry Pancake Muffins: Stir in 1/3 cup (75 mL) blueberries or raspberries at the end of step 2.

Sweet and Savory Pancake Muffins: Stir in 1/4 cup (60 mL) crumbled cooked bacon or 2 cooked breakfast sausages, chopped or crumbled, at the end of step 2. If desired, sprinkle each muffin with 1 tbsp (15 mL) shredded Cheddar cheese at the end of step 3.

Chocolate Chip Pancake Muffins: Stir in 3 tbsp (45 mL) miniature semisweet chocolate chips at the end of step 2.

Cinnamon Twists

MAKES 12 PASTRIES

Light and flaky, these delicate twists are irresistible, thanks to the aromatic nuances of cinnamon, butter and caramelizing sugar.

TIP

These twists are best eaten very soon after they are air-fried.

• Preheat air fryer to 360°F (180°C)

2 tbsp	granulated sugar	30 mL
1 tsp	ground cinnamon	5 mL
1	can (8 oz/250 g) refrigerated crescent dinner rolls	1
2 tbsp	butter, melted	30 mL

1. In a small bowl, whisk together sugar and cinnamon.

2. Remove dough from packaging and unroll onto a work surface. Separate dough into 4 equal rectangles (each made of two triangular shapes). Using your fingertips, press together the perforations on each rectangle.

3. Brush tops of two rectangles with half the butter. Evenly sprinkle half the cinnamon sugar over butter; position the remaining rectangles on top, gently pressing edges together to seal. Brush with the remaining butter and sprinkle with the remaining cinnamon sugar.

4. Using a sharp knife, cut each rectangle lengthwise into 6 equal strips. Twist each strip 3 times.

5. Place half the pastries in air fryer basket, spacing them 2 inches (5 cm) apart (refrigerate the remaining pastries). Air-fry for 8 to 12 minutes or until puffed and golden brown. Transfer pastries to a wire rack. Repeat with the remaining pastries. Serve warm.

Variation

An equal amount of pumpkin pie spice or ground ginger, or ¾ tsp (3 mL) ground cardamom, can be used in place of the cinnamon.

Buttery Almond Croissants

Improving the flavor of buttery croissants is no easy feat, but these pastries prove it is possible by adding a double dose of almonds.

TIPS

The sheet of puff pastry should be about 9 inches (23 cm) square for this recipe. If your sheets are a different size, or the pastry comes in a block, roll or trim it into a 9-inch (23 cm) square as necessary.

Commercial puff pastry loses it crispness quickly, so it is best to eat the croissants shortly after air-frying.

Look for canned almond filling online and where pie fillings are shelved in the supermarket. The filling is loose and spreadable (not to be confused with almond paste or marzipan).

- Preheat air fryer to 390°F (200°C)

	All-purpose flour	
1	sheet (9 inches/23 cm square) frozen puff pastry (half a 17.3-oz/ 490 g package), thawed	1
4 tbsp	canned almond cake and pastry filling	60 mL
2 tbsp	butter, melted	30 mL
2 tbsp	sliced almonds, coarsely chopped	30 ml
1½ tbsp	granulated sugar	22 mL

1. On a lightly floured work surface, unfold pastry sheet. Cut sheet into 4 equal squares.

2. Spread 1 tbsp (15 mL) almond filling on each pastry square to within ¼ inch (1 cm) of the edge.

3. Fold squares in half, enclosing filling, to form triangles. Starting at the wide side, roll up triangles toward the point. Curve ends in slightly to form a crescent shape. Brush with butter and sprinkle with almonds and sugar, dividing evenly.

4. Place 2 croissants, point side down, in air fryer basket, leaving 1 inch (2.5 cm) space in between (refrigerate the remaining croissants). Air-fry for 12 to 17 minutes or until croissants are puffed and golden brown. Transfer to a wire rack and let cool for 15 minutes. Repeat with the remaining croissants.

Variation

Chocolate Hazelnut Croissants: Replace the almond filling with chocolate hazelnut spread. Omit the almonds or replace them with chopped hazelnuts.

Pull-Apart Cranberry Coffee Cake

Cranberries, almonds and melted butter form an irresistible trinity in this quick and easy coffee cake. Pulling it apart to eat each bite ups the pleasure factor!

TIP

Hot air and steam will release from the air fryer throughout the cooking cycle. If your face is in close proximity to the appliance during the cooking cycle or when you are opening the basket, you risk being scalded by the release of accumulated steam.

- Preheat air fryer to 360°F (180°C)
- 6-inch (15 cm) round metal cake pan, sprayed with nonstick cooking spray

2 tbsp	granulated sugar	30 mL
2 tbsp	dried cranberries, chopped	30 mL
2 tbsp	sliced almonds, chopped	30 mL
2 tbsp	butter, melted	30 mL
1	can (6 oz/250 g) refrigerated small dinner biscuits	1

1. In a small, shallow dish, stir together sugar, cranberries and almonds.
2. Place butter in another small, shallow dish.
3. Remove dough from packaging and separate into biscuits. Cut each biscuit into quarters.
4. Dip each dough piece in butter and dredge in sugar mixture, pressing gently to adhere. Arrange dough pieces in prepared pan, overlapping if needed. Drizzle any remaining butter and sprinkle any remaining sugar mixture over dough.
5. Air-fry for 18 to 23 minutes or until golden brown. Transfer pan to a wire rack and let cool for at least 10 minutes. Run knife around edge of pan to loosen and invert cake onto a serving platter.

Variations

Replace the dried cranberries with an equal amount of other dried fruit (such as raisins, chopped dried apricots or dried cherries).

Replace the almonds with an equal amount of other chopped nuts (such as walnuts or pecans).

Strawberry Jam Breakfast Tarts

Pastry, strawberry jam and an old-fashioned icing add up to a breakfast or brunch treat you are guaranteed to love.

STORAGE TIP

Store the cooled iced tarts in an airtight container in the refrigerator for up to 3 days.

- Preheat air fryer to 360°F (180°C)

Tarts

1	package (15 oz/425 g) refrigerated rolled pie crusts	1
4 tbsp	strawberry jam or preserves	60 mL

Icing

1/2 cup	confectioners' (icing) sugar	125 mL
1 1/2 tsp	milk	7 mL
1	drop almond extract	1

1. *Tarts:* On work surface, unroll pie crust. Cut into 4 equal wedges. Spread 2 tbsp (30 mL) jam on each of 2 wedges, leaving a 1/2-inch (1 cm) border. Brush crust edges with water. Top with the 2 remaining wedges. Press edges firmly with a fork to seal.

2. Place tarts in air fryer basket, spacing them evenly. Air-fry for 12 to 17 minutes or until crust is golden brown. Transfer to a wire rack to cool completely.

3. *Icing:* In a small bowl or cup, stir together confectioners' sugar, milk and almond extract until blended and smooth. Spoon icing over the cooled tarts.

Variations

Chocolate Hazelnut Tarts: Replace the jam with chocolate hazelnut spread.

PB&J Tarts: Use 1 tbsp (15 mL) creamy peanut butter and 1 tbsp (15 mL) strawberry jam or preserves in each tart.

Almost Effortless Donuts

A quick spell in the air fryer, a dip in melted butter and a tumble in sugar produces puffy, home-style donuts everyone will fawn over. Variations are as easy as adding an icing or a hint of spice to the sugar.

Variations

Chocolate or Vanilla Sprinkles Donuts: Prepare donuts as directed, omitting the sugar, and let cool for 3 minutes. While donuts air-fry, microwave 1 cup (250 mL) ready-to-use chocolate or vanilla frosting in a microwave-safe bowl until melted (about 15 to 30 seconds on High power). Dip one side of each donut in frosting and sprinkle with multicolor candy sprinkles.

Sugar and Spice Donuts: Stir 1¼ tsp (6 mL) ground cinnamon or pumpkin pie spice into the granulated sugar in step 1.

- Preheat air fryer to 360°F (180°C)
- 1-inch (2.5 cm) biscuit or cookie cutter

⅓ cup	granulated sugar	75 mL
¼ cup	butter, melted	60 mL
1	can (17.3 oz/490 g) refrigerated large dinner biscuits	1

1. Place sugar in a small, shallow dish.
2. Place butter in another small, shallow dish.
3. Remove dough from packaging and separate into biscuits. Flatten each biscuit slightly with your palm. Using the biscuit cutter, cut out circles from the centers of the dough. Place donuts and holes on a piece of parchment paper, keeping them separate.
4. Working with one donut at a time, dip in butter, coating all sides, then dredge in sugar, gently shaking off excess. Place 2 to 3 donuts in air fryer basket, leaving 1 inch (2.5 cm) space in between.
5. Air-fry for 9 to 13 minutes or until golden brown. Transfer to a wire rack and let cool for at least 3 minutes. Repeat with the remaining donuts.
6. Dip and dredge the donut holes in butter and sugar. Place in basket, leaving space in between. Air-fry for 3 to 6 minutes or until golden brown. Transfer to wire rack and let cool for at least 3 minutes. Discard any excess sugar and melted butter.

Lemon Ricotta Donut Bites

**MAKES
8 DONUT BITES**

Delivering the nuanced flavor of deep-fried Italian donuts, but with a fraction of the fat, time and effort, these lemony donuts are small bites of bliss.

TIP

Choose a pancake mix that calls for the addition of eggs and milk, rather than a "complete" pancake mix that calls for only the addition of water or milk.

⅓ cup	granulated sugar	75 mL
1½ tsp	finely grated lemon zest	7 mL
1	large egg	1
½ cup	ricotta cheese	125 mL
⅓ cup	pancake mix (see tip)	75 mL

1. In a medium bowl, whisk together sugar, lemon zest, egg and ricotta cheese. Stir in pancake mix until blended and no lumps remain.

2. Scoop about 1½ tbsp (22 mL) dough and, using your hands, roll into a ball. Repeat with the remaining dough. Place balls on a plate, cover loosely with plastic wrap and refrigerate for 15 minutes.

3. Preheat air fryer to 360°F (180°C).

4. Place half the dough balls in air fryer basket, spacing them evenly. Air-fry for 14 to 18 minutes or until tops are golden and a tester inserted in the center of a donut bite comes out clean. Transfer to a wire rack and let cool completely. Repeat with the remaining dough balls.

Variation

Replace the lemon zest with an equal amount of orange zest, ½ tsp (2 mL) vanilla extract or ¼ tsp (1 mL) almond extract.

Chocolate Chip Peanut Butter Breakfast Cookies

MAKES 16 COOKIES

Humble banana is at the heart of these nourishing, on-the-go breakfast cookies, lending moistness and natural sweetness in one fell swoop.

TIP

Quick-cooking oats work best in this recipe; thanks to their smaller size, they absorb liquids more quickly than large-flake (old-fashioned) rolled oats. If large-flake rolled oats are all you have, place the same amount in a food processor and pulse 3 or 4 times to break up the oats before adding them to the recipe.

STORAGE TIP

Store the cooled cookies in an airtight container at room temperature for up to 3 days or in the refrigerator for up to 1 week.

- Preheat air fryer to 360°F (180°C)
- 32 miniature foil or paper muffin cup liners

1	very ripe large banana	1
3 tbsp	creamy peanut butter	45 mL
1 tsp	vanilla extract	5 mL
1/8 tsp	salt	0.5 mL
1 cup	quick-cooking rolled oats	250 mL
3 tbsp	miniature semisweet chocolate chips	45 mL

1. Place one muffin cup liner inside another. Repeat to create 16 doubled liners.

2. In a medium bowl, finely mash banana. Stir in peanut butter, vanilla and salt until blended. Stir in oats and chocolate chips.

3. Divide batter equally among the doubled liners (about a heaping tablespoon/15 mL in each).

4. Place half the cookies in air fryer basket, spacing them evenly. Air-fry for 7 to 10 minutes or until tops are golden brown. Transfer to a wire rack and let cool completely. Repeat with the remaining cookies.

Variations

Other varieties of nut or seed butter (such as almond, cashew or sunflower seed) can be used in place of the peanut butter.

An equal amount of chopped dried fruit (such as raisins, apricots, cherries or cranberries) can be used in place of the chocolate chips.

Chunky Trail Mix Granola

Oats are a great cereal on their own, but they also love to mingle with countless other flavors. Case in point, this honey-sweetened granola. Trail mix — a mixture of nuts, seeds and dried fruits — makes the cereal taste complex without the addition of a laundry list of ingredients.

STORAGE TIP

Store the cooled granola in an airtight container at room temperature for up to 3 weeks or in the freezer for up to 3 months.

- Preheat air fryer to 300°F (150°C)

1/4 cup	liquid honey	60 mL
2 tbsp	butter, melted	30 mL
1/8 tsp	salt	0.5 mL
1 cup	large-flake (old-fashioned) rolled oats	250 mL
1 cup	trail mix, coarsely chopped	250 mL

1. In a large bowl, whisk together honey, butter and salt. Add oats and trail mix, tossing to coat.

2. Spread mixture in a single layer in air fryer basket. Air-fry for 13 to 18 minutes, stirring twice, until oats are golden brown.

3. Transfer granola to a medium bowl and let cool completely.

Variations

An equal amount of virgin coconut oil, melted, vegetable oil or olive oil can be used in place of the butter.

An equal amount of pure maple syrup can be used in place of the honey.

Snacks

Cinnamon Sugar Tortilla Chips

Cinnamon sugar is a nostalgic flavor, no matter how, or on what, it is sprinkled. These quick and simple chips will renew — and perhaps double — everyone's affection.

TIP

For gluten-free chips, use a gluten-free flour tortilla.

STORAGE TIP

Store the cooled chips in an airtight container at room temperature for up to 5 days.

• Preheat air fryer to 360°F (180°C)

1	10-inch (25 cm) flour tortilla	1
1 tbsp	granulated sugar	15 mL
¾ tsp	ground cinnamon	3 mL
Pinch	salt	Pinch
1 tbsp	butter, melted	15 mL
	Nonstick cooking spray	

1. Cut tortilla in half. Stack the two halves and cut crosswise into 1-inch (2.5 cm) strips. Place in a medium bowl.

2. In a small cup, stir together sugar, cinnamon and salt.

3. Drizzle butter over tortilla strips and sprinkle with cinnamon sugar, tossing to coat. Transfer to air fryer basket, spacing them evenly, and spray with cooking spray.

4. Air-fry for 4 to 7 minutes, shaking basket twice, until chips are browned and crisp. Transfer to a wire rack and let cool for at least 5 minutes. Serve warm or let cool completely.

Variations

Pumpkin Spice Tortilla Chips: Use an equal amount of pumpkin pie spice in place of the cinnamon.

Spicy Cinnamon Tortilla Chips: Add a large pinch of cayenne pepper along with the cinnamon in step 2.

Cinnamon–Brown Sugar Tortilla Chips: Replace the granulated sugar with packed brown sugar.

Fried Apple Rings

Brown sugar has a caramel profile that, when combined with apple, inevitably invokes apple pie. These easy apple rings are sweet and delicious proof.

TIPS

Choose a pancake mix that calls for the addition of eggs and milk, rather than a "complete" pancake mix that calls only for the addition of water or milk.

These treats are best eaten very soon after they are air-fried.

Air fryers become very hot, especially when heated to maximum temperature. Use oven pads or mitts when touching the appliance and when opening and closing the basket.

- Preheat air fryer to 390°F (200°C)

2	medium-large tart-sweet apples (such as Gala, Golden Delicious or Braeburn)	2
⅓ cup	pancake mix (see tip)	75 mL
1½ tbsp	packed brown sugar	22 mL
1	large egg	1
3 tbsp	water	45 mL
1½ cups	graham cracker crumbs	375 mL
	Nonstick cooking spray	

1. Peel apples and cut each crosswise into 6 slices. Using a small sharp knife, remove seeds and core from each apple ring.

2. In a shallow dish, whisk together pancake mix, brown sugar, egg and water until blended and smooth.

3. Spread graham cracker crumbs in another shallow dish.

4. Working with 1 apple ring at a time, dip in batter, shaking off excess, then dredge in crumbs, pressing gently to adhere. As they are dredged, place 4 to 6 apple rings (depending on size) in air fryer basket, leaving space in between. Spray with cooking spray.

5. Air-fry for 5 to 8 minutes or until golden brown. Serve immediately.

6. Repeat steps 4 and 5 with the remaining apple rings, batter and crumbs. Discard any excess batter and crumbs.

Banana Oat Snack Cookies

Kudos to bananas for enhancing so many home-baked treats, such as these three-ingredient snack cookies, but also for making it a cinch to get a day's supply of potassium.

TIPS

For best results, choose a banana that is extremely soft, with lots of brown spots on the peel.

When adding the stir-ins, use no more than 6 tbsp (90 mL) total.

If you have large-flake (old-fashioned) rolled oats (rather than quick-cooking), pulse them several times in a food processor before using.

Variation

Gluten-Free Banana Oat Snack Cookies: Use oats that are certified gluten-free.

- Preheat air fryer to 330°F (165°C)
- 8 standard-size foil or paper muffin cup liners

½ cup	mashed very ripe banana (about 1 large)	125 mL
½ cup	quick-cooking rolled oats	125 mL
Pinch	salt	Pinch

Suggested Stir-Ins (see tip)

¼ tsp	vanilla extract	1 mL
2 to 3 tbsp	chocolate chips	30 to 45 mL
2 to 3 tbsp	chopped dried fruit (such as raisins, cherries or cranberries)	30 to 45 mL
2 to 3 tbsp	chopped nuts or seeds (such as walnuts, pecans or sunflower seeds)	30 to 45 mL
2 tbsp	peanut butter or other nut butter	30 mL
2 tbsp	chocolate hazelnut spread	30 mL
1 tbsp	ground flax seeds (flaxseed meal), wheat germ or chia seeds	15 mL

1. Place one muffin cup liner inside another. Repeat to create 4 doubled liners.

2. In a small bowl, stir together banana, oats and salt until well blended. Stir in any of the suggested stir-ins, if desired.

3. Divide batter equally among the doubled liners, smoothing tops with the back of a spoon or your fingers.

4. Place filled liners in air fryer basket, spacing them evenly. Air-fry for 6 to 9 minutes or until edges are golden and centers appear dry. Transfer to a wire rack and let cool completely.

Berry Pancake Muffins
(variation, page 35)

Almost Effortless Donuts (page 40)

Banana Oat Snack Cookies (page 48)

Pimento Cheese Pinwheels (page 51)

Fried Ricotta Cheese Balls (page 66),
Tex-Mex Mini Pepper Poppers (page 73)
and Artichoke Dip Bites (page 70)

Baked Potato Dip (page 69)

Asian Barbecue Chicken Wings (page 81)

Crispy, Spicy Baby Bok Choy (page 89)
and Popcorn Cauliflower (page 92)

Fried Onion Biscuit Bites

A cross between onion rings and biscuits, these savory bites are ready in minutes — without fuss or deep-frying.

TIP

Air fryers become very hot, especially when heated to maximum temperature. Use oven pads or mitts when touching the appliance and when opening and closing the basket.

• Preheat air fryer to 390°F (200°C)

1	can (12 oz/375 g) refrigerated large dinner biscuits	1
1 tbsp	butter, melted	15 mL
½ cup	crushed canned French-fried onions	125 mL

1. Remove dough from packaging and separate into biscuits. Using scissors or a knife, cut each biscuit into quarters.

2. In a medium bowl, toss together biscuit pieces and butter until coated. Add onions, tossing to coat.

3. Place half the biscuit bites in air fryer basket, spacing them evenly. Air-fry for 4 to 7 minutes or until puffed and golden brown. Serve immediately. Repeat with the remaining biscuit bites.

Variation

Crunchy Biscuit Bites: Replace the onions with crushed corn chips.

Blooming Green Onion Bread

Cheesy, crispy and studded with green onions, this easy appetizer is the bread cousin of the blooming onion. It can be varied in countless ways, with different shredded cheeses and herbs.

TIP

For best results, select a crusty, rustic style of bread.

- Preheat air fryer to 360°F (180°C)
- Large square of foil

1	small (6 inches/15 cm in diameter) bread round/ boule (unsliced)	1
1 cup	shredded Italian cheese blend	250 mL
2/3 cup	finely chopped green onions	150 mL
1/4 cup	freshly grated Parmesan cheese	60 mL
	Nonstick cooking spray	

1. Cut bread in one direction into 1-inch (2.5 cm) slices, cutting to within $1/2$ inch (1 cm) of bottom of loaf. Repeat cuts in opposite direction.

2. Gently open cuts in bread and sprinkle Italian cheese, green onions and Parmesan cheese in between cuts, dividing evenly. Generously spray with cooking spray. Wrap in foil, completely enclosing bread.

3. Place package in air fryer basket. Air-fry for 15 minutes. Unwrap foil to expose top of bread. Air-fry for 5 to 7 minutes or until cheese is melted and top is golden brown. Serve immediately.

Variations

Blooming Herb Bread: Replace the green onions with $1 1/2$ tsp (7 mL) dried Italian seasoning and $1/3$ cup (75 mL) fresh flat-leaf (Italian) parsley leaves, chopped.

For a more decadent appetizer, drizzle bread all over with $1/4$ cup (60 mL) melted butter instead of spraying with nonstick cooking spray.

Pimento Cheese Pinwheels

**MAKES
16 PINWHEELS**

The sharp, nutty flavor of Cheddar cheese, the fresh bite of green onions and the hint of sweetness from pimentos are all anchored by flaky swirls of dough in these pinwheels.

Variation

An equal amount of chopped roasted red bell peppers can be used in place of the pimentos.

- Preheat air fryer to 360°F (180°C)
- 6-inch (15 cm) round metal cake pan, sprayed with nonstick cooking spray

1 cup	shredded sharp (old) Cheddar cheese	250 mL
1/3 cup	finely chopped green onions	75 mL
1/3 cup	drained jarred pimentos, chopped	75 mL
3 oz	brick-style cream cheese, softened	90 g
1/4 tsp	freshly cracked black pepper	1 mL
1	can (8 oz/250 g) refrigerated crescent dinner rolls	1
	Nonstick cooking spray	

1. In a medium bowl, combine Cheddar cheese, green onions, pimentos, cream cheese and pepper until well blended.

2. Remove dough from packaging and unroll onto work surface (do not separate into triangles). Using your fingertips, gently press seams together. Spread cheese mixture on dough, leaving a 1/4-inch (0.5 cm) border. Beginning with a long side, roll dough back up into a cylinder. Cut crosswise into 16 equal pieces.

3. Place half the pinwheels in prepared pan, spacing them evenly (refrigerate the remaining pinwheels).

4. Place pan in air fryer basket. Air-fry for 8 to 12 minutes or until puffed and golden brown. Transfer pinwheels to a wire rack to cool slightly. Serve warm.

5. Wipe out pan and respray with cooking spray. Repeat steps 3 and 4 with the remaining pinwheels.

Buffalo Chickpea Bites

MAKES 16 BITES

Humble chickpeas and carrots, spiffed up to taste like mini Buffalo wing bites? It's true! Even meat lovers will reach for seconds.

TIP

Air fryers become very hot, especially when heated to maximum temperature. Use oven pads or mitts when touching the appliance and when opening and closing the basket.

Variation

Gluten-Free Buffalo Chickpea Bites: Replace the panko with gluten-free bread crumbs or crushed gluten-free crackers or corn flakes cereal.

- Preheat air fryer to 380°F (190°C)
- Food processor

2	large carrots, peeled and chopped	2
1	can (14 to 15 oz/398 to 425 mL) chickpeas, drained and rinsed	1
⅔ cup	chopped green onions	150 mL
1 cup	panko (Japanese bread crumbs), divided	250 mL
¼ cup	Buffalo-style wing sauce	60 mL
½ tsp	salt	2 mL
	Nonstick cooking spray	

Suggested Accompaniment
    Ranch or blue cheese dressing

1. In food processor, process carrots until finely chopped. Transfer to a large bowl.

2. Add chickpeas and green onions to food processor; pulse until a chunky paste forms. Transfer to the bowl.

3. Add half the panko, the wing sauce and salt to the carrot mixture, stirring until well blended.

4. Spread the remaining panko in a shallow dish.

5. Using your hands, roll chickpea mixture into 16 balls (about 1 heaping tablespoon/15 mL per ball). Roll balls in panko, gently pressing to adhere.

6. Place half the balls in air fryer basket, spacing them evenly. Spray with cooking spray. Air-fry for 13 to 17 minutes or until golden brown and coating appears crispy. Serve immediately with suggested accompaniment, if desired. Repeat with the remaining balls. Discard any remaining panko.

PB&J "Fries"

Get ready to feel like a kid again! These peanut butter and jelly treats have nothing to do with potato french fries except for their shared shape and their irresistibility.

TIPS

The "fries" can be assembled through step 1 up to 2 days in advance. Wrap in plastic wrap and refrigerate until ready to proceed with steps 2 through 4.

Other varieties of creamy nut or seed butter (such as almond, cashew or sunflower seed) can be used in place of the peanut butter. If using a natural-style butter, use at room temperature for easier spreading.

If desired, omit the peanuts.

• Preheat air fryer to 360°F (180°C)

1	package (15 oz/425 g) refrigerated rolled pie crusts	1
¾ cup	creamy peanut butter	175 mL
⅓ cup	raspberry jam or preserves	75 mL
1	large egg	1
2 tsp	water	10 mL
½ cup	finely chopped roasted peanuts	125 mL

1. On work surface, unroll pie crusts. On 1 pie crust, spread peanut butter to within ⅛ inch (3 mm) of the edge. On second pie crust, spread jam to within ⅛ inch (3 mm) of the edge. Place second crust, jam side down, on first crust and gently press them together.

2. In a small cup, whisk together egg and water. Brush egg mixture evenly over the top crust and sprinkle with peanuts.

3. Using a sharp knife or pizza cutter, cut pie crust into eighteen ½-inch (1 cm) strips. Make 3 cuts crosswise, creating 4 rows, for a total of 72 "fries."

4. Place 18 "fries," peanut side up, in air fryer basket, spacing them evenly (refrigerate the remaining "fries"). Air-fry for 8 to 12 minutes or until golden brown. Using a pancake turner, transfer to a wire rack and let cool for 5 minutes. Serve warm or let cool completely. Repeat three times with the remaining "fries."

Variation

Chocolate Hazelnut "Fries": Omit the jam and peanuts. Replace the peanut butter with chocolate hazelnut spread.

Spicy Tuna Melt Wedges

Zesty salsa and pepper Jack cheese balance the rich flavors of mayonnaise and tuna in these anytime tuna melt snacks.

TIPS

For best results, do not use fat-free mayonnaise.

Either regular or whole wheat pitas can be used.

• Preheat air fryer to 390°F (200°C)

2	cans (each 5 oz/150 g) water-packed flaked tuna, drained	2
3 tbsp	mayonnaise	45 mL
3 tbsp	salsa	45 mL
	Salt and freshly cracked black pepper	
2	6-inch (15 cm) pitas	2
1½ cups	shredded pepper Jack cheese	375 mL

1. In a medium bowl, combine tuna, mayonnaise and salsa. Season to taste with salt and pepper.
2. Place 1 pita in air fryer basket. Air-fry for 1 to 2 minutes or until golden and slightly crisp.
3. Remove pita from air fryer and spread with half the tuna mixture. Sprinkle with half the cheese.
4. Return pita to air fryer basket. Air-fry for 4 to 7 minutes or until cheese is melted and bubbly. Transfer to a cutting board and cut into 6 wedges.
5. Repeat steps 2 to 4 with the remaining pita, tuna mixture and cheese.

Variations

Cheddar Tuna Melt Wedges: Increase the mayonnaise to ¼ cup (60 mL) and omit the salsa. Use shredded Cheddar cheese in place of the pepper Jack cheese.

An equal amount of canned chicken, shrimp or backfin (lump) crabmeat can be used in place of the tuna.

Zucchini Pizza Bites

**MAKES 2 TO
3 SERVINGS**

Pizza recipes are copious, but these petite, zucchini-based bites are standouts because of their fresh, clean flavors and lightning-fast preparation.

TIPS

Use either regular beef and pork pepperoni or turkey pepperoni.

Air fryers become very hot, especially when heated to maximum temperature. Use oven pads or mitts when touching the appliance and when opening and closing the basket.

• Preheat air fryer to 390°F (200°C)

1	medium zucchini	1
	Nonstick cooking spray	
	Salt and freshly cracked black pepper	
2 tbsp	marinara sauce	30 mL
½ cup	shredded Italian blend or mozzarella cheese	125 mL
8	small slices pepperoni, halved	8

1. Cut zucchini crosswise into $\frac{1}{4}$-inch (0.5 cm) thick slices. Spray both sides with cooking spray and season to taste with salt and pepper.

2. Arrange zucchini slices in a single layer in air fryer basket, spacing them evenly. Air-fry for 4 to 6 minutes or until beginning to brown.

3. Open basket and top each zucchini slice with $\frac{1}{4}$ tsp (1 mL) sauce, 2 tsp (10 mL) cheese and 1 half slice pepperoni. Air-fry for 1 to 2 minutes or until cheese is melted and bubbly. Serve immediately.

Variation

Zucchini Pesto Pizza Bites: Replace the marinara sauce with prepared basil pesto. Omit the pepperoni.

Salami Chips

Introducing your new favorite chip — no dip required!

TIP

It is okay if the salami edges overlap slightly in the basket.

STORAGE TIP

Store the cooled chips in an airtight container at room temperature for up to 5 days.

- Preheat air fryer to 300°F (150°C)

8	thin slices hard salami (about 2½ inches/6 cm in diameter)	8

1. Arrange salami slices in a single layer in air fryer basket.
2. Air-fry for 10 to 12 minutes or until edges begin to curl. Transfer slices to a wire rack and let cool completely (chips will crisp as they cool).

Bacon-Wrapped Potato Tots

MAKES 2 SERVINGS

Bacon's smoky, salty charms shine in this easy snack. Be sure to make a second batch if you plan to share with more than one friend!

TIP

For best results, use regular, not thick-cut, bacon.

- Preheat air fryer to 360°F (180°C)

| 8 | slices thick-cut bacon, halved crosswise | 8 |
| 16 | frozen potato tots | 16 |

1. Wrap 1 piece of bacon around each potato tot, overlapping ends.
2. Place wrapped tots, seam side down, in air fryer basket, spacing them evenly. Air-fry for 20 to 25 minutes or until bacon is cooked and crisp and tots are golden brown. Serve immediately.

Variations

Barbecue Bacon Tots: Brush one side of each bacon piece with about $\frac{1}{2}$ tsp (2 mL) barbecue sauce before wrapping it around potato tot.

Blazing Bacon Tots: Generously brush one side of each bacon piece with about $\frac{1}{8}$ tsp (0.5 mL) hot pepper sauce (such as Tabasco) before wrapping it around potato tot.

Brown Sugared Bacon–Wrapped Dogs

Always a favorite, these salty-sweet bites are also a snap to prepare.

TIPS

Turkey or pork hot dogs can be used in place of the beef hot dogs.

Air fryers become very hot, especially when heated to maximum temperature. Use oven pads or mitts when touching the appliance and when opening and closing the basket.

• Preheat air fryer to 390°F (200°C)

4	slices bacon (not thick-cut), halved crosswise	4
¼ cup	packed brown sugar	60 mL
2	all-beef hot dogs, each cut crosswise into 4 pieces	2

1. Sprinkle 1 side of each bacon piece with brown sugar. Wrap 1 bacon piece around each hot dog piece, overlapping ends.
2. Arrange hot dogs, seam side down, in air fryer basket, leaving space in between. Air-fry for 12 to 17 minutes or until bacon is cooked crisp. Serve immediately.

Variations

Spicy Bacon-Wrapped Dogs: Omit the brown sugar. Brush each bacon piece with ⅛ tsp (0.5 mL) hot pepper sauce before wrapping it around hot dog.

Maple Bacon-Wrapped Dogs: Omit the brown sugar. Brush each bacon piece with ⅛ tsp (0.5 mL) pure maple syrup before wrapping it around hot dog.

Bite-Size Beef Tacos

MAKES 1 TO 2 SERVINGS

Meaty, cheesy, hand-held and easy to make, these are everything a hearty snack should be.

TIP

Hot air and steam will release from the air fryer throughout the cooking cycle. If your face is in close proximity to the appliance during the cooking cycle or when you are opening the basket, you risk being scalded by the release of accumulated steam.

- Preheat air fryer to 360°F (180°C)

4	frozen cooked beef meatballs, thawed and crumbled	4
$\frac{1}{2}$ cup	shredded pepper Jack or Cheddar cheese	125 mL
2 tbsp	salsa	30 mL
8	scoop-shaped tortilla chips	8
1 tbsp	minced fresh cilantro or green onions	15 mL

1. In a small bowl, combine meatballs, cheese and salsa. Divide mixture evenly among tortilla chips.
2. Arrange filled chips in air fryer basket, spacing them evenly. Air-fry for 3 to 6 minutes or until heated through and cheese is melted. Sprinkle with cilantro and serve immediately.

Variations

Bite-Size Black Bean Tacos: Replace the meatballs with $\frac{1}{3}$ cup (75 mL) rinsed drained canned black beans, slightly mashed.

Bite-Size Chicken Tacos: Replace the meatballs with $\frac{1}{3}$ cup (75 mL) chopped cooked chicken.

Burgers and Fries Bites

Go ahead: eat one or two, even three burgers and fries, without blowing your diet! Just make sure they are in the form of these two-bite snacks, which are as cute as they are crave-worthy.

TIP

Air fryers become very hot, especially when heated to maximum temperature. Use oven pads or mitts when touching the appliance and when opening and closing the basket.

- Preheat air fryer to 390°F (200°C)
- Toothpicks

4 oz	lean ground beef	125 g
	Salt and freshly cracked black pepper	
6	frozen waffle-cut fries	6
6	small slices Cheddar cheese (about 3 inches/7.5 cm square)	6
6	slices bread-and-butter or dill pickle	6
6	small cherry or grape tomatoes	6

1. Shape beef into 6 small patties, each about ½ inch (1 cm) thick. Season with salt and pepper.

2. Place waffle fries in a single layer on one side of air fryer basket. Air-fry for 6 minutes. Open basket and position mini burgers on the other side of basket, spacing them evenly. Air-fry for 4 to 7 minutes or until burgers are no longer pink inside and an instant-read thermometer inserted horizontally into the center of a patty registers 165°F (74°C).

3. Remove fries and burgers from air fryer. Place 1 burger atop each fry, followed by a cheese slice, pickle slice and tomato. Secure with toothpicks. Serve immediately.

Variations

An equal amount of lean ground turkey can be used in place of the ground beef.

Other varieties of sliced cheese (such as Swiss, provolone or Monterey Jack) can be used in place of the Cheddar.

Mozzarella Meatball Bites

A trio of Italian favorites —
meatballs, mozzarella and
Parmesan — team up in
tender biscuits for a hearty
home-style snack.

Variation

Replace the mozzarella stick
with a Cheddar or marbled
cheese stick of equal size.

- Preheat air fryer to 360°F (180°C)
- 6-inch (15 cm) round metal cake pan, sprayed
  with nonstick cooking spray

1	mozzarella stick (1 oz/28 g)	1
1	can (6 oz/175 g) refrigerated flaky-style dinner biscuits	1
5	frozen cooked beef meatballs, thawed and halved	5
	Nonstick cooking spray	
3 tbsp	freshly grated Parmesan cheese	45 mL
	Marinara sauce, warmed, or basil pesto (optional)	

1. Remove mozzarella cheese from packaging and cut crosswise into 10 equal pieces.

2. Remove dough from packaging and separate into biscuits. Using your fingertips, split each biscuit crosswise into 2 layers.

3. Place 1 meatball half, cut side up, in center of each dough circle. Top meatball with one mozzarella piece. Fold biscuit up and around filling, shaping into a ball and pressing edges together to seal. Place in prepared pan, seam side down, spacing them evenly. Spray meatball bites with cooking spray and sprinkle evenly with Parmesan.

4. Place pan in air fryer basket. Air-fry for 11 to 15 minutes or until golden brown. Serve warm with marinara sauce or pesto for dipping, if desired.

Appetizers

Quick and Easy Onion Rings

MAKES 4 SERVINGS

The simplified preparation for these onion rings has an additional bonus: all of the ingredients are pantry-friendly (no eggs or dairy). In other words, you'll likely have everything you need to whip up a batch anytime!

TIP

If you do not have self-rising flour, use the following ratio to make your own. For every 1 cup (250 mL) all-purpose flour, whisk in 1½ tsp (7 mL) baking powder and ½ tsp (2 mL) salt. Measure the amount for your recipe and store the extra in an airtight container at room temperature for up to 6 months.

• Preheat air fryer to 390°F (200°C)

1	large Vidalia onion	1
⅔ cup	self-rising flour (see tip)	150 mL
2 tbsp	cornstarch	30 mL
1 tsp	garlic powder	5 mL
½ tsp	salt	2 mL
¼ tsp	freshly ground black pepper	1 mL
¾ cup	water	175 mL
1⅓ cups	dry bread crumbs with Italian seasoning	325 mL
	Nonstick cooking spray	

1. Cut onion into ¼-inch (0.5 cm) slices and separate into rings.
2. In a shallow dish, whisk together flour, cornstarch, garlic powder, salt, pepper and water.
3. Spread bread crumbs in another shallow dish.
4. Working with 1 onion ring at a time, dip in batter, shaking off excess, then dredge in bread crumbs, pressing gently to adhere. As they are dredged, place 4 to 7 onion rings (depending on size) in air fryer basket, leaving space in between. Spray with cooking spray.

Other varieties of sweet onions can be used in place of the Vidalia onion.

An equal amount of arrowroot can be used in place of the cornstarch.

Air fryers become very hot, especially when heated to maximum temperature. Use oven pads or mitts when touching the appliance and when opening and closing the basket.

5. Air-fry for 5 to 7 minutes or until golden brown. Serve immediately.

6. Repeat steps 4 and 5 with the remaining onion rings, batter and bread crumbs. Discard any excess batter and bread crumbs.

Variations

Parmesan Onion Rings: Stir $1/2$ cup (125 mL) finely grated Parmesan cheese into the bread crumbs in step 3.

Cheezy Vegan Onion Rings: Stir $1/4$ cup (60 mL) nutritional yeast into the bread crumbs in step 3.

Gluten-Free Onion Rings: Replace the self-rising flour with self-rising flour substitute (see tip, page 64) made with a gluten-free all-purpose flour blend.

Fried Ricotta Cheese Balls

MAKES 30 BALLS

It turns out that the most delicious fried ricotta cheese balls aren't deep-fried at all! Crispy and crunchy outside, creamy and cheesy inside, they will please one and all.

TIPS

Cold eggs will separate more easily than room temperature eggs.

To get the cleanest break, crack eggs against the counter, not on the edge of the bowl.

Any variety of ricotta cheese — full-fat, lower-fat or fat-free — can be used in this recipe.

¼ cup	freshly grated Parmesan cheese	60 mL
⅓ cup	packed fresh flat-leaf (Italian) parsley leaves, chopped, divided	75 mL
⅛ tsp	freshly cracked black pepper	0.5 mL
2	large eggs, separated	2
1 cup	ricotta cheese	250 mL
1 cup	dry bread crumbs with Italian seasoning, divided	250 mL
	Nonstick cooking spray	

1. In a medium bowl, stir together Parmesan cheese, half the parsley, pepper, egg yolks and ricotta cheese until blended. Stir in half the bread crumbs until combined. Form into 1-inch (2.5 cm) balls. Place on a plate and freeze for 20 to 30 minutes or until firm (but not frozen).

2. Meanwhile, preheat air fryer to 390°F (200°C).

3. In a shallow dish, vigorously whisk egg whites with a fork until frothy.

4. Spread the remaining bread crumbs in another shallow dish.

5. Remove half the cheese balls from the freezer. (Keep the remaining cheese balls in freezer until ready to coat and air-fry.) Working with 1 ball at a time, dip in egg whites, shaking off excess, then roll in bread crumbs, pressing gently to adhere. As they are coated, place cheese balls in air fryer basket, leaving space in between. Spray with cooking spray.

6. Air-fry for 5 to 9 minutes or until golden brown. Serve immediately, sprinkled with half the remaining parsley.

7. Repeat steps 5 and 6 with the remaining cheese balls, egg whites, bread crumbs and parsley. Discard any excess egg whites and bread crumbs.

Variation

Gluten-Free Ricotta Cheese Balls: Replace the bread crumbs with an equal amount of gluten-free bread crumbs or crushed gluten-free crackers, and add $\frac{1}{4}$ tsp (1 mL) dried Italian seasoning.

Fried Pesto Mozzarella "Cigars"

Ready-to-use basil pesto is the sophisticated surprise in these crispy-gooey cheese appetizers. They are equally at home as fancy appetizers as they are game-day snacks.

TIP

Air fryers become very hot, especially when heated to maximum temperature. Use oven pads or mitts when touching the appliance and when opening and closing the basket.

- Preheat air fryer to 390°F (200°C)

12	refrigerated or thawed frozen 6½-inch (16 cm) square egg roll wrappers	12
¼ cup	basil pesto	60 mL
1	package (12 oz/375 g) mozzarella string cheese (about 12 sticks)	1
	Nonstick cooking spray	

1. Place 1 wrapper on work surface, with an edge facing you. Brush with 1 tsp (5 mL) pesto and place cheese stick on bottom third. Fold the sides of the wrapper in toward the center and roll tightly away from you, enclosing cheese stick. Repeat with the remaining wrappers, pesto and cheese sticks.

2. Place 4 "cigars," seam side down, in air fryer basket, spacing them evenly (refrigerate the remaining "cigars"). Spray generously with cooking spray. Air-fry for 5 to 7 minutes or until golden brown. Serve immediately. Repeat with the remaining "cigars."

Variation

Plain Mozzarella "Cigars": Prepare as directed, omitting the pesto. Serve with warm marinara sauce for dipping, if desired.

Baked Potato Dip

MAKES 4 SERVINGS

A variety of your favorite baked potato toppings come together as one in this hot, bubbling, crowd-pleasing dip. You can dip whatever you like, but for the full potato experience, use your favorite potato chips — or french fries!

TIP

For a lighter dip, use reduced-fat cream cheese, Cheddar cheese and sour cream, and reduce the bacon by half.

- Preheat air fryer to 360°F (180°C)
- 6-inch (15 cm) round metal cake pan, sprayed with nonstick cooking spray

8 oz	brick-style cream cheese, softened	250 g
½ cup	sour cream	125 mL
1 cup	shredded sharp (old) Cheddar cheese, divided	250 mL
¼ cup	crumbled cooked bacon, divided	60 mL
3 tbsp	finely chopped green onions, divided	45 mL

Suggested Accompaniment

Potato chips

1. In a medium bowl, combine cream cheese and sour cream, stirring until blended. Stir in half the Cheddar, half the bacon and half the green onions.

2. Spoon and spread dip into prepared pan. Sprinkle with the remaining Cheddar and bacon.

3. Place pan in air-fryer basket. Air-fry for 13 to 16 minutes or until cheeses are melted and dip is heated through. Transfer to a wire rack and let cool for 5 minutes. Sprinkle with the remaining green onions. Serve with potato chips.

Variation

An equal amount of Monterey Jack or Gouda cheese can be used in place of the Cheddar cheese.

Artichoke Dip Bites

With the help of a short list of pantry and refrigerator ingredients, these poppable appetizers taste just like your favorite hot artichoke dip — all in one bite! Best of all, they are fast and simple to prepare.

TIP

An equal amount of thawed frozen artichoke hearts can be used in place of canned artichoke hearts.

- Preheat air fryer to 390°F (200°C)
- 24 standard-size foil or paper muffin cup liners

1	tube (13 oz/369 g) refrigerated pizza dough	1
1 cup	chopped drained canned artichoke hearts	250 mL
1 cup	shredded Italian cheese blend	250 mL
1/3 cup	finely chopped green onions	75 mL
1/2 cup	creamy Caesar salad dressing	125 mL

1. Place one muffin cup liner inside another. Repeat to create 12 doubled liners.

2. On work surface, unroll dough. Cut into 12 equal squares. Place 1 square in each doubled liner, gently pressing dough into bottom of liner.

3. In a medium bowl, stir together artichoke hearts, cheese, green onions and dressing until blended. Divide mixture equally among doubled liners.

4. Place 4 filled liners in air fryer basket, spacing them evenly (refrigerate the remaining filled liners). Air-fry for 7 to 10 minutes or until golden brown. Transfer to a wire rack and let cool for at least 5 minutes. Serve warm. Repeat with the remaining bites.

Variations

Spinach Dip Bites: Replace the artichokes with 10 oz (300 g) chopped frozen spinach, thawed and squeezed of excess liquid.

An equal amount of ranch salad dressing can be used in place of the creamy Caesar salad dressing.

Broccoli Cheddar Crispy Bites

MAKES 12 BITES

Buttery, cheesy, crispy broccoli bites are sure to please eaters of all ages, not to mention you.

STORAGE TIP

Store the cooled broccoli bites in an airtight container in the refrigerator for up to 2 days or in the freezer for up to 3 months. Let thaw at room temperature for 1 to 2 hours before serving.

- Preheat air fryer to 360°F (180°C)
- 24 miniature foil or paper muffin cup liners
- Food processor

	Nonstick cooking spray	
12 oz	frozen chopped broccoli, thawed, drained and patted dry	375 g
1 cup	shredded Cheddar cheese	250 mL
8 tbsp	crushed round buttery crackers (about 12 crackers), divided	125 mL
1	large egg	1
⅛ tsp	freshly cracked black pepper	0.5 mL

1. Place one muffin cup liner inside another. Repeat to create 12 doubled liners. Lightly spray inside of liners with cooking spray.

2. In food processor, combine broccoli, cheese, 6 tbsp (90 mL) crushed crackers, egg and pepper; pulse until chopped and blended (but not a purée). Divide mixture equally among doubled liners and sprinkle with the remaining crushed crackers.

3. Place half the filled liners in air fryer basket, spacing them evenly. Air-fry for 8 to 11 minutes or until golden brown and egg is set. Transfer to a wire rack and let cool for at least 3 minutes. Serve warm. Repeat with the remaining bites.

Variation

Cheesy Cauliflower Crispy Bites: Replace the broccoli with an equal amount of frozen chopped cauliflower florets, thawed, drained and patted dry.

Cauliflower Parmesan Puffs

The sweet-salty umami flavor of Parmesan is a perfect match for nutty cauliflower in these easy-peasy puffs.

TIP

Choose a pancake mix that calls for the addition of eggs and milk, rather than a "complete" pancake mix that calls for only the addition of water or milk.

STORAGE TIP

Store the cooled cauliflower puffs in an airtight container in the refrigerator for up to 2 days or in the freezer for up to 3 months. Let thaw at room temperature for 1 to 2 hours before serving.

- Preheat air fryer to 360°F (180°C)
- 24 miniature foil or paper muffin cup liners

	Nonstick cooking spray	
⅓ cup	pancake mix (see tip)	75 mL
1	large egg	1
⅓ cup	milk	75 mL
⅛ tsp	salt	0.5 mL
⅛ tsp	freshly cracked black pepper	0.5 mL
12 oz	frozen chopped cauliflower, thawed, drained and patted dry	375 g
½ cup	freshly grated Parmesan cheese	125 mL

1. Place one muffin cup liner inside another. Repeat to create 12 doubled liners. Lightly spray inside of liners with cooking spray.

2. In a large bowl, stir together pancake mix, egg, milk, salt and pepper until blended and no lumps remain. Stir in cauliflower and cheese. Divide mixture equally among doubled liners.

3. Place half the filled liners in air fryer basket, spacing them evenly. Air-fry for 8 to 11 minutes or until golden brown. Transfer to a wire rack and let cool for at least 3 minutes. Serve warm. Repeat with the remaining puffs.

Tex-Mex Mini Pepper Poppers

Sweet peppers taste like something new when they are miniature in size and stuffed full of Southwestern-style ingredients. Heat lovers can get their fix by swapping the sweet peppers for jalapeño peppers (see variation).

TIP

Miniature sweet bell peppers are typically sold in bags in the produce department of supermarkets.

Variations

Gluten-Free Tex-Mex Mini Pepper Poppers: Replace the panko with gluten-free bread crumbs or crushed gluten-free crackers or corn flakes cereal.

Tex-Mex Jalapeño Poppers: Replace the miniature bell peppers with an equal number of large jalapeño peppers or 16 medium jalapeños.

- Preheat air fryer to 360°F (180°C)

10	miniature sweet bell peppers	10
1 cup	shredded pepper Jack cheese	250 mL
8 oz	brick-style reduced-fat cream cheese, softened	250 g
½ cup	black bean and corn salsa	125 mL
½ cup	panko (Japanese bread crumbs)	125 mL
	Nonstick cooking spray	

1. Cut each pepper in half lengthwise. Using a spoon, scoop out any seeds and ribs. (If the peppers have stems, leave them intact.)

2. In a medium bowl, combine pepper Jack cheese, cream cheese and salsa. Spoon cheese mixture into peppers, dividing evenly and mounding as necessary.

3. Spread panko in a shallow dish. Press cheese side of each filled pepper into panko.

4. Place 5 to 8 filled peppers (depending on size), filling side up, in air fryer basket, leaving space in between. Spray with cooking spray. Air-fry for 10 to 12 minutes or until cheese is melted and bread crumbs are golden. Serve immediately. Repeat with the remaining filled peppers. Discard any excess panko.

Bacon-Wrapped Cheddar Jalapeños

This streamlined jalapeño popper recipe is a surefire way to get the party started. It has just three ingredients and three steps, so you'll have plenty of time to relax and enjoy the fun.

TIPS

Cold-pack sharp Cheddar cheese spread is usually available in 8-oz (250 g) and 1-lb (500 g) tubs and can be found in the deli section or the refrigerated cheese case.

For spicier appetizers, leave some of the ribs inside the jalapeños.

• Preheat air fryer to 390°F (200°C)

10	medium jalapeño peppers	10
8 oz	refrigerated cold-pack sharp Cheddar cheese spread, softened	250 g
10	slices bacon (not thick-cut), halved crosswise	10

1. Cut each jalapeño in half lengthwise. Using a spoon, scoop out any seeds and ribs. (If the peppers have stems, leave them intact.)
2. Spoon cheese spread into jalapeños, dividing evenly. Wrap 1 piece of bacon around each filled jalapeño, overlapping ends.
3. Arrange 5 to 8 filled jalapeños (depending on size), filling side up, in air fryer basket, leaving space in between. Air-fry for 12 to 17 minutes or until bacon is cooked crisp. Serve immediately. Repeat with the remaining filled jalapeños.

Salmon Croquettes

**MAKES 2 TO
3 SERVINGS
(8 CROQUETTES)**

The rich flavor of salmon
is best accented by easy
preparations, such as these
super-fast croquettes.
Sour cream and onion
chips add both crunch and
classic flavor without any
fussy steps.

TIPS

Whole-grain or brown mustard
can be used in place of the
Dijon mustard.

Air fryers become very hot,
especially when heated to
maximum temperature. Use
oven pads or mitts when
touching the appliance and
when opening and closing
the basket.

• Preheat air fryer to 360°F (180°C)

½ cup	finely crushed sour cream and onion potato chips	125 mL
2 tbsp	finely chopped green onions	30 mL
⅓ cup	mayonnaise	75 mL
1 tbsp	Dijon mustard	15 mL
⅛ tsp	freshly cracked black pepper	0.5 mL
2	cans (each 5 oz/142 g) boneless skinless salmon, drained and flaked	2
	Nonstick cooking spray	

1. In a medium bowl, gently combine chips,
   green onions, mayonnaise, mustard and
   pepper. Gently stir in salmon. Form into
   eight ¾-inch (2 cm) thick patties.

2. Place 4 patties in air fryer basket, leaving
   space in between. Spray with cooking spray.
   Air-fry for 4 minutes. Open basket and,
   using a spatula, carefully turn patties over.
   Air-fry for 4 to 7 minutes or until golden
   brown. Serve immediately. Repeat with the
   remaining patties.

Variations

An equal amount of plain potato chips can be
used in place of the sour cream and onion chips.

Replace the salmon with an equal amount
of canned tuna or backfin (lump) crabmeat,
picked over.

Crab-Stuffed Mushrooms

Regardless of how many versions of stuffed mushrooms you have had before now, this crab-rich recipe needs to go on your must-make list. They are so good, you may even fool yourself into thinking they were a time-consuming preparation!

TIP

Air fryers become very hot, especially when heated to maximum temperature. Use oven pads or mitts when touching the appliance and when opening and closing the basket.

- Preheat air fryer to 390°F (200°C)
- Food processor

8 oz	medium-large cremini mushrooms (about 10)	250 g
4 oz	drained canned backfin (lump) crabmeat, picked over	125 g
½ cup	packed fresh flat-leaf (Italian) parsley leaves	125 mL
3 tbsp	dry bread crumbs with Italian seasoning	45 mL
1 tsp	Old Bay or other seafood seasoning	5 mL
	Salt and freshly cracked black pepper	
	Nonstick cooking spray	

1. Remove mushroom stems and set the caps aside.
2. In food processor, combine mushroom stems, crab, parsley, bread crumbs and Old Bay seasoning. Pulse until finely ground. Season to taste with salt and pepper.
3. Place mushroom caps, hollow side up, on work surface. Divide filling equally among mushrooms, mounding it in the center of each. Spray with cooking spray.
4. Place mushrooms in air fryer basket, spacing them evenly. Air-fry for 9 to 12 minutes or until filling is golden brown and mushrooms are tender. Serve immediately.

Variations

Shrimp-Stuffed Mushrooms: Replace the crab with an equal amount of cooked peeled deveined shrimp, chopped.

Gluten-Free Crab-Stuffed Mushrooms: Replace the bread crumbs with an equal amount of crushed gluten-free corn flakes cereal.

Easiest Shrimp Egg Rolls

Freshly prepared egg rolls are terrific, but the thought of making them is terrifying for many home chefs. Fear no more: with an air fryer, four readily available ingredients and just a few short steps, homemade egg rolls can be made in minutes with minimal fuss and muss but all of the great crunch and flavor you crave.

TIPS

The egg rolls can be assembled up to 1 day in advance. Store in an airtight container in the refrigerator until ready to air-fry. Increase the cooking time by 1 to 2 minutes for chilled egg rolls.

Any variety of stir-fry sauce will work in this recipe. A general-purpose Chinese-style stir-fry sauce was used for testing.

While assembling the egg rolls, keep the stack of wrappers moist by covering them with a damp dish towel.

1 lb	thawed frozen stir-fry vegetables, drained	500 g
12 oz	cooked peeled deveined shrimp, chopped	375 g
2 tbsp	bottled stir-fry sauce	30 mL
10	refrigerated or thawed frozen 6½-inch (16 cm) square egg roll wrappers	10
	Nonstick cooking spray	

1. Using paper towels, pat vegetables dry to remove as much excess moisture as possible. Chop vegetables and place in a large bowl. Add shrimp and stir-fry sauce, stirring until combined.

2. Preheat air fryer to 390°F (200°C).

3. Place 1 wrapper on work surface, with an edge facing you. Spoon ¼ cup (60 mL) shrimp-vegetable mixture onto bottom third. Fold the sides of the wrapper in toward the center and roll tightly away from you, enclosing filling. Repeat with the remaining wrappers and filling.

4. Place 3 to 4 egg rolls, seam side down, in air fryer basket, spacing them evenly. Spray generously with cooking spray. Air-fry for 5 to 7 minutes or until golden brown. Serve immediately. Repeat with the remaining egg rolls.

Variation

Replace the shrimp with an equal amount of chopped cooked chicken, cooked ground pork, chopped cooked pork sausage or chopped drained extra-firm tofu.

Teriyaki Shrimp Balls

Shrimp lovers will find these balls — bite-size versions of teriyaki shrimp takeout — irresistible.

TIP

Choose teriyaki sauce that is about the same viscosity as soy sauce, rather than a thicker teriyaki glaze or barbecue sauce.

Variations

Gluten-Free Shrimp Balls: Replace the panko with an equal amount of gluten-free bread crumbs or crushed gluten-free crackers or corn flakes cereal.

Teriyaki Chicken Balls: Replace the shrimp with 12 oz (375 g) uncooked chicken breast, chopped into 1-inch (2.5 cm) pieces before adding to food processor. Cook balls as directed until an instant-read thermometer inserted into a chicken ball registers 165°F (74°C).

- Preheat air fryer to 380°F (190°C)
- Food processor

1 lb	shrimp, peeled and deveined	500 g
1	can (12 oz/375 mL) sliced water chestnuts, drained and finely chopped	1
½ cup	finely chopped green onions	125 mL
½ cup	garlic-flavored teriyaki sauce, divided	125 mL
⅛ tsp	freshly ground black pepper	0.5 mL
⅔ cup	panko (Japanese bread crumbs)	150 mL
	Nonstick cooking spray	

1. In food processor, pulse shrimp until chopped (but not a paste). Transfer to a large bowl.

2. Add water chestnuts, green onions, 3 tbsp (45 mL) teriyaki sauce and pepper to shrimp, stirring until well blended. Stir in panko until blended. Form into 1-inch (2.5 cm) balls. Spray generously with cooking spray.

3. Arrange half the balls in air fryer basket, spacing them evenly. Air-fry for 8 to 12 minutes or until balls are browned and firm to the touch. Serve immediately with the remaining teriyaki sauce. Repeat with the remaining balls.

Double Barbecue Chicken Bites

Here's the answer to great barbecue chicken, any time of year, with no grilling required!

TIP

It will take approximately 4 cups (1 L) potato chips to yield ¾ cup (175 mL) finely crushed potato chips.

• Preheat air fryer to 390°F (200°C)

1	large egg	1
5 tbsp	barbecue sauce, divided	75 mL
1 tbsp	water	15 mL
¾ cup	finely crushed barbecue-flavored potato chips	175 mL
8 oz	boneless skinless chicken breasts, cut into 1½-inch (4 cm) chunks	250 g
	Nonstick cooking spray	

1. In a shallow dish, whisk together egg, 1 tbsp (15 mL) barbecue sauce and water.

2. Spread crushed potato chips in another shallow dish.

3. Working with 1 chicken chunk at a time, dip in egg mixture, shaking off excess, then dredge in chips, pressing gently to adhere. As they are dredged, arrange in air fryer basket, spacing them evenly. Spray with cooking spray. Discard any excess egg mixture and chips.

4. Air-fry for 8 to 12 minutes or until chicken is no longer pink inside. Serve immediately with the remaining barbecue sauce for dipping.

Variation

Salt and Vinegar Chicken Bites: Replace the crushed barbecue chips with an equal amount of crushed salt and vinegar chips. Replace the barbecue sauce with an equal amount of creamy Caesar or ranch salad dressing.

Buffalo Chicken Wontons

MAKES
20 WONTONS

A riff on one of the most popular appetizers of all time, these crunchy "Buffalo" wontons have chicken, hot sauce and blue cheese packed into each and every bite.

TIPS

While assembling the chicken wontons, keep the stack of wrappers moist by covering them with a damp towel.

The chicken wontons can be assembled up to 1 day in advance. Refrigerate in an airtight container until ready to air-fry. Increase the cooking time by 1 to 2 minutes for chilled chicken wontons.

- Preheat air fryer to 390°F (200°C)

⅓ cup	crumbled blue cheese	75 mL
1 tbsp	Buffalo-style wing sauce	15 mL
1 cup	finely chopped cooked chicken	250 mL
	Salt and freshly ground black pepper	
20	3-inch (7.5 cm) square wonton wrappers	20
3 tbsp	butter, melted	45 mL

1. In a medium bowl, using a fork, mash together blue cheese and wing sauce until blended. Gently stir in chicken until combined. Season with salt and pepper.
2. Place 7 wrappers on work surface. Spoon 2 tsp (10 mL) chicken mixture into the center of each wrapper. Using a brush or fingertip, brush the edges of each wrapper with butter. Fold wontons in half to make a triangle shape. Press edges together to seal. Brush tops of wontons with more butter.
3. Place wontons in a single layer in air fryer basket, leaving about 1 inch (2.5 cm) space in between. Air-fry for 8 to 12 minutes or until golden brown.
4. Repeat steps 2 and 3 in two more batches with the remaining wonton wrappers, chicken mixture and butter.

Variation

Replace the blue cheese with an equal amount of shredded Cheddar, mozzarella or Monterey Jack cheese.

Asian Barbecue Chicken Wings

Bold spices and the savory umami of soy sauce are wonderful foils for the honey sweetness of barbecue sauce in this super-simple rendition of Asian-style chicken wings.

TIP

Air fryers become very hot, especially when heated to maximum temperature. Use oven pads or mitts when touching the appliance and when opening and closing the basket.

- Preheat air fryer to 360°F (180°C)

6	chicken wings, tips removed and wings cut into drumettes and flats	6
1/8 tsp	freshly ground black pepper	0.5 mL
1/4 cup	honey barbecue sauce	60 mL
2 tsp	soy sauce	10 mL
1/2 tsp	ground ginger	2 mL
1/4 tsp	garlic powder	1 mL

1. Sprinkle chicken wings with pepper. Place wings in a single layer (with some overlap) in air fryer basket. Air-fry for 24 to 28 minutes, shaking basket twice, until skin is browned and crisp and juices run clear when chicken is pierced.
2. Meanwhile, in a medium bowl, combine barbecue sauce, soy sauce, ginger and garlic powder.
3. Transfer wings to a bowl. Add sauce and toss to coat. Serve immediately.

Variations

Jamaican Jerk Chicken Wings: Replace the soy sauce with 1 tsp (5 mL) finely grated lime zest, 1 tbsp (15 mL) freshly squeezed lime juice and 1/4 tsp (1 mL) freshly ground black pepper. Replace the ginger with an equal amount of ground allspice.

Fiery Curry Chicken Wings: Replace the soy sauce with 1 tbsp (15 mL) hot pepper sauce. Replace the ginger and garlic powder with 1 1/2 tsp (7 mL) curry powder.

For spicier wings, add 1/2 tsp (2 mL) hot pepper sauce to the barbecue sauce mixture in step 2.

Fried Sausage Chips with Honey Mustard Dip

Wow everyone at your next game-day gathering with this easy, entertaining and addictive take on chips and dip.

TIP

Any variety of cooked sausage (such as kielbasa or garlic sausage) can be used in place of the smoked sausage.

STORAGE TIP

Cooled leftover sausage chips can be stored in an airtight container in the refrigerator for up to 3 days. Air-fry for 3 to 5 minutes at 330°F (165°C) to warm through.

• Preheat air fryer to 300°F (150°C)

¼ cup	mayonnaise	60 mL
3 tbsp	spicy brown mustard	45 mL
1 tbsp	liquid honey	15 mL
8 oz	cooked smoked sausage	250 g

1. In a small cup, whisk together mayonnaise, mustard and honey.
2. Very thinly slice sausage on the diagonal.
3. Place half the sausage slices in air fryer basket, spacing them evenly. Air-fry for 20 to 25 minutes or until lightly browned. Transfer to paper towels to drain. Serve warm with dip. Repeat with the remaining sausage slices.

Variations

An equal amount of packed brown sugar can be used in place of the honey.

An equal amount of Dijon or yellow mustard can be used in place of the spicy brown mustard.

Bacon Cheeseburger Bombs

This rendition of bacon cheeseburgers will bowl you over with its deliciousness, ease of preparation and bite-size fun.

TIP

Choose a pancake mix that calls for the addition of eggs and milk, rather than a "complete" pancake mix that calls only for the addition of water or milk.

- Preheat air fryer to 360°F (180°C)
- 6-inch (15 cm) round metal cake pan, sprayed with nonstick cooking spray

1 cup	shredded sharp (old) Cheddar cheese	250 mL
½ cup	pancake mix (see tip)	125 mL
4 oz	lean ground beef	125 g
¼ cup	crumbled cooked bacon	60 mL
1½ tsp	steak seasoning	7 mL
1 tbsp	water	15 mL

1. In a medium bowl, combine cheese, pancake mix, ground beef, bacon, steak seasoning and water until blended.

2. Form mixture into 1-inch (2.5 cm) balls and place in prepared pan, spacing them evenly.

3. Place pan in air fryer basket. Air-fry for 10 to 12 minutes or until an instant-read thermometer inserted in a burger bomb registers 165°F (74°C). Serve immediately.

Variation

Italian Sausage Bombs: Omit the bacon. Replace the ground beef with Italian sausage (bulk or casings removed). Use Italian cheese blend in place of the Cheddar cheese. Replace the steak seasoning with an equal amount of dried Italian seasoning.

Reuben Egg Rolls

The charms of a New York deli favorite shine in these crispy, crunchy egg rolls.

TIPS

The egg rolls can be assembled up to 1 day in advance. Store in an airtight container in the refrigerator until ready to air-fry. Increase the cooking time by 1 to 2 minutes for chilled egg rolls.

While assembling the egg rolls, keep the stack of wrappers moist by covering them with a damp towel.

6 oz	sliced deli corned beef, chopped	175 g
1½ cups	shredded Swiss cheese	375 mL
¾ cup	sauerkraut, drained and chopped	175 mL
¾ cup	Thousand Island dressing, divided	175 mL
12	refrigerated or thawed frozen 6½-inch (16 cm) square egg roll wrappers	12
	Nonstick cooking spray	

1. In a large bowl, combine corned beef, cheese, sauerkraut and half the dressing.

2. Preheat air fryer to 390°F (200°C).

3. Place 1 wrapper on work surface, with an edge facing you. Spoon ¼ cup (60 mL) corned beef mixture onto bottom third. Fold the sides of the wrapper in toward the center and roll tightly away from you, enclosing filling. Repeat with the remaining wrappers and filling.

4. Place 3 to 4 egg rolls, seam side down, in air fryer basket, spacing them evenly. Spray generously with cooking spray. Air-fry for 5 to 7 minutes or until golden brown. Serve immediately with the remaining dressing. Repeat with the remaining egg rolls.

Meatball Parmesan Puffs

Here, I've pepped up store-bought meatballs with flaky puff pastry, Parmesan cheese and some warm marinara sauce for dipping. The delectable result is a great appetizer by any measure, but three or four of these can easily move into the main-dish category.

TIPS

The sheet of puff pastry should be about 9 inches (23 cm) square for this recipe. If your sheets are a different size, or the pastry comes in a block, roll or trim it into a 9-inch (23 cm) square as necessary.

Commercial puff pastry loses it crispness quickly, so it is best to eat the puffs shortly after air-frying.

- Preheat air fryer to 360°F (180°C)
- 36 miniature foil or paper muffin liners

	All-purpose flour	
1	sheet (9 inches/23 cm square) frozen puff pastry (half a 17.3-oz/490 g package), thawed	1
	Nonstick cooking spray	
½ cup	finely grated Parmesan cheese	125 mL
18	frozen fully cooked beef meatballs, thawed	18
1 cup	marinara sauce, warmed	250 mL

1. Place one muffin cup liner inside another. Repeat to create 18 doubled liners.

2. On a lightly floured work surface, unfold puff pastry sheet. Spray with cooking spray and sprinkle evenly with cheese.

3. Cut sheet into 3 equal strips. Cut each strip lengthwise into 6 strips, making 18 strips in total. With the cheese side facing in, wrap 1 strip around 1 meatball. Place puff, seam side down, in a doubled liner. Repeat with the remaining strips and meatballs.

4. Place half the puffs in air fryer basket, spacing them 1 inch (2.5 cm) apart (refrigerate the remaining puffs). Air-fry for 10 to 15 minutes or until puffed and golden brown. Serve warm, with marinara sauce for dipping. Repeat with the remaining puffs.

Vegetables

Fried Artichoke Hearts

In this air-fryer spin on Roman fried artichokes, panko, Parmesan cheese and a bit of olive oil stand in for deep-frying. It's a mini feast! Best of all, they are ready in a flash.

TIP

Air fryers become very hot, especially when heated to maximum temperature. Use oven pads or mitts when touching the appliance and when opening and closing the basket.

• Preheat air fryer to 390°F (200°C)

½ cup	panko (Japanese bread crumbs)	125 mL
3 tbsp	freshly grated Parmesan cheese	45 mL
1 tbsp	olive oil	15 mL
⅛ tsp	freshly cracked black pepper	0.5 mL
1	large egg	1
1	can (14 oz/398 g) artichoke hearts, drained and patted dry	1
	Nonstick cooking spray	

Suggested Accompaniment
Lemon wedges

1. In a shallow dish, combine panko, Parmesan, oil and pepper until blended.

2. In another shallow dish, whisk egg until blended.

3. Working with 1 artichoke heart at a time, dip in egg, shaking off excess, then dredge in panko mixture, pressing gently to adhere. As they are dredged, place artichoke hearts in a single layer in air fryer basket, leaving space in between. Discard any excess egg and panko mixture. Spray artichokes generously with cooking spray.

4. Air-fry for 5 to 8 minutes or until golden brown. Serve immediately with lemon wedges, if desired.

Variation

Gluten-Free Fried Artichoke Hearts: Replace the panko with an equal amount of gluten-free bread crumbs or crushed gluten-free crackers or corn flakes cereal.

Crispy, Spicy Baby Bok Choy

Here's an excellent reason to make a beeline for the produce section of the supermarket: crisp-tender baby bok choy, speckled with hot pepper flakes. Air-frying removes all of the cooking guesswork, as well as excess oil.

TIP

If baby bok choy are not available, substitute half of one regular bunch of bok choy, trimmed, cut crosswise into 2-inch (5 cm) lengths and separated.

• Preheat air fryer to 390°F (200°C)

2	heads baby bok choy (about 8 to 10 oz/250 to 300 g total)	2
1 tbsp	vegetable oil	15 mL
¼ tsp	salt	1 mL
¼ tsp	hot pepper flakes	1 mL

1. Trim bok choy and separate the leaves. In a medium bowl, toss together bok choy, oil, salt and hot pepper flakes.

2. Arrange bok choy in air fryer basket (it will overlap somewhat). Air-fry for 10 to 14 minutes, shaking basket once halfway through, until leaves look crispy and edges are browned. Serve immediately.

Variation

Add more or less hot pepper flakes according to taste.

Broccoli Divine

A stalwart side dish, broccoli is too often taken for granted. Here it gets the "divine" treatment it deserves, with a creamy sauce and crisp Cheddar topping — which draw out every ounce of flavor from the florets. And it's so easy!

TIP

Panko (Japanese bread crumbs) or regular (unseasoned) bread crumbs can be used in place of the bread crumbs with Italian seasoning.

- Preheat air fryer to 390°F (200°C)
- 6-inch (15 cm) round metal cake pan, sprayed with nonstick cooking spray

8 oz	frozen broccoli florets (about 1 cup/250 mL), thawed	250 g
¼ cup	sour cream	60 mL
1 tbsp	butter, melted	15 mL
⅛ tsp	freshly cracked black pepper	0.5 mL
¼ cup	shredded sharp (old) Cheddar cheese	60 mL
2 tbsp	dry bread crumbs with Italian seasoning	30 mL

1. Arrange broccoli in prepared pan, spacing evenly.
2. In a small bowl or cup, stir together sour cream, butter and pepper; spoon over broccoli. Sprinkle with cheese and bread crumbs.
3. Place pan in air fryer basket. Air-fry for 10 to 14 minutes or until cheese is melted and bread crumbs are golden brown. Transfer to a wire rack and let cool for 5 minutes before serving.

Variations

Cauliflower Divine: Replace the broccoli with an equal amount of thawed frozen cauliflower florets.

Gluten-Free Broccoli Divine: Replace the bread crumbs with an equal amount of gluten-free bread crumbs or crushed gluten-free crackers or corn flakes cereal, and stir in a pinch of dried Italian seasoning.

Bacon-Wrapped Brussels Sprouts

MAKES 2 SERVINGS

You can never have enough bacon, especially when it is used to perk up Brussels sprouts, which are infused with smoky richness and extra tenderness as a result.

TIP

For best results, use regular, not thick-cut, bacon.

- Preheat air fryer to 390°F (200°C)

6	slices bacon, halved crosswise	6
1½ tbsp	honey mustard	22 mL
6	large Brussels sprouts, halved lengthwise	6

1. Spread one side of each bacon piece with mustard, dividing evenly. Wrap 1 piece of bacon around each Brussels sprout half, overlapping ends.

2. Arrange half the wrapped Brussels sprouts, seam side down, in air fryer basket, leaving space in between (refrigerate the remaining wrapped Brussels sprouts). Air-fry for 12 to 17 minutes or until bacon is cooked crisp. Serve immediately. Repeat with the remaining wrapped Brussels sprouts.

Variations

Use other varieties of mustard (such as Dijon, spicy brown or whole-grain) in place of the honey mustard, or simply omit the mustard.

Use pure maple syrup in place of the honey mustard.

Popcorn Cauliflower

Here comes healthy comfort! Sprinkled with crispy panko following a quick bath in ranch dressing, these popcorn-like cauliflower pieces are a crave-worthy, homey delight.

TIP

One medium head of cauliflower will yield approximately 3 cups (750 mL) florets.

• Preheat air fryer to 390°F (200°C)

1	medium head cauliflower, cut into bite-size florets, divided	1
²/₃ cup	ranch dressing, divided	150 mL
1 cup	panko (Japanese bread crumbs), divided	250 mL
	Nonstick cooking spray	
	Salt and freshly cracked pepper	

1. In a medium bowl, combine half the cauliflower florets and half the ranch dressing, gently tossing to coat. Add half the panko, tossing to coat.

2. Spread cauliflower in a single layer in air fryer basket and spray with cooking spray. Air-fry for 10 to 14 minutes or until deep golden brown. Transfer to a serving dish and season to taste with salt and pepper. Serve immediately.

3. Repeat steps 1 and 2 with the remaining cauliflower, ranch dressing and panko.

Variations

Popcorn Broccoli: Replace the cauliflower with a medium head of broccoli.

Parmesan Popcorn Cauliflower: Reduce the panko to ¾ cup (175 mL) and add ⅓ cup (75 mL) freshly grated Parmesan cheese.

Cheezy Vegan Popcorn Cauliflower: Reduce the panko to ¾ cup (175 mL) and add ¼ cup (60 mL) nutritional yeast.

Gluten-Free Popcorn Cauliflower: Replace the panko with an equal amount of gluten-free bread crumbs or crushed gluten-free crackers or corn flakes cereal.

Mexican Corn on the Cob

Street corn — roasted in the husks, then slathered in butter and topped with cheese and spices — is a beloved treat in Mexico and parts of the American Southwest, but you can recreate the flavor (without the extra fat) with the power of your air fryer.

TIP

If cotija cheese is unavailable, use an equal amount of freshly grated Parmesan cheese.

- Preheat air fryer to 390°F (200°C)

2	medium ears corns, husked, halved crosswise	2
	Nonstick cooking spray	
	Salt and freshly ground black pepper	
1	lime, halved	1
1 tsp	chili powder	5 mL
2 tbsp	grated cotija cheese	30 mL
2 tbsp	chopped fresh cilantro	30 mL

1. Spray corn with cooking spray and season to taste with salt and pepper. Arrange corn in air fryer basket, spacing them evenly.

2. Air-fry for 7 to 11 minutes or until corn kernels are beginning to get brown spots. Squeeze lime juice over corn and sprinkle with chili powder, cheese and cilantro. Serve immediately.

Variation

An equal amount of ground cumin can be used in place of the chili powder.

Eggplant Parmesan Fries

Typical renditions of
eggplant Parmesan
are heavy and rich
with oil. This playful
"fries" interpretation of
the dish is a light and
healthy departure that
highlights the flavor of star
ingredients: fresh eggplant
and Parmesan cheese.
Bonus: this may be the
easiest eggplant Parmesan
recipe you ever encounter.

TIPS

Room temperature eggs
will whisk more easily than
cold eggs.

Although freshly grated
Parmesan has the best flavor,
an equal amount of pre-grated
Parmesan cheese can be used
in its place.

• Preheat air fryer to 390°F (200°C)

1	small eggplant (about 10 oz/300 g), trimmed	1
	Salt and freshly ground black pepper	
1	large egg	1
1 tbsp	water	15 mL
2/3 cup	dry bread crumbs with Italian seasoning	150 mL
1/2 cup	freshly grated Parmesan cheese	125 mL
	Nonstick cooking spray	
1 cup	marinara sauce, warmed	250 mL

1. Cut eggplant lengthwise into 1/2-inch (1 cm)
   slices. Cut each slice lengthwise into 1/2-inch
   (1 cm) strips, then cut the strips crosswise
   into 2- to 3-inch (5 to 7.5 cm) long pieces.
   Season to taste with salt and pepper.

2. In a shallow dish, whisk together egg and
   water.

3. In another shallow dish, combine bread
   crumbs and cheese.

4. Working with 1 eggplant strip at a time, dip in
   egg mixture, shaking off excess, then dredge
   in bread crumb mixture, pressing gently to
   adhere. As they are dredged, arrange 8 to
   10 eggplant strips in air fryer basket, leaving
   space in between. Spray with cooking spray.

Air fryers become very hot, especially when heated to maximum temperature. Use oven pads or mitts when touching the appliance and when opening and closing the basket.

5. Air-fry for 7 to 9 minutes or until coating is golden brown. Serve immediately with warm marinara sauce for dipping.

6. Repeat steps 4 and 5 with the remaining eggplant strips, egg mixture and bread crumb mixture. Discard any excess egg mixture and bread crumb mixture.

Variations

Gluten-Free Eggplant Parmesan Fries: Replace the bread crumbs with an equal amount of gluten-free bread crumbs or crushed gluten-free crackers or corn flakes cereal, and add $\frac{1}{8}$ tsp (0.5 mL) dried Italian seasoning.

Vegan Eggplant Fries: In place of the egg mixture, whisk together 2 tsp (10 mL) ground flax seeds (flaxseed meal) and $\frac{1}{4}$ cup (60 mL) water. Let stand for 5 minutes before use. Replace the Parmesan with 3 tbsp (45 mL) nutritional yeast.

Crispy Panko Sweet Onions

If the mere mention of onion rings makes your mouth water, then these swift and simple sweet onions may be your new favorite side dish.

TIPS

Other varieties of sweet onions can be used in place of the Vidalia onion.

Although freshly grated Parmesan has the best flavor, an equal amount of pre-grated Parmesan cheese can be used in its place.

An equal amount of olive oil can be used in place of the butter.

• Preheat air fryer to 390°F (200°C)

1	large sweet onion (such as Vidalia)	1
	Nonstick cooking spray	
	Salt and freshly cracked black pepper	
1/3 cup	panko (Japanese bread crumbs)	75 mL
1 tbsp	freshly grated Parmesan cheese	15 mL
1 tbsp	butter, melted	15 mL
1/4 tsp	dried thyme	1 mL

1. Cut onion in half horizontally. Spray all over with cooking spray and season to taste with salt and pepper.

2. Place onion halves, cut side up, in air fryer basket. Air-fry for 25 to 30 minutes or until golden.

3. Meanwhile, in a small bowl, stir together panko, cheese, butter, thyme, a pinch of salt and a pinch of pepper.

4. Open basket and spoon panko mixture evenly on top of each onion half. Air-fry for 10 to 12 minutes or until topping is golden brown.

TIPS

You can use $\frac{1}{2}$ tsp (2 mL) fresh thyme leaves in place of the dried thyme.

Air fryers become very hot, especially when heated to maximum temperature. Use oven pads or mitts when touching the appliance and when opening and closing the basket.

Variations

Vegan Crispy Panko Sweet Onions: Replace the butter with olive oil and either omit the Parmesan or replace it with an equal amount of nutritional yeast.

Gluten-Free Crispy Sweet Onions: Replace the panko with an equal amount of gluten-free bread crumbs or crushed gluten-free crackers or corn flakes cereal.

An equal amount of crumbled dried rosemary or dried Italian seasoning can be used in place of the thyme.

An equal amount of plain dry bread crumbs or dry bread crumbs with Italian seasoning can be used in place of the panko.

Rosemary Roasted Mushrooms

This satisfying dish is the essence of an easy, yet impressive, side dish: everyday mushrooms, plus a few basic pantry seasonings, are given depth of flavor with speedy air-fryer roasting and a sprinkle of rosemary.

TIP

You can use $\frac{1}{2}$ tsp (2 mL) crumbled dried rosemary in place of the fresh rosemary.

- Preheat air fryer to 390°F (200°C)

8 oz	mushrooms, trimmed	250 g
1 tbsp	olive oil	15 mL
1 tsp	minced fresh rosemary	5 mL
$\frac{1}{4}$ tsp	salt	1 mL
$\frac{1}{8}$ tsp	freshly cracked black pepper	0.5 mL
	Chopped fresh parsley (optional)	

1. Slice mushrooms in half lengthwise. In a medium bowl, toss together mushrooms, oil, rosemary, salt and pepper.

2. Arrange mushrooms in air-fryer basket, spacing them evenly. Air-fry for 5 to 7 minutes or until browned and tender. Transfer to a serving dish and sprinkle with parsley, if desired.

Blistered Baby Bell Peppers

It's the spicy, smoky sweetness of the paprika that really sells these addictive mini peppers. A sprinkle of flaky sea salt heightens the vibrancy of their flavor.

TIPS

Miniature sweet bell peppers are typically sold in bags in the produce department of supermarkets.

Table salt can be used in place of the flaky sea salt.

- Preheat air fryer to 390°F (200°C)

8 oz	miniature sweet bell peppers	250 g
2 tsp	olive oil	10 mL
1/4 tsp	smoked paprika	1 mL
1/8 tsp	salt	0.5 mL
	Flaky sea salt	

1. Halve peppers lengthwise. Using a spoon, scoop out and discard seeds and veins.

2. In a medium bowl, stir together peppers, oil, paprika and salt.

3. Transfer peppers to air fryer basket, spacing them evenly. Air-fry for 7 to 12 minutes, shaking the basket every 3 minutes, until skins are blistered and flesh is softened. Serve immediately, sprinkled with sea salt to taste.

Variation

An equal amount of ground cumin can be used in place of the smoked paprika.

Dijon Rutabaga Fries

Related to turnips, rutabagas, with their firm, orange flesh, make sensational (and colorful!) fries. Piquant Dijon mustard provides an excellent foil to their subtle sweetness.

TIP

Air fryers become very hot, especially when heated to maximum temperature. Use oven pads or mitts when touching the appliance and when opening and closing the basket.

- Preheat air fryer to 390°F (200°C)

2 tsp	olive oil	10 mL
1 tsp	Dijon mustard	5 mL
1/4 tsp	dried thyme	1 mL
1/4 tsp	salt	1 mL
1/8 tsp	freshly ground black pepper	0.5 mL
8 oz	rutabaga, cut into 3-inch (7.5 cm) long by 1/4-inch (0.5 cm) thick sticks	250 g

1. In a large bowl, whisk together oil, mustard, thyme, salt and pepper. Add rutabaga sticks, tossing to coat.

2. Spread half the rutabaga sticks in a single layer in air fryer basket, spacing them apart. Air-fry for 5 minutes, then shake the basket. Air-fry for 4 to 8 minutes or until rutabaga sticks are golden brown. Serve immediately. Repeat with the remaining rutabaga sticks.

Variations

You can use an equal amount of dried rosemary in place of the thyme.

An equal amount of spicy brown mustard or prepared horseradish can be used in place of the Dijon mustard.

Spiced Acorn Squash Wedges

Acorn squash and brown sugar have a natural affinity, which is amplified by the addition of subtle spice and heat from chili powder and black pepper.

TIP

An equal amount of olive oil or vegetable oil can be used in place of the butter.

• Preheat air fryer to 390°F (200°C)

1	acorn squash, halved and seeded	1
1 tbsp	packed brown sugar	15 mL
1 tbsp	butter, melted	15 mL
1½ tsp	chili powder	7 mL
¼ tsp	salt	1 mL
⅛ tsp	freshly cracked black pepper	0.5 mL

1. Cut each squash half into 4 equal wedges.

2. In a medium bowl, stir together brown sugar, butter, chili powder, salt and pepper. Add squash, rubbing cut sides all over with butter mixture.

3. Transfer squash to air fryer basket and arrange in an even layer. Air-fry for 25 to 30 minutes, shaking the basket every 10 minutes, until squash is fork-tender. Serve immediately.

Variation

You can use ¾ tsp (3 mL) ground cumin in place of the chili powder.

Air-Fried Spaghetti Squash

Staggeringly simple, and versatile enough to go with a broad range of toppings or flavor additions, this delicious play on "noodles" may become one of your go-to vegetable dishes.

TIPS

If you prefer to prepare one squash half at a time, the second half, unsprayed and uncooked, can be stored in an airtight container or wrapped in plastic wrap in the refrigerator for up to 3 days.

An equal amount of melted butter can be used in place of the olive oil.

• Preheat air fryer to 390°F (200°C)

1	small spaghetti squash (about 1½ lbs/750 g)	1
	Nonstick cooking spray	
	Salt and freshly cracked black pepper	
2 tsp	olive oil	10 mL

Suggested Accompaniments

Freshly grated Parmesan cheese

Chopped fresh herbs (such as parsley, rosemary, basil or thyme)

Marinara sauce, warmed

1. Cut squash in half lengthwise. Using a spoon, scoop out and discard seeds. Spray cut sides of squash with cooking spray and season with salt and pepper.
2. Place one squash half, cut side down, in air fryer basket. Air-fry for 25 to 30 minutes or until flesh is very easily pierced with a fork.
3. Repeat step 2 with the remaining squash half. Let cool slightly.
4. Scrape out squash pulp into a medium bowl (discard peel). Using a fork, rake pulp into strands. Drizzle with oil and season to taste with salt and pepper. Serve with any of the suggested accompaniments, as desired.

Pecan Streusel Sweet Potatoes

Ready-to-use sweet potatoes, a bit of butter and a dose of pumpkin pie spice are blended here to create an almost impossibly perfect side dish for cold-weather eating. The quick crumble of gingersnaps and pecans on top clinches it.

TIPS

You can use 4 to 5 vanilla wafers in place of the gingersnaps. Add $1/8$ tsp (0.5 mL) pumpkin pie spice to the wafer mixture in step 2.

For a gluten-free side dish, make sure to use gluten-free gingersnaps.

- Preheat air fryer to 330°F (165°C)
- 6-inch (15 cm) round metal cake pan, sprayed with nonstick cooking spray

1	can (15 oz/425 g) sweet potatoes in syrup, drained	1
2 tbsp	butter, melted, divided	30 mL
$1/2$ tsp	pumpkin pie spice	2 mL
4	hard gingersnap cookies, finely crushed (about $1/3$ cup/ 75 mL)	4
3 tbsp	chopped pecans	45 mL

1. In a medium bowl, mash sweet potatoes. Stir in half the butter and the pumpkin pie spice until blended and mostly smooth (some small lumps will remain). Spoon into prepared pan, smoothing top.

2. In a small bowl or cup, stir together crushed gingersnaps, pecans and the remaining butter; sprinkle evenly over sweet potatoes.

3. Place pan in air fryer basket. Air-fry for 14 to 18 minutes or until potatoes are heated through and topping is golden brown and appears crispy. Transfer to a wire rack and let cool for 5 minutes before serving.

Variation

Coconut-Pecan Streusel Sweet Potatoes:
Replace the gingersnaps with $1/4$ cup (60 mL) sweetened flaked coconut.

Fried Pesto Cherry Tomatoes

These pesto- and crumb-coated tomatoes are positively addictive, whether as a side dish, appetizer or snack.

TIPS

Choose a pancake mix that calls for the addition of eggs and milk, rather than a "complete" pancake mix that calls for only the addition of water or milk.

Air fryers become very hot, especially when heated to maximum temperature. Use oven pads or mitts when touching the appliance and when opening and closing the basket.

- Preheat air fryer to 390°F (200°C)

¾ cup	panko (Japanese bread crumbs)	175 mL
½ cup	pancake mix (see tip)	125 mL
1	large egg	1
2 tbsp	basil pesto	30 mL
2 cups	cherry tomatoes	500 mL
	Nonstick cooking spray	

1. In a shallow dish, combine panko and pancake mix until blended.

2. In another shallow dish, whisk together egg and pesto until blended.

3. Working with 1 tomato at a time, dip in egg mixture, shaking off excess, then dredge in panko mixture, pressing gently to adhere. Repeat process to double-coat tomatoes. As they are double-dredged, place half the tomatoes in air fryer basket, leaving space in between. Spray generously with cooking spray.

4. Air-fry for 5 to 8 minutes or until golden brown. Serve immediately.

5. Repeat steps 3 and 4 with the remaining tomatoes, egg mixture and panko mixture. Discard any excess egg and panko mixtures.

Variations

Fried Cherry Tomatoes: Replace the pesto with an equal amount of milk.

Gluten-Free Fried Pesto Cherry Tomatoes: Replace the panko with an equal amount of gluten-free bread crumbs or crushed gluten-free crackers or corn flakes cereal. Use a gluten-free pancake mix.

Garlicky Roasted Roma Tomatoes

Garlic and tomatoes melt into each other with the help of a small amount of olive oil and a blast of heat from the air fryer.

TIP

You can use $\frac{1}{2}$ tsp (2 mL) garlic powder in place of the fresh garlic.

• Preheat air fryer to 390°F (200°C)

4	plum (Roma) tomatoes	4
1	large clove garlic, minced	1
1 tbsp	olive oil	15 mL
$\frac{1}{4}$ tsp	salt	1 mL
$\frac{1}{8}$ tsp	freshly ground black pepper	0.5 mL

1. Cut tomatoes in half lengthwise. Using a spoon or your fingers, scoop out and discard seeds and pulp.
2. In a medium bowl, toss together tomatoes, garlic, oil, salt and pepper.
3. Arrange tomatoes, cut side up, in a single layer in air fryer basket, spacing them evenly. Air-fry for 13 to 18 minutes or until tomatoes have begun to shrivel and edges are browned. Serve warm or let cool completely.

Blue Cheese–
Stuffed Tomatoes

This decadent side dish delivers a lot of flavor and sophistication for very little work.

TIP

Air fryers become very hot, especially when heated to maximum temperature. Use oven pads or mitts when touching the appliance and when opening and closing the basket.

• Preheat air fryer to 390°F (200°C)

2	medium-large tomatoes	2
⅓ cup	dry bread crumbs with Italian seasoning	75 mL
3 tbsp	crumbled blue cheese	45 mL
2 tbsp	chopped fresh parsley	30 mL
¼ tsp	garlic powder	1 mL
⅛ tsp	salt	0.5 mL
⅛ tsp	freshly cracked black pepper	0.5 mL
	Nonstick cooking spray	

1. Cut tops off tomatoes; discard tops. Using a spoon or your fingers, scoop out seeds and pulp; roughly chop pulp and place pulp and seeds in a small bowl. Stir in bread crumbs, cheese, parsley, garlic powder, salt and pepper until blended. Spoon bread crumb mixture into tomatoes.

2. Place stuffed tomatoes in air fryer basket, spacing them evenly. Spray with cooking spray. Air-fry for 8 to 11 minutes or until stuffing is browned and tomatoes are tender.

Variations

Vegan Stuffed Tomatoes: Replace the blue cheese with 2 tbsp (30 mL) chopped toasted walnuts and 2 tsp (10 mL) nutritional yeast.

Gluten-Free Stuffed Tomatoes: Replace the bread crumbs with an equal amount of gluten-free bread crumbs or crushed gluten-free crackers or corn flakes cereal, and add ⅛ tsp (0.5 mL) dried Italian seasoning.

An equal amount of crumbled feta cheese or freshly grated Parmesan cheese can be used in place of the blue cheese.

Zucchini Tots

Here, I've recast an all-time potato favorite with zucchini. These tots will disappear as fast as you can make them!

TIP

To shred the zucchini, use the large holes of a box grater.

- Preheat air fryer to 390°F (200°C)

1	medium zucchini (unpeeled), shredded	1
¼ cup	finely chopped green onions	60 mL
¼ cup	freshly grated Parmesan cheese	60 mL
¼ cup	dry bread crumbs with Italian seasoning	60 mL
1	large egg, lightly beaten	1
¼ tsp	salt	1 mL
⅛ tsp	freshly cracked black pepper	0.5 mL

1. Place shredded zucchini in center of a clean dish towel. Working over the sink, gather the ends of the towel together and twist tightly around the zucchini. Squeeze out as much liquid as possible.

2. Transfer zucchini to a medium bowl. Stir in green onions, cheese, bread crumbs, egg, salt and pepper until well blended.

3. Scoop dough by heaping tablespoonfuls (15 mL) and form into short logs (about 1½ inches/4 cm long).

4. Arrange half the logs in air fryer basket, spacing them evenly. Air-fry for 14 to 18 minutes or until golden brown. Serve immediately. Repeat with the remaining logs.

Variations

Gluten-Free Zucchini Tots: Replace the bread crumbs with an equal amount of gluten-free bread crumbs or crushed gluten-free crackers, and add a pinch of dried Italian seasoning.

An equal amount of yellow crookneck summer squash or yellow zucchini can be used in place of the zucchini.

Tex-Mex Zucchini Boats

The fresh, clean flavor of zucchini makes a delicious — as well as convenient — base for bold Southwestern flavors. Although this is a great side dish for two, it's also a filling, nutritious main dish for one.

TIP

Look for zucchini that are about 5 to 6 inches (12.5 to 15 cm) long and about $1\frac{1}{2}$ inches (4 cm) thick for this recipe.

- Preheat air fryer to 390°F (200°C)

2	small zucchini (see tip), halved lengthwise	2
	Salt and freshly cracked black pepper	
$\frac{1}{2}$ cup	rinsed drained canned black beans	125 mL
2 tbsp	salsa	30 mL
1 tbsp	chopped fresh cilantro	15 mL
$\frac{1}{2}$ cup	shredded pepper Jack cheese	125 mL
	Nonstick cooking spray	

1. Using a metal spoon, scoop and scrape out seeds from each zucchini half, leaving a $\frac{1}{4}$-inch (0.5 cm) shell; discard seeds. Sprinkle cut sides with salt and pepper.

2. In a small bowl, using a fork, coarsely mash beans. Stir in salsa and cilantro until blended. Spoon bean mixture into hollowed-out zucchini, dividing evenly. Sprinkle cheese over stuffing and spray with cooking spray.

3. Place zucchini halves, cheese side up, in air fryer basket, spacing them evenly. Air-fry for 15 to 20 minutes or until zucchini are tender and cheese is melted and golden brown in spots. Serve immediately.

Horseradish Roasted Root Vegetables

Straight horseradish can be intense, but when used in moderation as a quick coating for root vegetables, it is a lively counterpoint, making the vegetables taste clean and bright, not heavy.

TIP

Air fryers become very hot, especially when heated to maximum temperature. Use oven pads or mitts when touching the appliance and when opening and closing the basket.

- Preheat air fryer to 390°F (200°C)

2	carrots, cut into ½-inch (1 cm) thick slices	2
1	parsnip, cut into ½-inch (1 cm) thick slices	1
1	beet, cut into ½-inch (1 cm) thick slices	1
1 tbsp	olive oil	15 mL
1 tsp	prepared horseradish	5 mL
¼ tsp	salt	1 mL
⅛ tsp	freshly cracked black pepper	0.5 mL

1. In a medium bowl, toss together carrots, parsnip, beet, oil, horseradish, salt and pepper.
2. Transfer vegetables to air fryer basket and arrange in an even layer. Air-fry for 16 to 21 minutes, shaking the basket once or twice, until vegetables are fork-tender. Serve immediately.

Variation

An equal amount of mustard (such as Dijon or spicy brown) can be used in place of the horseradish. Alternatively, simply omit the horseradish.

Potatoes

Rustic Gold Potato Chips

These light, crisp and golden chips will make you glow with pleasure — in part from the high levels of copper, vitamin C and zinc, all of which are beneficial to a healthy complexion.

TIPS

Make sure the potato slices are of even thickness, or some will be overdone before others are cooked.

It's okay for the potato slices to overlap slightly in the basket.

Check the chips frequently as they air-fry; they can quickly turn from golden brown to burned.

STORAGE TIP

Store potato chips in an airtight container at room temperature for up to 1 week.

1	large yellow-fleshed potato (unpeeled)	1
	Ice water	
2 tsp	olive oil	10 mL
$\frac{1}{4}$ tsp	garlic salt	1 mL
$\frac{1}{8}$ tsp	freshly ground black pepper	0.5 mL

1. Using a very sharp knife or a mandoline, cut potatoes into $\frac{1}{8}$-inch (3 mm) thick slices. Place potato slices in a large bowl of ice water and let stand for 15 minutes to remove excess starch.

2. Preheat air fryer to 330°F (165°C).

3. Drain potatoes, then pat dry with paper towels. In a medium bowl, toss together potatoes, oil, garlic salt and pepper until potatoes are coated.

4. Spread coated potatoes in air fryer basket. Air-fry for 18 to 22 minutes, shaking basket two or three times, until edges are golden brown and chips appear crisp. Transfer chips to a wire rack and let cool completely (they will crisp more as they cool).

Variation

An equal amount of plain salt can be used in place of the garlic salt.

Provençal Potato Wedges

Herbes de Provence, olive oil and a hint of garlic give these crispy wedges their South of France flavor.

TIP

Air fryers become very hot, especially when heated to maximum temperature. Use oven pads or mitts when touching the appliance and when opening and closing the basket.

3	medium yellow-fleshed potatoes (each about 5 oz/ 150 g)	3
2 tsp	herbes de Provence	10 mL
1½ tsp	garlic powder	7 mL
½ tsp	salt	2 mL
⅛ tsp	freshly ground black pepper	0.5 mL
2 tbsp	olive oil	30 mL

1. Place potatoes in a medium saucepan and add enough water to cover by 1 inch (2.5 cm). Bring to a boil over medium-high heat. Reduce heat to low and boil gently for 35 to 40 minutes or until fork-tender. Drain potatoes, transfer to a plate and let stand until cool enough to handle.

2. Preheat air fryer to 390°F (200°C).

3. In a small cup, combine herbes de Provence, garlic powder, salt and pepper.

4. Pour oil into a shallow dish.

5. Cut cooled potatoes into quarters. Dip potatoes into oil, turning to coat, and sprinkle with herb mixture.

6. Arrange potatoes in air fryer basket, leaving space in between. Air-fry for 12 to 15 minutes, gently shaking the basket after 8 minutes, until potatoes are golden brown. Serve immediately.

Variations

An equal amount of dried Italian seasoning can be used in place of the herbes de Provence.

An equal number of red-skinned potatoes can be used in place of the yellow-fleshed potatoes.

Extra-Crispy French Fries

These fries garner their extra-crispy status from two key steps: first, a quick water bath removes some of their starch, allowing for enhanced browning and crisping, and second, a coating of panko bread crumbs. The results? Extra amazing!

TIPS

A single large russet potato may weigh 1 lb (500 g).

Soaking the potato sticks in hot water before roasting removes some of the starch, ensuring extra-crisp fries without deep-frying.

Room temperature eggs will whisk more easily than cold eggs.

1 lb	russet potatoes	500 g
	Hot (not boiling) water	
	Nonstick cooking spray	
3/4 tsp	salt, divided	3 mL
1/4 tsp	freshly ground black pepper, divided	1 mL
1/2 cup	all-purpose flour	125 mL
1 1/2 cups	panko (Japanese bread crumbs)	375 mL
2	large eggs	2

1. Peel potatoes and cut lengthwise into 1/4-inch (0.5 cm) thick sticks. Place in a large bowl and add enough hot water to cover. Let stand for 10 minutes. Drain, pat dry and return to dry bowl. Spray with nonstick cooking spray and sprinkle with 1/2 tsp (2 mL) salt and half the pepper, tossing to coat.
2. Preheat air fryer to 360°F (180°C).
3. Place flour in a large sealable plastic bag.
4. Spread panko in a shallow dish.
5. In another shallow bowl, whisk together eggs and the remaining salt and pepper.
6. Add half the potatoes to the bag of flour, seal and toss until coated. Working with 1 potato stick at a time, remove from flour, shaking off excess. Dip in egg mixture, shaking off excess, then dredge in panko, pressing gently to adhere. As they are dredged, place potato sticks in air fryer basket, leaving space in between. Spray with cooking spray.

TIP

Hot air and steam will release from the air fryer throughout the cooking cycle. If your face is in close proximity to the appliance during the cooking cycle or when you are opening the basket, you risk being scalded by the release of accumulated steam.

7. Air-fry for 14 to 18 minutes or until golden brown. Serve immediately.
8. Repeat steps 6 and 7 with the remaining potato sticks, flour, egg mixture and panko. Discard any excess flour, egg mixture and panko.

Variations

Italian Crispy Fries: Add $1\frac{1}{2}$ tsp (7 mL) dried Italian seasoning and 1 tsp (5 mL) garlic powder when tossing the potatoes with salt and pepper in step 1.

Gluten-Free Crispy French Fries: Replace the all-purpose flour with a gluten-free all-purpose flour blend and replace the panko with crushed gluten-free corn flakes cereal.

Hash Browns for One

Ready for the best hash browns ever? The air fryer and ready-to-use hash browns lead the way to crispy, golden-brown perfection.

TIPS

An equal amount of vegetable oil or melted butter can be used in place of the olive oil.

Air fryers become very hot, especially when heated to maximum temperature. Use oven pads or mitts when touching the appliance and when opening and closing the basket.

- Preheat air fryer to 360°F (180°C)
- 6-inch (15 cm) round metal cake pan, sprayed with nonstick cooking spray

1⅓ cups	frozen shredded hash brown potatoes	325 mL
2 tsp	olive oil	10 mL
⅛ tsp	salt	0.5 mL
Pinch	freshly ground black pepper	Pinch

1. Spread hash browns in an even layer in prepared pan. Drizzle with oil and season with salt and pepper. Toss to combine and spread evenly in pan.
2. Place pan in air fryer basket. Air-fry for 10 minutes. Open basket and toss hash browns; spread evenly in pan. Air-fry for 8 to 12 minutes or until golden brown and crispy at edges. Serve immediately.

Variation

Replace the shredded hash browns with an equal amount of frozen diced hash brown potatoes with peppers and onions. This variety of hash browns is often labeled "O'Brien" potatoes.

Hash Brown Nests

Crisp hash browns are the ideal crust for a quick filling of eggs, bell peppers and cheese. The results make any weekday breakfast feel like a leisurely brunch.

TIP

Air fryers become very hot, especially when heated to maximum temperature. Use oven pads or mitts when touching the appliance and when opening and closing the basket.

Variation

Other varieties of shredded cheese, such as pepper Jack, Cheddar, Gouda or provolone, can be used in place of the Swiss.

- Preheat air fryer to 390°F (200°C)
- 8 standard-size foil or paper muffin cup liners

	Nonstick cooking spray	
1 cup	refrigerated or thawed frozen shredded hash brown potatoes	250 mL
	Salt and freshly cracked black pepper	
3	large eggs	3
1/2 cup	shredded Swiss cheese	125 mL
1/3 cup	chopped red bell pepper	75 mL
2 tbsp	finely chopped green onions	30 mL

1. Place one muffin cup liner inside another. Repeat to create 4 doubled liners. Spray insides of liners with cooking spray.

2. Scoop 1/4 cup (60 mL) hash browns into each prepared double liner, using a spoon or fingers to create an indentation in each. Season to taste with salt and pepper and spray with cooking spray.

3. Place filled liners in air fryer basket, spacing them evenly. Air-fry for 20 minutes.

4. Meanwhile, in a small bowl, whisk together eggs, 1/4 tsp (1 mL) salt and 1/8 tsp (0.5 mL) pepper until blended. Stir in cheese, red pepper and green onions.

5. Open basket and divide egg mixture evenly among hash brown nests. Carefully close basket and air-fry for 5 to 8 minutes or until eggs are set. Transfer to a wire rack and let cool for 5 minutes before serving.

Air Fryer Baked Potatoes

Forget about heating the entire oven to bake a few potatoes. The air-fryer "bakes" potatoes to perfection — in less time, to boot.

TIPS

Air fryers become very hot, especially when heated to maximum temperature. Use oven pads or mitts when touching the appliance and when opening and closing the basket.

These potatoes can also be used to make Stuffed Potato Skins (page 128).

• Preheat air fryer to 390°F (200°C)

4	medium russet potatoes	4
	Nonstick cooking spray	
	Salt and freshly cracked black pepper	

Suggested Accompaniments

Butter

Sour cream

Shredded Cheddar cheese

Minced fresh chives

Crumbled cooked bacon

1. Spray potatoes with cooking spray and season to taste with salt and pepper. Using a fork, pierce all sides of potatoes.

2. Place potatoes in air fryer basket, spacing them evenly. Air-fry for 20 minutes. Open basket and, using tongs, turn potatoes over. Air-fry for 15 to 20 minutes or until skin appears crispy and potatoes give very easily when pierced with a fork.

3. Serve potatoes with any of the suggested accompaniments, as desired.

Variation

Air Fryer Baked Sweet Potatoes: Replace the russet potatoes with 2 medium-large sweet potatoes. Air-fry for 25 minutes, then turn sweet potatoes over and air-fry for 15 to 20 minutes. Cut in half to serve.

Fried Smashed Potatoes

One simple two-part technique — pre-boiling followed by smashing — prior to air-frying results in the most incredible potato dish, replete with ultra-crispy edges and creamy centers. You can vary the seasonings to your heart's content, but plain salt and pepper is really all you need.

TIPS

Choose potatoes that are no more than 2 inches (5 cm) in diameter.

An equal amount of small yellow-fleshed potatoes can be used in place of the red-skinned potatoes.

8	small red-skinned potatoes (about 12 oz/375 g total)	8
	Salt	
2 tbsp	olive oil, divided	30 mL
	Freshly cracked black pepper	
	Minced fresh parsley (optional)	

1. Place potatoes in a medium saucepan and add enough water to cover by 1 inch (2.5 cm). Add $1/2$ tsp (2 mL) salt. Bring to a boil over medium-high heat, then reduce heat to low and boil gently for 25 to 30 minutes or until very tender. Drain and let cool for 10 minutes.

2. Preheat air fryer to 390°F (200°C).

3. On work surface, lightly press down on each potato with your palm or a pancake turner to smash to about $1/2$ inch (1 cm) thickness, keeping each potato in one piece. Brush tops with half the oil and season with salt and pepper.

4. Using a pancake turner, transfer half the potatoes to air fryer basket, placing them oiled side down and spacing them evenly. Brush with half the remaining oil and season with salt and pepper. Air-fry for 13 to 17 minutes or until browned and crispy at edges. Serve immediately, sprinkled with parsley (if using). Repeat with the remaining potatoes and oil, seasoning with salt and pepper.

Variation

Parmesan Fried Smashed Potatoes: Open basket during the last 3 minutes of cooking and sprinkle each potato with 2 tsp (10 mL) grated Parmesan cheese (about $1/3$ cup/75 mL total).

Scalloped Potatoes

Introducing scalloped potatoes, simplified. No flour, no butter and no fuss, just rich flavor, tender potatoes and a golden-brown top.

TIP

An equal amount of yellow-fleshed potatoes can be used in place of the russet potatoes.

- Preheat air fryer to 390°F (200°C)
- 6-inch (15 cm) round metal cake pan, sprayed with nonstick cooking spray

2	medium russet potatoes (about 10 oz/300 g total), peeled and thinly sliced	2
$\frac{1}{4}$ tsp	salt	1 mL
$\frac{1}{8}$ tsp	freshly cracked black pepper	0.5 mL
$\frac{3}{4}$ cup	heavy or whipping (35%) cream	175 mL

1. Layer half the potatoes in prepared pan, overlapping as they are layered. Season with half the salt and pepper. Layer the remaining potatoes on top and season with the remaining salt and pepper. Pour cream over potatoes. Cover pan tightly with foil, sealing edges.

2. Place pan in air fryer basket. Air-fry for 20 minutes. Open basket and carefully remove foil. Air-fry for 5 to 8 minutes or until potatoes are golden brown and tender when pierced with a fork. Transfer to a wire rack and let cool for at least 10 minutes before serving.

TIP

Air fryers become very hot, especially when heated to maximum temperature. Use oven pads or mitts when touching the appliance and when opening and closing the basket.

Variations

Garlic Scalloped Potatoes: Add $\frac{1}{2}$ tsp (2 mL) garlic powder. Sprinkle half over the first layer of potatoes and sprinkle the remaining half over the second layer.

Cheesy Scalloped Potatoes: Add $\frac{1}{2}$ cup (125 mL) shredded cheese (such as Cheddar, Swiss or Monterey Jack). Sprinkle half the cheese over the first layer of potatoes and sprinkle the remaining cheese over the second layer.

Parmesan Scalloped Potatoes: Add $\frac{1}{4}$ cup (60 mL) freshly grated Parmesan cheese. Sprinkle half the Parmesan over the first layer of potatoes and sprinkle the remaining Parmesan over the second layer.

Easy Garlic Roasted Potatoes

No trip to the supermarket required: this restaurant-worthy side dish is made with staple pantry items. Mayonnaise is the secret ingredient, contributing a rich flavor and optimal browning in one easy step.

TIPS

You can use 2 cloves garlic, minced, in place of the garlic powder.

An equal weight of small red-skinned potatoes can be used in place of the yellow-fleshed potatoes.

• Preheat air fryer to 360°F (180°C)

1½ tbsp	mayonnaise	22 mL
1 tsp	garlic powder	5 mL
¼ tsp	salt	1 mL
⅛ tsp	freshly cracked black pepper	0.5 mL
12 oz	small yellow-fleshed potatoes, quartered	375 g
	Chopped fresh parsley (optional)	

1. In a medium bowl, stir together mayonnaise, garlic powder, salt and pepper. Add potatoes, tossing to coat.

2. Spread potatoes in an even layer in air fryer basket. Air-fry for 10 minutes, then shake the basket.

3. Increase temperature to 390°F (200°C) and air-fry for 5 minutes, then shake the basket again. Air-fry for 4 to 8 minutes or until potatoes are golden brown and fork-tender. Serve immediately, sprinkled with parsley, if desired.

Potatoes Bravas

A splash of sherry vinegar and a sprinkle of smoked paprika transform everyday potatoes into a classic Spanish side dish.

TIP

An equal weight of yellow-fleshed potatoes can be used in place of the russet potato.

- Preheat air fryer to 360°F (180°C)

1	large russet potato (about 12 oz/375 g), peeled and cut into 1-inch (2.5 cm) cubes	1
1	small onion, cut into 1-inch (2.5 cm) pieces	1
1½ tbsp	olive oil	22 mL
1 tsp	smoked paprika	5 mL
½ tsp	salt	2 mL
⅛ tsp	freshly cracked black pepper	0.5 mL
1½ tsp	sherry vinegar	7 mL

1. In a medium bowl, toss together potato and onion. Pour in oil and season with paprika, salt and pepper, tossing to coat.

2. Spread potato mixture in an even layer in air fryer basket. Air-fry for 10 minutes, then shake the basket.

3. Increase temperature to 390°F (200°C) and air-fry for 5 minutes, then shake the basket again. Air-fry for 4 to 8 minutes or until potatoes are fork-tender. Serve immediately, drizzled with vinegar.

Variations

Regular paprika or ground cumin can be used in place of the smoked paprika.

An equal amount of red wine vinegar or cider vinegar can be used in place of the sherry vinegar.

Crispy-Top Parmesan Mashed Potatoes

Parmesan's flavorful charms shine in this homey side dish, both in the potatoes and on top in the crisp, buttery topping.

TIPS

Packaged mashed potatoes can often be found in the refrigerated deli or produce section of the supermarket. This works equally well with leftover homemade mashed potatoes.

The potatoes can be assembled through step 3 up to 1 day in advance. Cover and refrigerate until ready to air-fry. Increase the air-frying time by 3 to 4 minutes.

- Preheat air fryer to 360°F (180°C)
- 6-inch (15 cm) round metal cake pan, sprayed with nonstick cooking spray

1¾ cups	mashed potatoes (packaged or homemade)	425 mL
½ cup	shredded Italian cheese blend	125 mL
6 tbsp	freshly grated Parmesan cheese, divided	90 mL
	Salt and freshly cracked black pepper	
3 tbsp	panko (Japanese bread crumbs)	45 mL
1 tbsp	butter, melted	15 mL

1. In a medium bowl, stir together potatoes, Italian cheese blend and 4 tbsp (60 mL) Parmesan. Season to taste with salt and pepper.
2. Spread potatoes in prepared pan, smoothing top.
3. In a small bowl, stir together panko, the remaining Parmesan and butter. Sprinkle evenly over potatoes.
4. Place pan in air fryer basket. Air-fry for 16 to 20 minutes or until potatoes are heated through and topping is golden brown. Serve immediately.

Variation

Crispy Blue Cheese Mashed Potatoes: Replace the Italian cheese blend with ⅓ cup (75 mL) crumbled blue cheese.

Potato Croquettes

Creamy mashed potatoes, enriched with two cheeses, chives and a potato-chip coating, hold their own as the star of this delectable dish.

TIP

Packaged mashed potatoes can often be found in the refrigerated deli or produce section of the supermarket. You'll need a 24-oz (750 g) package for this recipe. This works equally well with leftover homemade mashed potatoes.

Variations

Jalapeño Croquettes: Replace the chives with ¼ cup (60 mL) chopped drained canned jalapeño peppers.

Bacon Croquettes: Replace the chives with ½ cup (125 mL) crumbled cooked bacon or ready-to-use bacon pieces.

- Large rimmed baking sheet, lined with parchment paper

8 oz	kettle-cooked potato chips, crushed	250 g
2½ cups	mashed potatoes (packaged or homemade)	625 mL
1½ cups	shredded sharp (old) Cheddar cheese	375 mL
½ cup	freshly grated Parmesan cheese	125 mL
3 tbsp	minced fresh chives	45 mL
¼ tsp	salt	1 mL
¼ tsp	freshly ground black pepper	1 mL
	Nonstick cooking spray	

1. Spread crushed chips in a shallow dish.
2. In a large bowl, combine potatoes, Cheddar cheese, Parmesan cheese, chives, salt and pepper, stirring until completely blended. Form potato mixture into 1-inch (2.5 cm) balls.
3. Working with 1 potato ball at a time, roll in chips to coat, pressing gently to adhere. Place balls on prepared baking sheet, loosely cover and refrigerate for 20 to 30 minutes. (Discard any excess chips.)
4. Preheat air fryer to 390°F (200°C).
5. Remove 9 to 10 balls from the refrigerator and spray all over with cooking spray. Place in a single layer in air fryer basket, leaving space in between. Air-fry for 5 to 8 minutes or until coating is golden brown and insides are hot. Serve immediately.
6. Repeat step 5 with the remaining potato balls.

Potato Taquitos

MAKES 4 SERVINGS

The nutty flavor of corn tortillas plays well with the spicy, cheesy potato filling of these taquitos. Enjoy them as a side, snack or appetizer — anytime.

TIP

Packaged mashed potatoes can often be found in the refrigerated deli or produce section of the supermarket. You'll need half a 24-oz (750 g) package for this recipe. This works equally well with leftover homemade mashed potatoes.

Variations

Add 2 tbsp (30 mL) chopped fresh cilantro or $1/4$ cup (60 mL) finely chopped green onions in step 1.

Other varieties of shredded cheese, such as provolone or Cheddar, can be used in place of the pepper Jack.

Flour tortillas can be used in place of the corn tortillas.

• Preheat air fryer to 390°F (200°C)

1¼ cups	mashed potatoes (packaged or homemade)	300 mL
1 cup	shredded pepper Jack cheese	250 mL
1 tsp	ground cumin	5 mL
	Salt and freshly cracked black pepper	
12	6-inch (15 cm) corn tortillas	12
	Nonstick cooking spray	
	Salsa	

1. In a medium bowl, stir together potatoes, cheese and cumin until blended. Season to taste with salt and pepper.

2. Place half the tortillas between 2 damp paper towels. Microwave on High for 15 to 30 seconds or until warm and pliable.

3. Working with 1 tortilla at a time, spread about 3 tbsp (45 mL) potato mixture onto tortilla to within $1/2$ inch (1 cm) of the edge. Roll into a tube and place, seam side down, in air fryer basket. Repeat with 5 more tortillas and potato filling, spacing tortillas evenly. Spray with cooking spray.

4. Air-fry for 8 to 11 minutes or until golden brown and edges appear crispy. Serve immediately with salsa for dipping.

5. Repeat steps 2 to 4 with the remaining tortillas and potato filling.

Double-Cheese Hasselback Potatoes

Hasselback potatoes may look complex, but preparing them is little more than straightforward slicing followed by some seasoning. Air-frying guarantees that they will be cooked to perfection.

TIPS

The Cheddar cheese slices should be roughly 1½ to 2 inches (4 to 5 cm) square. Do not worry about cutting the exact number of slits in the potatoes for the cheese.

Air fryers become very hot, especially when heated to maximum temperature. Use oven pads or mitts when touching the appliance and when opening and closing the basket.

• Preheat air fryer to 390°F (200°C)

2	medium russet or yellow-fleshed potatoes (each about 6 oz/175 g), peeled	2
2 tbsp	butter, melted, divided	30 mL
	Salt and freshly cracked black pepper	
4 oz	sharp (old) Cheddar cheese	125 g
2 tbsp	freshly grated Parmesan cheese	30 mL
1 tbsp	minced fresh chives	15 mL

1. Slice each potato crosswise at $\frac{1}{8}$-inch (3 mm) intervals, cutting to within $\frac{1}{4}$ inch (0.5 cm) of the bottom. Brush with half the butter and season with salt and pepper.

2. Place potatoes, cut side up, in air fryer basket. Air-fry for 20 minutes.

3. Meanwhile, cut the Cheddar cheese into 30 small, very thin slices.

4. Open basket and, using tongs, carefully transfer potatoes to a cutting board. Insert a piece of Cheddar into each slice in the potatoes. Drizzle potatoes with the remaining butter and sprinkle with Parmesan cheese and chives.

5. Using tongs, return potatoes to basket. Air-fry for 5 to 7 minutes or until potatoes are tender and cheese is melted and bubbly. Serve immediately.

Variation

Other varieties of shredded cheese, such as pepper Jack, Swiss, Gouda or provolone, can be used in place of the Cheddar.

Stuffed Potato Skins

This rendition of an appetizer classic is supremely satisfying — especially because making a batch doesn't require a crowd!

TIPS

If desired, reserve the scooped cooked potato to make mashed potatoes for any of the recipes in this chapter that call for packaged or homemade mashed potatoes.

Air fryers become very hot, especially when heated to maximum temperature. Use oven pads or mitts when touching the appliance and when opening and closing the basket.

• Preheat air fryer to 390°F (200°C)

1	large Air Fryer Baked Potato (page 118), cooled slightly	1
	Nonstick cooking spray	
	Salt and freshly cracked black pepper	
½ cup	shredded Cheddar cheese	125 mL
3 tbsp	crumbled cooked bacon	45 mL
3 tbsp	sour cream	45 mL
2 tbsp	minced chives or green onions	30 mL

1. Halve potato lengthwise. Scoop out potato flesh, leaving a ¼-inch (0.5 cm) thick shell (reserve scooped potato for another use). Quarter each potato skin half.

2. Spray potato shells with cooking spray and season to taste with salt and pepper. Arrange shells, skin side down, in a single layer in air fryer basket (it is okay if they are touching). Air-fry for 12 to 16 minutes or until golden brown and crispy.

3. Open basket and sprinkle shells with cheese and bacon. Air-fry for 1 to 2 minutes or until cheese is melted. Transfer potato shells to a platter, dollop with sour cream and sprinkle with chives. Serve immediately.

Variations

Vegan Potato Skins: Omit the bacon. Use Cheddar-style vegan cheese in place of the Cheddar cheese, and use nondairy sour cream in place of the sour cream.

Other varieties of shredded cheese, such as pepper Jack, Gouda or provolone, can be used in place of the Cheddar.

Loaded Pizza Potato Tots

Although these over-the-top tots teeter on the side of decadence, everyone will be too busy licking their plates to worry.

TIP

Air fryers become very hot, especially when heated to maximum temperature. Use oven pads or mitts when touching the appliance and when opening and closing the basket.

- Preheat air fryer to 390°F (200°C)
- 6-inch (15 cm) round metal cake pan, sprayed with nonstick cooking spray

1⅓ cups	frozen potato tots	325 mL
3 tbsp	marinara sauce	45 mL
⅔ cup	shredded Italian cheese blend	150 mL
8	slices pepperoni, halved	8

1. Arrange potato tots in prepared pan, spacing them evenly.
2. Place pan in air fryer basket. Air-fry for 17 to 21 minutes or until golden brown.
3. Open basket and dollop tots with marinara sauce. Using a spoon, gently spread sauce over tots. Sprinkle with cheese and pepperoni.
4. Air-fry for 4 to 5 minutes or until cheese is melted.

Variations

Loaded Nacho Tots: Replace the marinara sauce with an equal amount of thick and chunky salsa. Use Cheddar or pepper Jack cheese in place of the Italian cheese blend. Omit the pepperoni. If desired, top with 1 tbsp (15 mL) sour cream and 1 tbsp (15 mL) finely chopped green onions.

Other favorite pizza toppings, such as cooked crumbled Italian sausage, chopped cooked ham, crumbled cooked bacon, chopped onions or sliced olives can be added or used in place of the pepperoni.

Vegan Mains

Buffalo Cauliflower Wings

MAKES 2 SERVINGS

This plant-based play on wings features plenty of authentic Buffalo flavor, but the cauliflower "drumsticks" are what set the dish apart. Warning: the meat eaters in the room will devour these, too.

TIP

One medium head of cauliflower will yield approximately 3 cups (750 mL) florets.

• Preheat air fryer to 390°F (200°C)

¾ cup	all-purpose flour	175 mL
¾ cup	plain nondairy milk (such as almond, hemp, cashew or soy)	175 mL
1 tsp	salt	5 mL
¼ tsp	freshly ground black pepper	1 mL
1	medium head cauliflower, cut into medium-sized florets (leave some stem attached)	1
	Nonstick cooking spray	
⅓ cup	vegan Buffalo wing sauce	75 mL
1 tbsp	vegan margarine	15 mL

1. In a large bowl, whisk together flour, milk, salt and pepper until blended and smooth. Add cauliflower, gently tossing to coat.

2. Using a slotted spoon, lift cauliflower florets from batter, shaking off excess, and place in air fryer basket. Arrange in an even layer (florets may overlap slightly). Spray with cooking spray.

3. Air-fry for 20 minutes. Shake basket. Air-fry for 5 to 10 minutes or until deep golden brown.

4. Meanwhile, in a small saucepan set over medium heat, combine wing sauce and margarine. Cook, stirring, until margarine is melted and mixture comes to a low boil. Remove from heat.

5. Transfer cauliflower to a medium bowl. Pour in sauce and toss to coat. Serve immediately.

Variation

Gluten-Free Buffalo Cauliflower Wings: Replace the all-purpose flour with a gluten-free all-purpose flour blend.

Eggplant Steaks with Tahini and Pomegranate

MAKES 2 SERVINGS

Despite the modern assemblage of flavors, these eggplant steaks, drizzled with tahini and flecked with pomegranate jewels, taste like comfort food.

TIP

Reserve the remaining eggplant for another use, such as soups or stir-fries.

• Preheat air fryer to 390°F (200°C)

1	eggplant (about 1 lb/ 500 g), stem trimmed	1
	Nonstick cooking spray	
½ tsp	salt, divided	2 mL
3 tbsp	tahini	45 mL
1 tbsp	freshly squeezed lemon juice	15 mL
⅛ tsp	freshly cracked black pepper	0.5 mL
½ cup	pomegranate seeds	125 mL
2 tbsp	chopped fresh mint	30 mL

1. Position eggplant on a cutting board with the stem side up; using a large knife, cut two 1-inch (2.5 cm) thick slices from the largest part of the eggplant; reserve the remaining eggplant for another use.

2. Spray both sides of eggplant steaks with cooking spray. Sprinkle with ¼ tsp (1 mL) salt, dividing evenly.

3. Place steaks in air fryer basket, overlapping slightly if needed. Air-fry for 12 to 16 minutes or until browned in multiple spots and very tender when pierced with a fork.

4. Meanwhile, in a small bowl, combine tahini, lemon juice, the remaining salt and pepper.

5. Serve eggplant drizzled with tahini sauce and sprinkled with pomegranate seeds and mint.

Crispy Cauliflower Steaks

MAKES 2 SERVINGS

Cauliflower takes to high heat beautifully, the air fryer concentrating its natural sweetness. The results are crispy, caramelized and irresistible.

TIP

Air fryers become very hot, especially when heated to maximum temperature. Use oven pads or mitts when touching the appliance and when opening and closing the basket.

• Preheat air fryer to 390°F (200°C)

1	medium head cauliflower, trimmed, core intact	1
¼ cup	vegan mayonnaise	60 mL
3 tbsp	water	45 mL
⅛ tsp	salt	0.5 mL
⅛ tsp	freshly cracked black pepper	0.5 mL
⅓ cup	all-purpose flour	75 mL
1 cup	panko (Japanese bread crumbs)	250 mL
3 tbsp	nutritional yeast	45 mL
	Nonstick cooking spray	

Suggested Accompaniments

Chopped fresh parsley or chives

Warmed marinara sauce

Prepared olive or sun-dried tomato tapenade

1. Position cauliflower on a cutting board with the core side down; using a large knife and starting in the center, cut four ½-inch (1 cm) thick slices from the largest part of the head to make "steaks"; reserve the remaining cauliflower for another use.

2. In a large shallow dish, whisk together mayonnaise, water, salt and pepper.

3. Spread flour on a large plate. On another large plate, combine panko and nutritional yeast; spread into a single layer.

Variation

Gluten-Free Crispy Cauliflower Steaks: Replace the all-purpose flour with a gluten-free all-purpose flour blend and replace the panko with crushed gluten-free corn flakes cereal.

4. Dredge a cauliflower steak in flour; shake off excess. Dip in mayonnaise mixture, then press into panko mixture, using your hands to fully coat the steak. Repeat with a second steak, flour, mayonnaise mixture and panko mixture.

5. Place steaks in air fryer basket and spray generously with cooking spray. Air-fry for 12 to 16 minutes or until steaks are golden brown and fork-tender. Serve immediately with any of the suggested accompaniments, as desired.

6. Repeat steps 4 and 5 with the remaining cauliflower steaks, flour, mayonnaise mixture and panko mixture. Discard any remaining flour, mayonnaise mixture and panko mixture.

Hearts of Palm "Crab" Cakes

Canned hearts of palm — made with the crunchy vegetable harvested from the centers of cabbage palm trees — have a delicious secret: when shredded, they have a texture and taste that is remarkably like crabmeat. Making them into crunchy "crab" cakes is the natural next step!

TIP

Spraying the patties with a light coating of nonstick cooking spray helps them achieve a light, crispy, crunchy texture. Don't skip this step!

- Preheat air fryer to 375°F (180°C)

1	can (14 to 15 oz/398 to 425 mL) hearts of palm, drained and rinsed	1
$\frac{1}{4}$ cup	vegan mayonnaise	60 mL
1 tsp	Old Bay or other seafood seasoning	5 mL
$\frac{1}{8}$ tsp	salt	0.5 mL
$\frac{1}{8}$ tsp	freshly cracked black pepper	0.5 mL
$\frac{1}{4}$ cup	finely chopped green onions	60 mL
1 cup	panko (Japanese bread crumbs), divided	250 mL
	Nonstick cooking spray	

Suggested Accompaniments

Lemon wedges

Chopped fresh parsley

Cocktail sauce

1. Thinly slice hearts of palm lengthwise; cut slices crosswise into ¾-inch (2 cm) lengths. Transfer to a medium bowl and, using your fingers, gently press and break apart into shreds.

2. In another medium bowl, whisk together mayonnaise, Old Bay seasoning, salt and pepper until well blended. Gently stir in hearts of palm and green onions until well combined, being careful not to overmix.

Hot air and steam will release from the air fryer throughout the cooking cycle. If your face is in close proximity to the appliance during the cooking cycle or when you are opening the basket, you risk being scalded by the release of accumulated steam.

3. Sprinkle half the panko over hearts of palm mixture and mix in gently but thoroughly (do not mash). Form into four ¾-inch (2 cm) thick patties.

4. Spread the remaining panko in a small dish. Dredge patties in panko, pressing gently to adhere. As they are dredged, place patties in air fryer basket, spacing them evenly. Spray with cooking spray. Discard any excess panko.

5. Air-fry for 8 to 12 minutes or until golden brown. Serve immediately with any of the suggested accompaniments, as desired.

Variation

Gluten-Free Hearts of Palm "Crab" Cakes: Replace the panko with an equal amount of gluten-free bread crumbs or crushed gluten-free crackers.

Mediterranean Stuffed Sweet Potatoes

Drawing flavor inspiration from the Mediterranean region, this satisfying main dish makes dinner easy and enticing in one fell swoop.

TIP

Air fryers become very hot, especially when heated to maximum temperature. Use oven pads or mitts when touching the appliance and when opening and closing the basket.

Variations

An equal amount of fresh mint or cilantro can be used in place of the parsley.

Russet potatoes can be used in place of the sweet potatoes; reduce the air-frying time in step 2 to 20 minutes.

- Preheat air fryer to 390°F (200°C)

2	medium-large sweet potatoes (about 12 oz/375 g total)	2
	Nonstick cooking spray	
	Salt and freshly cracked black pepper	
1	can (14 to 15 oz/398 to 425 mL) chickpeas, drained and rinsed	1
¼ cup	hummus	60 mL
2 tbsp	water	30 mL
1 cup	cherry or grape tomatoes, halved	250 mL
¼ cup	packed fresh parsley, chopped	60 mL

1. Spray potatoes with cooking spray and season to taste with salt and pepper. Using a fork, pierce all sides of potatoes.

2. Place potatoes in air fryer basket. Air-fry for 25 minutes. Open basket and add chickpeas, spreading them in and around sweet potatoes. Spray chickpeas with cooking spray. Air-fry for 15 to 20 minutes or until sweet potatoes are very tender.

3. Meanwhile, whisk together hummus, water, ⅛ tsp (0.5 mL) salt and ⅛ tsp (0.5 mL) pepper until blended and smooth.

4. Transfer sweet potatoes to dinner plates and let cool for 5 minutes. Slit potatoes lengthwise and press to open. Spoon air-fried chickpeas and tomatoes into the center of each sweet potato. Drizzle with hummus sauce and sprinkle with parsley.

Southwestern Falafel

With a few simple swaps and a few delicious detours, Middle Eastern falafel takes a bold, Tex-Mex turn.

TIPS

If you can find only larger 19-oz (540 mL) cans of beans, you will need about 1½ cups (375 mL) drained.

For easier shaping, use moist hands to form the bean mixture into patties.

- Preheat air fryer to 390°F (200°C)
- Food processor

¾ cup	coarsely crushed tortilla chips	175 mL
1	can (14 to 15 oz/398 to 425 mL) pinto beans, drained and rinsed, divided	1
½ cup	packed fresh cilantro leaves	125 mL
1 tsp	ground cumin	5 mL
⅓ cup	salsa	75 mL
	Nonstick cooking spray	

Suggested Accompaniments

Small flour tortillas

Guacamole

Plain Greek yogurt or sour cream

Salsa

1. In food processor, pulse chips into crumbs. Add half the beans, cilantro, cumin and salsa; pulse until a stiff, chunky purée forms.

2. Transfer purée to a medium bowl and stir in the remaining beans. Form into eight ½-inch (1 cm) thick patties. Place patties in air fryer basket, spacing them evenly, and spray with cooking spray.

3. Air-fry for 8 to 12 minutes or until patties are crispy on the outside and hot in the center. Serve with any of the suggested accompaniments, as desired.

Variation

An equal amount of black beans can be used in place of the pinto beans.

Poblano Peppers with Black Bean and Corn Risotto Stuffing

The mild zing of poblano peppers in this dish is complemented by an earthy, hearty filling. Choose the straightest chiles you can find — they are easier to peel and stuff.

TIP

For a short-cut, purchase frozen cooked rice or make extra rice when you're cooking another recipe, then freeze in airtight containers to have on hand; let thaw before using.

- Preheat air fryer to 390°F (200°C)

4	medium poblano peppers	4
1 cup	cooled cooked white or brown rice	250 mL
1 cup	black bean and corn salsa	250 mL
¼ cup	finely chopped green onions	60 mL
1 cup	shredded Cheddar-style vegan cheese, divided	250 mL
	Salt and freshly cracked black pepper	

1. Cut peppers in half lengthwise; scoop out and discard seeds, leaving stems intact. Place peppers, skin side up, in air fryer basket, spacing them evenly.

2. Air-fry for 10 to 12 minutes or until skins blister and darken in spots. Transfer peppers to a sheet of foil; lift foil up and around peppers, completely enclosing them. Let stand for 10 minutes or until cool enough to handle. While warm, lift, peel off and discard skins (use the tip of a knife, if necessary). Let peppers cool completely.

TIPS

If black bean and corn salsa is not available, make your own by combining $\frac{2}{3}$ cup (150 mL) salsa, $\frac{1}{4}$ cup (60 mL) rinsed drained canned black beans and 2 tbsp (30 mL) thawed frozen corn.

It will take 2 to 3 green onions (depending on size) to measure $\frac{1}{4}$ cup (60 mL) chopped.

3. In a medium bowl, combine rice, salsa, green onions and half the vegan cheese; season to taste with salt and pepper. Fill cooled roasted peppers with stuffing.

4. Transfer filled peppers to air fryer basket and sprinkle filling with the remaining vegan cheese. Air-fry for 8 to 11 minutes or until filling is heated and cheese is melted. Serve immediately.

Variations

An equal amount of mozzarella-style vegan cheese can be used in place of the Cheddar-style vegan cheese.

An equal amount of cooked quinoa can be used in place of the rice.

Spiced White Bean Eggplant Boats

MAKES 1 SERVING

The eggplant containers are as nutritious and delicious as the Moroccan-inspired filling with these hearty dinner "boats."

TIP

Canned chickpeas can be used in place of the white beans.

- Preheat air fryer to 390°F (200°C)

1	Japanese or Italian eggplant (about 8 oz/250 g), trimmed and halved lengthwise	1
¼ tsp	salt	1 mL
	Nonstick cooking spray	
½ cup	rinsed drained canned white beans (such as Great Northern, navy or cannellini)	125 mL
3 tbsp	thick and chunky marinara sauce	45 mL
2 tbsp	chopped fresh cilantro, divided	30 mL
¼ tsp	pumpkin pie spice	1 mL
⅛ tsp	freshly ground black pepper	0.5 mL

1. Scoop out centers of eggplant, leaving ¼-inch (0.5 cm) thick shells. Sprinkle cut sides of eggplant halves with salt and spray with cooking spray.

2. Place eggplant halves, cut side down, in air fryer basket, spacing them evenly. Air-fry for 8 minutes.

3. Meanwhile, in a medium bowl, coarsely mash beans with a fork. Stir in marinara sauce, half the cilantro, pumpkin pie spice and pepper.

Air fryers become very hot, especially when heated to maximum temperature. Use oven pads or mitts when touching the appliance and when opening and closing the basket.

4. Open basket and, using tongs, transfer eggplant halves to work surface; fill with bean mixture, dividing evenly. Return stuffed eggplant halves to air fryer basket, spacing evenly.

5. Air-fry for 6 to 9 minutes or until eggplant is tender and stuffing is heated through. Top with the remaining cilantro.

Variations

An equal amount of ground allspice or ground cinnamon can be used in place of the pumpkin pie spice.

An equal amount of chopped fresh parsley leaves can be used in place of the cilantro.

For spicier eggplant boats, use an equal amount of thick and chunky salsa (with the heat level of your choice) in place of the marinara sauce.

Hummus and Avocado Quesadillas

This nutritious take on quesadillas — loaded with creamy avocado and spicy hummus — is my idea of easy California living.

TIPS

For gluten-free quesidillas, use gluten-free flour tortillas.

Any other variety of hummus can be used in place of the red pepper hummus.

- Preheat air fryer to 390°F (200°C)

4	6-inch (15 cm) flour tortillas	4
½ cup	red pepper hummus	125 mL
1	small Hass avocado, sliced	1
⅔ cup	shredded mozzarella-style vegan cheese	150 mL
1 tbsp	chopped fresh cilantro	15 mL
	Nonstick cooking spray	

1. Place 2 tortillas on work surface. Spread half the hummus on each tortilla, spreading to the edges. Top with avocado, vegan cheese and cilantro, dividing evenly. Top with the remaining tortillas, pressing down gently. Spray both sides with cooking spray.

2. Place 1 quesadilla in air fryer basket. Air-fry for 7 to 10 minutes or until cheese is melted and tortillas are golden brown. Transfer to a cutting board and cut into quarters. Repeat with the remaining quesadilla. Serve immediately.

Variation

An equal amount of Cheddar-style vegan cheese can be used in place of the mozzarella-style vegan cheese.

Blue Cheese–Stuffed Tomatoes (page 106)

Horseradish Roasted Root Vegetables (page 109)

Crispy-Top Parmesan Mashed Potatoes (page 124)

Double-Cheese Hasselback Potatoes (page 127)

Hearts of Palm "Crab" Cakes (page 136)

Tapenade and Tomato Pizzas (variation, page 145)

Puffed Egg Tarts (page 161)

Sriracha and Honey Crispy Cod (page 175)

Personal Pan Pizzas

Here, a quick crust made from store-bought pizza dough is spiffed up with a slather of sauce, a generous toss of nondairy cheese and a sprinkle of fresh basil. The air fryer cooks the pies to perfection!

TIP

Air fryers become very hot, especially when heated to maximum temperature. Use oven pads or mitts when touching the appliance and when opening and closing the basket.

- Preheat air fryer to 390°F (200°C)
- 6-inch (15 cm) round metal cake pan, sprayed with nonstick cooking spray

All-purpose flour

8 oz	pizza dough (thawed if frozen), divided	250 g
¼ cup	marinara sauce, divided	60 mL
1⅓ cups	shredded mozzarella-style vegan cheese, divided	325 mL
2 tbsp	shredded fresh basil, divided (optional)	30 mL

1. On a lightly floured work surface, cut pizza dough in half.
2. Press half of dough into bottom and sides of prepared pan. Spread with half the marinara sauce and top with half the vegan cheese.
3. Place pan in air fryer basket. Air-fry for 10 to 12 minutes or until crust is golden brown. Using a spatula, slide pizza out of pan onto a wire rack and let cool for 5 minutes before serving topped with half the basil (if using).
4. Repeat steps 2 and 3 with the remaining dough, marinara sauce, cheese and basil.

Variations

Tapenade and Tomato Pizzas: Replace the marinara sauce with an equal amount of vegan olive tapenade. Top with 4 to 5 thin slices of plum (Roma) tomatoes before sprinkling with cheese.

Winter Squash and Rosemary Pizzas: Replace the marinara sauce with 3 tbsp (45 mL) thawed frozen winter squash purée or canned pumpkin purée (not pie filling) mixed with 1 tbsp (15 mL) olive oil, 1 tbsp (15 mL) nutritional yeast and 1 tsp (5 mL) chopped fresh rosemary, seasoned to taste with salt and pepper.

Meaty Quinoa Burgers

Canned beets are the stealth ingredient here, adding depth of flavor (but no beet taste — I promise!), moisture and a deep, "meaty" burger color. The combination of quinoa and beans in these plant-based burgers rivals the nutrition of meat burgers (think: high protein, iron and other minerals), but without the saturated fat and cholesterol.

TIPS

You can used fresh cooked or packaged cooked beets instead of canned in this recipe. Just make sure they are soft-cooked, not tender-crisp, so they purée.

If you can find only larger 19-oz (540 mL) cans of beans, you will need about $1\frac{1}{2}$ cups (375 mL) drained.

Variation

An equal amount of black beans can be used in place of the kidney beans.

- Preheat air fryer to 390°F (200°C)
- Food processor

$\frac{2}{3}$ cup	drained canned sliced beets, patted dry	150 mL
1	can (14 to 15 oz/398 to 425 mL) light red kidney beans, drained and rinsed, divided	1
2 tsp	chili powder	10 mL
1 tsp	ground cumin	5 mL
$\frac{1}{4}$ tsp	salt	1 mL
$\frac{1}{4}$ tsp	freshly cracked black pepper	1 mL
$\frac{3}{4}$ cup	cooled cooked quinoa	175 mL
	Nonstick cooking spray	

Suggested Accompaniments

Sliced tomatoes

Sliced avocado

Lettuce or spinach leaves

Hamburger buns, split and toasted

1. In food processor, combine beets, half the beans, chili powder, cumin, salt and pepper; pulse until a chunky purée forms.

2. In a medium bowl, coarsely mash the remaining beans with a fork. Add beet purée and quinoa, stirring until well blended. Form into two $\frac{3}{4}$-inch (2 cm) thick patties.

3. Place patties in air fryer basket, spacing them evenly. Spray with cooking spray. Air-fry for 8 minutes. Using a pancake turner, turn patties over. Air-fry for 4 to 6 minutes or until crispy on the outside and hot in the center.

4. Serve with any of the suggested accompaniments, as desired.

Vegetables and Tempeh with Black Bean Garlic Sauce

Here, the spicy, salty and umami flavors of black bean and garlic sauce deliver instant Asian oomph to vegetables and tempeh.

TIPS

Black bean and garlic sauce is a savory condiment made from fermented black soy beans, garlic and rice wine. It is available in the Asian foods section of well-stocked supermarkets alongside soy sauce, or at Asian grocery stores.

Air fryers become very hot, especially when heated to maximum temperature. Use oven pads or mitts when touching the appliance and when opening and closing the basket.

• Preheat air fryer to 390°F (200°C)

2 tbsp	black bean and garlic sauce	30 mL
1 tbsp	water	15 mL
1	medium zucchini, halved lengthwise and cut into ½-inch (1 cm) thick slices	1
1	Japanese eggplant, halved lengthwise and cut into ½-inch (1 cm) thick slices	1
1	orange or red bell pepper, cut into 8 pieces	1
	Nonstick cooking spray	
8 oz	tempeh, cut crosswise into 12 strips	250 g

1. In a large bowl, whisk together black bean sauce and water. Reserve 1 tbsp (15 mL) sauce mixture. Add zucchini, eggplant and orange pepper to the remaining sauce in bowl, gently tossing to combine.

2. Transfer vegetables to air fryer basket and spread in an even layer (do not clean bowl). Spray vegetables with cooking spray. Air-fry for 12 minutes, shaking basket once halfway through.

3. Meanwhile, in same large bowl used for vegetables, gently toss tempeh with the reserved sauce.

4. Add tempeh to air fryer basket, nestling it in between vegetables. Air-fry for 5 to 8 minutes or until vegetables are tender and tempeh is browned.

Garlicky Broccoli Rabe and Tempeh

Tempeh, made with fermented soy beans, is a great option for anyone who has difficulty digesting tofu and other plant-based proteins. The fermentation process leads to greater ease in digestion of proteins, as well as better absorption of minerals.

TIP

Nutritional yeast flakes are available in health food stores and the health food section of well-stocked supermarkets.

• Preheat air fryer to 390°F (200°C)

8 oz	broccoli rabe, tough, fibrous stems removed (keep tender stems)	250 g
8 oz	tempeh, cut crosswise into 12 strips	250 g
1 tbsp	olive oil	15 mL
1 tbsp	nutritional yeast	15 mL
½ tsp	garlic powder	2 mL
¼ tsp	salt	1 mL
⅛ tsp	freshly cracked black pepper	0.5 mL

1. Chop broccoli rabe into 1-inch (2.5 cm) long pieces.
2. In a medium bowl, toss together broccoli rabe, tempeh, oil, nutritional yeast, garlic powder, salt and pepper. Spread in an even layer in air fryer basket.
3. Air-fry for 10 to 12 minutes or until broccoli rabe stems are tender and leaves are crisp, and tempeh is warmed through and browned at the edges. Serve immediately.

Variations

An equal amount of baby broccoli (Broccolini) can be used in place of the broccoli rabe.

You can use 8 oz (250 g) drained extra-firm tofu, cut into cubes or strips, in place of the tempeh.

Potato Chip–Crusted Tofu Sticks

You can forgo fish sticks without giving up the fun, the crunch and the opportunity for some ketchup dunking. Simply sub tofu for the fish, add a crispy coating of salt and vinegar–flavored potato chips and keep the Old Bay seasoning.

TIPS

It is imperative to use tofu labeled "extra-firm." Anything less than extra-firm (including tofu labeled "firm") contains too much water and will explode in the microwave.

If you prefer, you can drain tofu the traditional way (rather than the quick method in step 2). Wrap the block of tofu in four or five layers of paper towels. Place on a dinner plate. Cover with a second dinner plate. Place two or three heavy cans on top. Let drain for 30 minutes. Remove cans, plates and paper towels. Repeat the process once more. Cut tofu into sticks as directed.

1 lb	extra-firm tofu, packing water poured off	500 g
	Salt and freshly ground black pepper	
1 cup	finely crushed salt and vinegar–flavored kettle-style potato chips	250 mL
¼ cup	vegan mayonnaise	60 mL
2 tbsp	water	30 mL
2 tsp	Old Bay or other seafood seasoning	10 mL
	Nonstick cooking spray	

1. Cut tofu into 3- by 1-inch (7.5 by 2.5 cm) sticks that are ½ inch (1 cm) thick. (Depending on your block of tofu, the sticks may be a slightly different size.) Season lightly with salt and pepper.

2. Arrange sticks in a single layer on a microwave-safe plate. Microwave on High for 3 to 4 minutes or until surface of tofu appears dry. Remove from microwave and let cool slightly.

3. Preheat air fryer to 390°F (200°C).

4. Meanwhile, spread potato chips in a shallow dish.

5. In another shallow dish, whisk together mayonnaise, water and Old Bay seasoning.

6. Dip tofu sticks into mayonnaise mixture, shaking off excess, then in potato chips, pressing to adhere and shaking off excess. Discard any excess mayonnaise mixture and potato chip mixture.

7. Arrange sticks in a single layer in air fryer basket, spacing them evenly. Spray with cooking spray. Air-fry for 6 to 9 minutes or until coating is golden brown and tofu is heated through.

Tofu Kofta

Fragrant with lemon, as well as both savory and sweet spices, this plant-based riff on Middle Eastern kofta is a sure thing for everyone at the table.

TIPS

It is imperative to use tofu labeled "extra-firm." Anything less than extra-firm (including tofu labeled "firm") contains too much water and will explode in the microwave.

If you prefer, you can drain tofu the traditional way (rather than the quick method in step 1). Wrap the block of tofu in four or five layers of paper towels. Place on a dinner plate. Cover with a second dinner plate. Place two or three heavy cans on top. Let drain for 30 minutes. Remove cans, plates and paper towels. Repeat the process once more. Cut tofu into 1-inch (2.5 cm) cubes.

- Preheat air fryer to 390°F (200°C)

1 lb	extra-firm tofu, packing water poured off	500 g
2	lemons	2
1 tbsp	olive oil	15 mL
1½ tsp	pumpkin pie spice	7 mL
¾ tsp	ground cumin	3 mL
¼ tsp	salt	1 mL
⅛ tsp	freshly ground black pepper	0.5 mL

Suggested Accompaniments

Pita bread or naan

Chopped fresh cilantro or parsley

Chopped fresh tomatoes

Plain nondairy yogurt

1. Cut tofu into 1-inch (2.5 cm) cubes and arrange in a single layer on a microwave-safe plate. Microwave on High for 2 minutes. Stir tofu gently. Microwave on High for 1 to 2 minutes or until surface of tofu appears dry.

2. Cut one lemon in half crosswise. Squeeze enough juice to measure 1 tbsp (15 mL). In a medium bowl, combine lemon juice, oil, pumpkin pie spice, cumin, salt and pepper. Add tofu cubes and gently toss to coat. Let stand for 5 minutes.

TIP

Reserve any excess lemon juice for other uses; store in an airtight container in the refrigerator for up to 1 week.

STORAGE TIP

Store cooled tofu cubes in an airtight container in the refrigerator for up to 5 days.

3. Arrange tofu in a single layer in air fryer basket. Air-fry for 5 minutes, then shake the basket. Air-fry for another 5 minutes, then shake the basket again. Air-fry for 2 to 5 minutes or until tofu is golden brown and crispy.

4. Cut the remaining lemon into quarters. Serve tofu with lemon quarters and any of the suggested accompaniments, as desired.

Variations

Jerk Tofu Kebabs: Use an equal amount of salt-free jerk seasoning in place of the pumpkin pie spice and an equal amount of ground allspice in place of the cumin. Use fresh limes in place of the lemons.

Curry Tofu Kebabs: Use an equal amount of curry powder in place of the pumpkin pie spice and an equal amount of ground ginger in place of the cumin.

Eggs

Hard-Cooked Eggs

Hard-cooked eggs? Yes, your air fryer can do that, too! And it does it with ease and accuracy.

• Preheat air fryer to 300°F (150°C)

6	large eggs	6
	Ice water	

1. Arrange eggs in a single layer in air fryer basket. Air-fry for 13 minutes for a firm yolk (see variation).

2. Using tongs, transfer eggs to a medium bowl of ice water. Let eggs remain submersed in water for 20 to 30 minutes or until completely cool. Remove eggs from ice water. Use immediately or refrigerate until ready to serve.

Variation

For softer eggs to eat right away, air-fry for 7 minutes for a slightly runny yolk or 10 minutes for a medium-firm yolk. Skip transferring to ice water and enjoy hot.

Scotch Eggs

Scotch eggs are a gastropub delight: hard-cooked eggs that are swaddled in sausage meat before they are coated in bread crumbs and deep-fried to golden-brown perfection. This recipe, which replaces hot oil with hot air, is based on a version made by my Scotch-Irish grandmother.

STORAGE TIP

Store cooled Scotch eggs in an airtight container in the refrigerator for up to 3 days.

- Preheat air fryer to 360°F (180°C)

1 lb	Italian sausage (bulk or casings removed)	500 g
1 cup	dry bread crumbs, divided	250 mL
1	large egg, beaten	1
4	hard-cooked eggs (see page 154), peeled	4
	Nonstick cooking spray	

1. In a medium bowl, combine sausage, $1/3$ cup (75 mL) bread crumbs and beaten egg until blended. Divide into 4 equal portions.

2. Spread the remaining bread crumbs in a shallow dish.

3. Working with 1 hard-cooked egg at a time, wrap with 1 portion of sausage mixture, completely enclosing egg. Dredge in bread crumbs, pressing gently to adhere. As they are dredged, place eggs in air fryer basket, leaving space in between. Spray with cooking spray. Discard any excess bread crumbs.

4. Air-fry for 11 to 15 minutes or until golden brown and sausage is no longer pink. Using tongs, transfer eggs to a plate and let cool for at least 10 minutes before serving. Serve warm or chilled.

Variation

Gluten-Free Scotch Eggs: Replace the bread crumbs with an equal amount of gluten-free bread crumbs or crushed gluten-free crackers or corn flakes cereal, and make sure the sausage is gluten-free.

Air-Fried Omelet

MAKES 2 SERVINGS

Seasoned with nothing more than salt and pepper, then stuffed with cheese (or any additional ingredients that suit your fancy), this air-fryer take on an omelet works just as well for dinner as it does for breakfast.

TIPS

An equal amount of vegetable oil or olive oil can be used in place of the butter.

When adding fillings, use no more than 4 tbsp (60 mL) total.

Air fryers become very hot, especially when heated to maximum temperature. Use oven pads or mitts when touching the appliance and when opening and closing the basket.

- Preheat air fryer to 390°F (200°C)
- 6-inch (15 cm) round metal cake pan, sprayed with nonstick cooking spray

3	large eggs	3
⅛ tsp	salt	0.5 mL
Pinch	freshly ground black pepper	Pinch
2 tsp	butter, cut into small pieces	10 mL
½ cup	shredded cheese (such as Cheddar, Monterey Jack, Swiss or Gouda)	125 mL

Suggested Fillings (see tip)

¼ cup	chopped or crumbled cooked breakfast sausage, diced fully cooked smoked sausage or diced cooked ham	60 mL
2 to 3 tbsp	chopped roasted red bell peppers	30 to 45 mL
2 tbsp	salsa	30 mL
2 tbsp	crumbled cooked bacon	30 mL
	Chopped fresh herbs (such as parsley, chives, cilantro or rosemary)	

1. In a medium bowl, whisk together eggs, salt and pepper. Stir in any of the suggested fillings, as desired.
2. Place butter in prepared pan. Place pan in air fryer basket. Air-fry for 10 to 20 seconds or until butter is melted.
3. Open basket and pour egg mixture over butter. Air-fry for 3 to 5 minutes or until eggs are just set. Sprinkle with cheese. Using a spatula, transfer omelet to a plate, carefully folding omelet in half. Let stand for 1 minute to melt cheese. Serve immediately.

Egg Soufflé Bake

This air-fried version of a soufflé may not be traditional, but it is supremely satisfying — and nutritious, too. Great for breakfast or brunch, it is also ideal for a last-minute supper (just add salad or a cup of soup alongside).

TIPS

An equal amount of vegetable oil or olive oil can be used in place of the butter.

Choose a pancake mix that calls for the addition of eggs and milk, rather than a "complete" pancake mix that calls for only the addition of water or milk.

For a gluten-free soufflé, use a gluten-free pancake mix.

- Preheat air fryer to 390°F (200°C)
- Blender or food processor
- 6-inch (15 cm) round metal cake pan, sprayed with nonstick cooking spray

½ cup	pancake mix (see tip)	125 mL
3 tbsp	freshly grated Parmesan cheese	45 mL
⅛ tsp	freshly ground black pepper	0.5 mL
3	large eggs	3
¾ cup	milk	175 mL
2 tsp	butter, cut into small pieces	10 mL

1. In blender, process pancake mix, cheese, pepper, eggs and milk until blended and smooth.

2. Place butter in prepared pan. Place pan in air fryer basket. Air-fry for 10 to 20 seconds or until butter is melted.

3. Open basket and pour egg mixture over butter. Air-fry for 18 to 22 minutes or until puffed and golden brown. Serve immediately.

Variation

After adding the egg mixture to the pan in step 3, sprinkle with ⅓ cup (75 mL) crumbled cooked bacon or chopped cooked ham.

Baked Eggs in Spicy Tomato Sauce

MAKES 1 SERVING

Versions of eggs cooked in tomato sauce appear throughout the Mediterranean, North Africa and the Middle East. The popularity is easily understood upon indulging in such a dish. In addition, it's a fast, convenient, frugal and nutritious dinner option any time of the year.

TIP

Air fryers become very hot, especially when heated to maximum temperature. Use oven pads or mitts when touching the appliance and when opening and closing the basket.

- Preheat air fryer to 380°F (190°C)
- 6-inch (15 cm) round metal cake pan, sprayed with nonstick cooking spray

1 cup	thick and chunky marinara sauce	250 mL
¼ tsp	hot pepper sauce (such as Tabasco)	1 mL
2	large eggs	2
¼ cup	crumbled feta cheese	60 mL
2 tsp	chopped fresh parsley	10 mL

1. In prepared pan, stir together marinara sauce and hot pepper sauce.
2. Place pan in air fryer basket. Air-fry for 3 to 6 minutes or until sauce is very warm.
3. Open basket and carefully crack eggs into sauce, spacing evenly. Sprinkle with cheese. Air-fry for 8 to 12 minutes or until egg whites are set. Sprinkle with parsley and serve immediately.

Variations

For a milder dish, decrease the hot pepper sauce by half or omit it.

Other varieties of cheese, such as shredded Monterey Jack, freshly grated Parmesan or crumbled goat cheese, can be used in place of the feta cheese.

Easy Egg and Potato Casserole

Using your air fryer is the key to preparing egg casseroles with ease and efficiency, the hot circulating air cooking the eggs quickly without overcooking. This dish makes a hearty breakfast or, when paired with a salad, a satisfying supper.

TIP

Room temperature eggs will whisk more easily than cold eggs.

- Preheat air fryer to 360°F (180°C)
- 6-inch (15 cm) round metal cake pan, sprayed with nonstick cooking spray

3	large eggs	3
3 tbsp	milk	45 mL
¼ tsp	salt	1 mL
⅛ tsp	freshly cracked black pepper	0.5 mL
1⅓ cups	frozen potato tots	325 mL
½ cup	shredded cheese (such as Cheddar, Monterey Jack, pepper Jack or Swiss)	125 mL

1. In a small bowl, whisk together eggs, milk, salt and pepper.

2. Arrange potato tots in prepared pan. Pour egg mixture over top and sprinkle with cheese.

3. Place pan in air fryer basket. Air-fry for 20 to 25 minutes or until eggs are set and top is golden brown. Transfer to a wire rack and let cool for 10 minutes before serving.

No-Crust Quiche

The beauty of French quiche remains, even in the simplest renditions: humble ingredients morph into a velvety, sophisticated dish (no crust required).

TIPS

To get the cleanest break, crack eggs against the counter, not on the edge of the bowl.

Room temperature eggs will whisk more easily than cold eggs.

- Preheat air fryer to 330°F (165°C)
- 6-inch (15 cm) round metal cake pan, sprayed with nonstick cooking spray

3	large eggs	3
2/3 cup	light (5%) cream	150 mL
1/4 tsp	salt	1 mL
1/8 tsp	freshly cracked black pepper	0.5 mL
3/4 cup	shredded Italian cheese blend	175 mL
1/3 cup	chopped cooked ham	75 mL
1 tbsp	chopped fresh chives (optional)	15 mL

1. In a medium bowl, whisk eggs until blended. Whisk in cream, salt and pepper until blended and smooth. Stir in cheese, ham and chives (if using). Pour mixture into prepared pan.

2. Place pan in air fryer basket. Air-fry for 20 to 25 minutes or until golden brown and just set at the center. Transfer to a wire rack and let cool for at least 15 minutes before serving. Serve warm, at room temperature or chilled.

Variations

Florentine Quiche: Omit the ham and chives. Add 1 cup (250 mL) thawed frozen chopped spinach, squeezed of all excess liquid, and 3/4 tsp (3 mL) dried Italian seasoning along with the cheese in step 1.

Bacon and Cheddar Quiche: Replace the ham with 3 tbsp (45 mL) crumbled cooked bacon. Replace the Italian cheese blend with an equal amount of Cheddar cheese.

Puffed Egg Tarts

Simplicity reigns in this elegant, but still easy, dish. Puff pastry cooks up and around each egg, forming a perfect nest.

TIPS

The sheet of puff pastry should be about 9 inches (23 cm) square for this recipe. If your sheets are a different size, or the pastry comes in a block, roll or trim it into a 9-inch (23 cm) square as necessary.

Air fryers become very hot, especially when heated to maximum temperature. Use oven pads or mitts when touching the appliance and when opening and closing the basket.

To make adding the egg easier, crack the egg into a small cup before sliding it onto the puff pastry.

- Preheat air fryer to 390°F (200°C)

	All-purpose flour	
1	sheet frozen puff pastry (half a 17.3-oz/490 g package), thawed	1
¾ cup	shredded cheese (such as Gruyère, Cheddar or Monterey Jack), divided	175 mL
4	large eggs	4
1 tbsp	minced fresh parsley or chives (optional)	15 mL

1. On a lightly floured surface, unfold pastry sheet. Cut into 4 squares.

2. Place 2 squares in air fryer basket, spacing them apart. Air fry for 10 minutes or until pastry is light golden brown.

3. Open basket and, using a metal spoon, press down the centers of each square to make an indentation. Sprinkle 3 tbsp (45 mL) cheese into each indentation and carefully crack an egg into the center of each pastry.

4. Air-fry for 7 to 11 minutes or until eggs are cooked to desired doneness. Transfer to a wire rack set over waxed paper and let cool for 5 minutes. Sprinkle with half the parsley, if desired. Serve warm.

5. Repeat steps 2 to 4 with the remaining pastry squares, cheese, eggs and parsley.

Scrambled Egg "Muffins"

MAKES 4 "MUFFINS"

A savory take on morning muffins, this protein-packed breakfast answers the question of how to eat scrambled eggs on the go.

TIPS

For a smoother texture, blend the eggs and cottage cheese together in a blender or food processor until smooth. Stir in any additional ingredients, as desired.

When adding stir-ins, use no more than ¾ cup (175 mL) total.

- Preheat air fryer to 360°F (180°C)
- 8 standard-size foil or paper muffin cup liners

	Nonstick cooking spray	
4	large eggs	4
⅔ cup	cottage cheese	150 mL
⅛ tsp	salt	0.5 mL
⅛ tsp	freshly ground black pepper	0.5 mL

Suggested Stir-Ins (see tip)

¾ cup	shredded cheese (such as Cheddar, Monterey Jack, Swiss or Gouda)	175 mL
⅔ cup	chopped thawed frozen broccoli or spinach (squeezed dry)	150 mL
½ cup	chopped or crumbled cooked breakfast sausage, diced fully cooked smoked sausage or diced cooked ham	125 mL
½ cup	chopped roasted red bell peppers	125 mL
¼ cup	crumbled cooked bacon	60 mL
¼ cup	freshly grated Parmesan cheese	60 mL
	Chopped fresh herbs (such as parsley, chives, cilantro or rosemary)	

1. Place one muffin cup liner inside another. Repeat to create 4 doubled liners. Spray insides of liners with cooking spray.

2. In a medium bowl, whisk together eggs, cottage cheese, salt and pepper. Stir in any of the suggested stir-ins, as desired.

3. Place doubled liners in air fryer basket, spacing evenly. Divide egg mixture evenly among the doubled liners. Air-fry for 12 to 17 minutes or until centers are completely set. Transfer to a wire rack to cool slightly. Serve immediately or let cool completely and refrigerate until ready to serve.

Variation

Scrambled Egg White "Muffins": Replace the eggs with 1 cup (250 mL) egg whites (pasteurized liquid whites from a carton or fresh-cracked).

Egg, Waffle and Cheese Sandwich

Why use waffles for this breakfast sandwich? Because the eggs and cheese fill every nook and cranny for a unique crunchy, creamy and cheesy wakeup.

TIP

For a gluten-free sandwich, use gluten-free frozen waffles in place of regular waffles.

• Preheat air fryer to 390°F (200°C)

1	large egg	1
Pinch	salt	Pinch
Pinch	freshly cracked black pepper	Pinch
2	frozen plain waffles	2
¼ cup	shredded cheese (such as Cheddar, Monterey Jack or Swiss)	60 mL

1. In a small bowl, whisk together egg, salt and pepper.
2. Place one waffle in air fryer basket. Pour egg mixture over waffle, spreading with a spoon to fill cavities. Place second waffle in air fryer basket (it may overlap slightly). Sprinkle cheese over second waffle.
3. Air-fry for 4 to 7 minutes or until waffles are golden brown, egg is set and cheese is melted. Remove waffles and press together to form a sandwich.

Variation

Top the second waffle with 1 tbsp (15 mL) crumbled cooked bacon, 2 tbsp (30 mL) chopped or crumbled cooked breakfast sausage or 2 tbsp (30 mL) chopped cooked ham before sprinkling with cheese.

Egg and Avocado Tostado

The sum is far greater than the parts in this Southwestern breakfast for one. A combination of creamy avocado, rich egg and a crisp corn tortilla shell — paired with spicy salsa and salty queso fresco, which cut through the richness — this tostado will disappear almost before you finish air-frying it.

TIP

To get the loaded tortilla into the hot air fryer, place it on a piece of parchment paper or foil that is as wide as the tortilla in one direction and 3 to 4 inches (7.5 to 10 cm) longer in the opposite direction. Place the toppings on the tortilla, then use the longer sides of the paper or foil to lift the tortilla and lower it into the air fryer basket. Once the tortilla is in the basket, gently slide the paper or foil out from under it.

- Preheat air fryer to 390°F (200°C)

1	6-inch (15 cm) soft corn tortilla	1
	Nonstick cooking spray	
2 tbsp	thick and chunky salsa, divided	30 mL
½	Hass avocado, thinly sliced lengthwise	½
1	large egg	1
1 tbsp	crumbled queso fresco or mild feta cheese	15 mL

1. Lightly spray both sides of tortilla with cooking spray. Spread half the salsa on one side to within ½ inch (1 cm) of the edge. Arrange avocado slices around outer edge of tortilla to create a well in the center.

2. Carefully transfer tortilla to air fryer basket (see tip). Carefully break egg into well. Air-fry for 4 to 6 minutes or until egg white and yolk are firm, not runny. Serve sprinkled with queso fresco, with the remaining salsa on the side.

Variation

A flour tortilla of the same size can be used in place of the corn tortilla.

Avocado Egg Boats

If you are already partial to avocado in every way possible, you will swoon over this pairing with eggs. Adding a sprinkle of chives or parsley is optional, but worth it, as it contrasts with the rich goodness underneath.

TIP

Spread the scooped-out avocado flesh on toast for avocado toast.

- Preheat air fryer to 360°F (180°C)
- 6-inch (15 cm) round metal pan

1	large, firm-ripe Haas avocado, halved lengthwise and pitted	1
	Salt and freshly cracked black pepper	
2	large eggs	2
2 tsp	minced fresh chives or parsley (optional)	10 mL

1. Scoop out approximately 2 tbsp (30 mL) flesh around the cavity in each avocado half (save scooped-out avocado flesh for another use). Place avocado halves in pan, cut side up. Season to taste with salt and pepper.

2. Crack an egg into each avocado cavity, letting yolks drop into cavities and allowing some of the whites to settle on top. Season eggs with salt and pepper.

3. Carefully transfer pan to air fryer basket. Air-fry for 7 minutes for runny yolks; 10 minutes for firm, just-set yolks; 13 minutes for firm yolks. If desired, sprinkle with chives. Serve immediately.

Portobello Eggs with Pesto and Parmesan

This dish of earthy, meaty portobellos filled with eggs and seasoned with basil pesto and Parmesan cheese is full of favorite Italian flavors. It's a satisfying meal any time of the day.

TIP

If you can find only large or extra-large portobello mushrooms, simply air-fry one mushroom at a time.

- Preheat air fryer to 390°F (200°C)

2	medium portobello mushrooms, stems removed and dark gills scraped out	2
3 tbsp	basil pesto, divided	45 mL
2	large eggs	2
	Salt and freshly ground black pepper	
2 tbsp	freshly grated Parmesan cheese	30 mL

1. Spread stemmed side of each mushroom with 1 tbsp (15 mL) pesto. Place mushrooms, smooth side down and close together (but not touching), in air fryer basket. Crack 1 egg into each mushroom. Season to taste with salt and pepper. Sprinkle evenly with cheese.

2. Air-fry for 10 minutes or until mushrooms are tender and egg whites and yolks are firm, not runny (or cook longer to desired doneness). Drizzle with the remaining pesto.

Egg-Stuffed Baked Potatoes

Any excuse to stuff a baked potato is a good excuse, and here is one that can go from breakfast to dinner. You get to stuff it with eggs, not to mention melted cheese and fresh chives.

TIP

Hot air and steam will release from the air fryer throughout the cooking cycle. If your face is in close proximity to the appliance during the cooking cycle or when you are opening the basket, you risk being scalded by the release of accumulated steam.'

- Preheat air fryer to 360°F (180°C)

2	Air Fryer Baked Potatoes (see page 118; prepared through step 2), cooled slightly	2
1 tbsp	butter, softened	15 mL
	Salt and freshly cracked black pepper	
¾ cup	shredded cheese (such as Cheddar, Monterey Jack, Swiss or Gouda), divided	175 mL
2	large eggs	2
1 tbsp	minced fresh chives	15 mL

1. Cut off a ¼-inch (0.5 cm) thick slice from one long side (top) of each potato. Using a spoon, scoop out enough potato to leave a ¼-inch (0.5 cm) thick shell (be careful not to puncture skin).

2. In a small bowl, mash scooped potato with butter and season to taste with salt and pepper. Stir in ½ cup (125 mL) cheese. Season inside of potato shells with salt and pepper and stuff potato shells with filling.

3. Place potatoes, cut side up, in air fryer basket, leaving space in between. Carefully break egg into each potato and sprinkle with chives and the remaining cheese, dividing evenly. Air-fry for 7 minutes for runny yolks; 10 minutes for firm, just-set yolks; or 13 minutes for firm yolks. Serve immediately.

Egg and Cheese Stuffed Zucchini

Even if you eat eggs every day, they need never be tedious. Jazzing them up with a short list of fresh ingredients, as they are here — cottage cheese and Parmesan cheese for added protein, creaminess and flavor, and fresh zucchini "boats" for baking vessels — transforms them into something exciting and new.

TIP

Look for zucchini that are about 5 to 6 inches (12.5 to 15 cm) long and about $1\frac{1}{2}$ inches (4 cm) thick for this recipe.

• Preheat air fryer to 390°F (200°C)

2	small zucchini (see tip), halved lengthwise	2
	Salt and freshly cracked black pepper	
1	large egg	1
$\frac{1}{3}$ cup	cottage cheese	75 mL
$\frac{1}{4}$ cup	freshly grated Parmesan cheese, divided	60 mL
	Nonstick cooking spray	

1. Using a metal spoon, scoop and scrape out seeds from each zucchini half, leaving a $\frac{1}{4}$-inch (0.5 cm) shell; discard seeds. Sprinkle cut sides with salt and pepper.

2. In a medium bowl, whisk together egg, cottage cheese, half the Parmesan cheese, $\frac{1}{8}$ tsp (0.5 mL) salt and a pinch of pepper.

3. Place zucchini halves, cut side up, in air fryer basket, spacing them evenly. Spray with cooking spray. Spoon egg mixture into cavities and sprinkle with the remaining Parmesan cheese.

4. Air-fry for 15 to 20 minutes or until zucchini are tender and filling is set. Serve immediately.

Fish and Seafood

Southern Air-Fried Catfish

Although unconventional in preparation, the catfish fillets in this quick and easy recipe get authentic oomph from the toasted corn flavor of crushed tortilla chips.

TIP

For less spicy catfish, omit the black pepper.

- Preheat air fryer to 390°F (200°C)

1 cup	finely crushed tortilla chips	250 mL
3 tbsp	ranch dressing	45 mL
¼ tsp	freshly ground black pepper	1 mL
2	skinless catfish fillets (each 6 oz/175 g), patted dry	2
	Nonstick cooking spray	

1. Spread crushed chips in a shallow dish.
2. In another shallow dish, whisk together ranch dressing and pepper.
3. Working with 1 fish fillet at a time, dip in dressing, shaking off excess, then dredge in chips, pressing gently to adhere. As they are dredged, place fillets in a single layer in air fryer basket, spacing them evenly. Spray with cooking spray. Discard any excess chips and dressing.
4. Air-fry for 10 to 14 minutes or until coating is golden brown and fish flakes easily when tested with a fork. Serve immediately.

Variations

An equal amount of plain salted kettle-style potato chips can be used in place of the tortilla chips.

Tilapia fillets may be used in place of the catfish.

Spicy, Crispy Buttermilk Catfish

For this comforting meal, a spicy buttermilk mixture adds quick depth of flavor to frugal catfish fillets.

TIPS

Choose a pancake mix that calls for the addition of eggs and milk, rather than a "complete" pancake mix that calls for only the addition of water or milk.

For gluten-free catfish, make sure to use a gluten-free pancake mix.

The fish can be prepared through step 3 and frozen (this will work only with fresh fish, not fish that has been previously frozen and thawed). Wrap the fish pieces in plastic wrap, then foil, completely enclosing them, and freeze for up to 3 months. When ready to cook, unwrap the frozen fish (do not thaw), place in air fryer basket and air-fry at 390°F (200°C) for 12 to 16 minutes or until coating is golden brown and fish flakes easily when tested with a fork.

- Preheat air fryer to 390°F (200°C)

1 cup	pancake mix (see tip)	250 mL
1	large egg	1
1/3 cup	buttermilk	75 mL
2 tsp	hot pepper sauce	10 mL
1/4 tsp	salt	1 mL
2	skinless catfish fillets (each 6 oz/175 g), patted dry	2
	Nonstick cooking spray	

1. Spread pancake mix in a shallow dish.

2. In another shallow dish, whisk together egg, buttermilk, hot pepper sauce and salt. Transfer 2 tbsp (30 mL) egg mixture to pancake mix, stirring until only very fine lumps remain.

3. Working with 1 fish fillet at a time, dip in egg mixture, shaking off excess, then dredge in pancake mixture, pressing gently to adhere. Repeat dipping and dredging to double coat. As they are dredged, place fillets in a single layer in air fryer basket, spacing them evenly. Generously spray with cooking spray. Discard any excess pancake mixture and egg mixture.

4. Air-fry for 10 to 14 minutes or until coating is golden brown and fish flakes easily when tested with a fork. Serve immediately.

Variation

Tilapia fillets may be used in place of the catfish.

Parmesan-Crusted Cod Fillets

Fast-cooking, meaty cod is a great choice for a quick meal, and adding a Parmesan crust will guarantee a "thumbs up" from all.

TIP

The thickness of cod fillets can vary significantly. Reduce the minimum cooking time by 1 to 2 minutes for thinner fillets and add extra cooking time for thicker fillets as needed.

- Preheat air fryer to 390°F (200°C)

2 tsp	mayonnaise	10 mL
2	skinless cod fillets (each about 6 oz/175 g)	2
	Salt and freshly cracked black pepper	
2 tbsp	freshly grated Parmesan cheese	30 mL
1 tbsp	minced fresh chives (optional)	15 mL
¼ cup	panko (Japanese bread crumbs)	60 mL
	Nonstick cooking spray	

1. Spread mayonnaise on tops of fish fillets, dividing evenly. Season with salt and pepper. Top fillets with cheese and chives (if using), dividing evenly. Gently press panko on tops of each fillet.

2. Place fillets in air fryer basket, spacing them evenly. Spray with cooking spray. Air-fry for 7 to 10 minutes or until fish is opaque and flakes easily when tested with a fork.

Variations

Gluten-Free Parmesan-Crusted Cod Fillets: Replace the panko with gluten-free bread crumbs or crushed gluten-free crackers or corn flakes cereal.

Sea bass, halibut or any other firm white fish fillets may be used in place of the cod.

Sriracha and Honey Crispy Cod

Honey can be used for so much more than sweetening tea and drizzling on scones; here, it works in tandem with Sriracha, lending deep flavor to cod fillets.

TIPS

Other varieties of hot pepper sauce can be used in place of the Sriracha.

The thickness of cod fillets can vary significantly. Reduce the minimum cooking time by 1 to 2 minutes for thinner fillets and add extra cooking time for thicker fillets as needed.

- Preheat air fryer to 360°F (180°C)

¾ cup	panko (Japanese bread crumbs)	175 mL
2 tbsp	Sriracha	30 mL
2 tbsp	liquid honey	30 mL
2	skinless cod fillets (each about 6 oz/175 g)	2
	Nonstick cooking spray	

1. Spread panko in a shallow dish.
2. In another shallow dish, stir together Sriracha and honey until blended.
3. Working with 1 fillet at a time, dip in Sriracha mixture, shaking off excess, then dredge in panko until coated, shaking off excess. As they are dredged, place fillets in air fryer basket, spacing them evenly. Spray with cooking spray. Discard any excess Sriracha mixture and panko.
4. Air-fry for 9 to 13 minutes or until crust is golden brown and fish flakes easily when tested with a fork.

Variations

Gluten-Free Sriracha and Honey Crispy Cod: Replace the panko with an equal amount of gluten-free bread crumbs or crushed gluten-free crackers.

Other mild, lean white fish, such as orange roughy, snapper, tilefish or striped bass, may be used in place of the cod.

Greek Cod Cakes with Herb Mayonnaise

MAKES 2 SERVINGS

An ode to fine weather, these Greek-inspired, herb-seasoned cakes taste like summer on a plate.

TIP

Air fryers become very hot, especially when heated to maximum temperature. Use oven pads or mitts when touching the appliance and when opening and closing the basket.

- Preheat air fryer to 390°F (200°C)

12 oz	skinless cod fillets	375 g
	Nonstick cooking spray	
⅔ cup	panko (Japanese bread crumbs), divided	150 mL
1 tbsp	chopped fresh flat-leaf (Italian) parsley	15 mL
1 tsp	dried dillweed	5 mL
¼ tsp	fine sea salt	1 mL
⅛ tsp	freshly cracked black pepper	0.5 mL
2 tbsp	mayonnaise	30 mL

Herb Mayonnaise

¼ cup	mayonnaise	60 mL
1 tbsp	chopped fresh flat-leaf (Italian) parsley	15 mL
⅛ tsp	dried dillweed	0.5 mL
⅛ tsp	freshly cracked black pepper	0.5 mL

Suggested Accompaniment

Lemon wedges

1. Spray both sides of cod fillets with cooking spray; place in air fryer basket, spacing them evenly. Air-fry for 7 to 10 minutes or until fish is opaque and flakes easily when tested with a fork. Transfer to a plate and let cool slightly, then pat dry with paper towels. Flake fish into small pieces.

Variations

Gluten-Free Greek Cod Cakes:
Replace the panko with gluten-free bread crumbs or crushed gluten-free crackers or corn flakes cereal.

Sea bass, halibut or any other firm white fish fillets may be used in place of the cod. Reduce the minimum cooking time by 1 to 3 minutes for thinner fillets, as needed.

2. In a large bowl, gently combine flaked fish, $\frac{1}{4}$ cup (60 mL) panko, parsley, dill, salt, pepper and mayonnaise until ingredients just hold together. Form into eight $\frac{1}{2}$-inch (1 cm) thick cakes.

3. Spread the remaining panko in a shallow dish.

4. Dredge cakes in panko, gently pressing to adhere. Place cakes in air fryer basket, leaving space in between. Spray with cooking spray. Discard any excess panko.

5. Air-fry cakes for 11 to 15 minutes or until golden brown.

6. *Herb Mayonnaise:* Meanwhile, whisk together mayonnaise, parsley, dill and pepper.

7. Serve cakes immediately with mayonnaise dip and lemon wedges, if using.

Irish Fish Sticks

An Irish-inspired coating (potato-based and green-flecked) makes these crispy-on-the-outside, moist-on-the-inside fish sticks enticing to kids of all ages.

TIPS

The parsley can be omitted, if desired.

Air fryers become very hot, especially when heated to maximum temperature. Use oven pads or mitts when touching the appliance and when opening and closing the basket.

- Preheat air fryer to 390°F (200°C)

1 cup	instant potato flakes	250 mL
2 tbsp	minced fresh parsley	30 mL
3 tbsp	butter, melted	45 mL
1/2 tsp	chopped fresh thyme	2 mL
1/4 tsp	salt	1 mL
1/8 tsp	freshly cracked black pepper	0.5 mL
12 oz	skinless cod fillets, cut into 3-inch (7.5 cm) strips	375 g
	Nonstick cooking spray	

1. Combine potato flakes and parsley in a shallow dish; spread in a single layer.
2. In another shallow dish, stir together butter, thyme, salt and pepper until blended.
3. Dip fish strips in butter mixture, shaking off excess, then in potato flakes mixture, pressing to adhere and shaking off excess. Discard any excess butter mixture and potato flakes mixture.
4. Place strips in a single layer in air fryer basket, spacing them evenly. Spray with cooking spray. Air-fry for 5 minutes. Open basket and, using tongs or a spatula, carefully turn strips over. Air-fry for 3 to 7 minutes or until coating is golden brown and fish is opaque and flakes easily when tested with a fork.

Variation

Sea bass, halibut or any other firm white fish fillets may be used in place of the cod.

Brown Sugar and Butter Glazed Salmon

MAKES 2 SERVINGS

Basting salmon fillets with a quick glaze of brown sugar and butter elevates its flavor in one fell swoop.

TIPS

An equal amount of whole-grain mustard can be used in place of the Dijon mustard.

The thickness of salmon fillets can vary significantly. Reduce the minimum cooking time by 1 to 2 minutes for thinner fillets and add extra cooking time for thicker fillets as needed.

1½ tbsp	packed dark brown sugar	22 mL
1 tbsp	butter, melted	15 mL
2 tsp	Dijon mustard	10 mL
⅛ tsp	salt	0.5 mL
2	skinless salmon fillets (each about 6 oz/175 g)	2

1. In a small bowl, stir together brown sugar, butter, mustard and salt.
2. Place the salmon fillets on a small plate. Spoon and spread mustard mixture over top and sides of fillets. Refrigerate for 10 minutes.
3. Preheat air fryer to 390°F (200°C).
4. Place fillets in air fryer basket, spacing them evenly. Air-fry for 6 to 9 minutes or until fish is opaque and flakes easily when tested with a fork.

Smoked Salmon and Potato Perogies

MAKES 8 PEROGIES

Perogies may have their roots in Eastern Europe, but they take beautifully to all kinds of modern interpretations such as this.

TIPS

Packaged mashed potatoes can often be found in the refrigerated deli or produce section of the supermarket. This recipe works equally well with leftover homemade mashed potatoes.

The perogies are best eaten soon after they are made.

Variations

An equal amount of chive-flavored or plain cream cheese can be used in place of the herb-flavored cheese spread.

Other herbs, such as 1 tsp (5 mL) dried basil or $\frac{1}{2}$ tsp (2 mL) dried thyme or dried oregano, can be used in place of the dillweed.

• Preheat air fryer to 360°F (180°C)

¾ cup	cold mashed potatoes (packaged or homemade)	175 mL
⅓ cup	herb-flavored cheese spread (such as Boursin), softened	75 mL
1 tsp	dried dillweed	5 mL
⅛ tsp	freshly cracked black pepper	0.5 mL
4 oz	smoked salmon, chopped	125 g
1	can (17.3 oz/490 g) refrigerated large dinner biscuits	1
	Nonstick cooking spray	

1. In a small bowl, stir together potatoes, cheese, dill and pepper until blended. Gently stir in salmon until combined.

2. Remove dough from packaging and separate into biscuits. Using your fingertips or a rolling pin, press or roll each biscuit into a 5-inch (12.5 cm) circle.

3. Place 2½ tbsp (37 mL) salmon mixture slightly off-center on each dough circle. Fold biscuits over filling and press edges together with a fork to seal. Prick the top of each perogie three times with a fork. Spray perogies with cooking spray.

4. Place half the perogies in air fryer basket, spacing them 2 inches (5 cm) apart (refrigerate the remaining perogies). Air-fry for 10 to 14 minutes or until puffed and golden brown. Transfer to a wire rack and let cool for at least 10 minutes before serving. Repeat with the remaining perogies. Serve warm or at room temperature.

Herb-Crusted Tilapia

If you are stumped for a quick and easy tilapia recipe, this is your solution. Fresh parsley delivers bright, fresh flavor in the coating, producing a dish that will please one and all.

TIP

Air fryers become very hot, especially when heated to maximum temperature. Use oven pads or mitts when touching the appliance and when opening and closing the basket.

- Preheat air fryer to 390°F (200°C)

1 cup	panko (Japanese bread crumbs)	250 mL
2 tbsp	finely chopped fresh flat-leaf (Italian) parsley	30 mL
½ tsp	dried Italian seasoning	2 mL
⅛ tsp	freshly cracked black pepper	0.5 mL
4 tsp	mayonnaise	20 mL
2	skinless tilapia fillets (each 6 oz/175 g), patted dry	2
	Nonstick cooking spray	

1. In a shallow dish, combine panko, parsley, Italian seasoning and pepper.

2. Working with 1 fish fillet at a time, spread both sides with half the mayonnaise, then dredge in panko mixture, pressing gently to adhere. As they are dredged, place fillets in air fryer basket, spacing them evenly. Discard any excess panko mixture.

3. Air-fry for 10 to 14 minutes or until coating is golden brown and fish flakes easily when tested with a fork. Serve immediately.

Variations

Gluten-Free Herb-Crusted Tilapia: Replace the panko with gluten-free bread crumbs or crushed gluten-free crackers or corn flakes cereal.

An equal amount of dry bread crumbs with Italian seasoning (omit the ½ tsp/2 mL dried Italian seasoning) or plain bread crumbs can be used in place of the panko.

Catfish fillets may be used in place of the tilapia.

Baja Fish Tacos

Quickly cooked spiced tilapia combined with mango salsa and crunchy coleslaw in a tortilla makes for scrumptious taqueria-style tacos.

TIPS

To warm the tortillas, completely enclose them in foil. Place in the preheated air fryer before cooking the fish and air-fry for 5 minutes. Remove from air fryer but keep wrapped in foil until ready to use.

Air fryers become very hot, especially when heated to maximum temperature. Use oven pads or mitts when touching the appliance and when opening and closing the basket.

• Preheat air fryer to 390°F (200°C)

2	skinless tilapia fillets (each about 6 oz/175 g)	2
	Nonstick cooking spray	
2 tsp	taco seasoning	10 mL
4	6-inch (15 cm) corn or flour tortillas, warmed (see tip)	4
1 cup	coleslaw mix (shredded cabbage and carrots)	250 mL
¼ cup	mango salsa	60 mL

Suggested Accompaniments

Lime wedges

Diced avocado

Chopped fresh cilantro

1. Spray both sides of fish with cooking spray; sprinkle evenly with taco seasoning.

2. Place fillets in air fryer basket, spacing them evenly. Air-fry for 7 to 10 minutes or until fish is opaque and flakes easily when tested with a fork. Transfer fish to a medium bowl and flake into bite-size pieces.

3. Fill tortillas with fish, coleslaw mix and salsa. Serve with any of the suggested accompaniments, as desired.

Variation

Other mild, lean white fish, such as orange roughy, snapper, cod, tilefish or striped bass, may be used in place of the tilapia.

Tuscan Cannellini Tuna Cakes

Creamy cannellini beans and briny tuna yield fantastic seafood cakes, especially when they are seasoned with two classic Tuscan ingredients — garlic and rosemary.

TIPS

Other varieties of white beans, such as navy or Great Northern, can be used in place of the cannellini beans.

If you can find only larger 19-oz (540 mL) cans of beans, you will need about $1^1/_2$ cups (375 mL) drained.

If using water-packed tuna, discard packing liquid and add 3 tbsp (45 mL) olive oil in place of the tuna oil in step 1.

You can use 1 tsp (5 mL) dried rosemary, crumbled, or dried Italian seasoning in place of the fresh rosemary.

Variation

Gluten-Free Tuscan Tuna Cakes: Replace the panko with an equal amount of gluten-free bread crumbs or crushed gluten-free crackers or corn flakes cereal.

• Preheat air fryer to 360°F (180°C)

1	can (14 to 15 oz/398 to 425 mL) cannellini (white kidney) beans, drained and rinsed	1
$1^1/_4$ cups	panko (Japanese bread crumbs), divided	300 mL
2 tsp	minced fresh rosemary	10 mL
1 tsp	garlic powder	5 mL
$^1/_4$ tsp	freshly cracked black pepper	1 mL
2	cans (each 6 oz/170 g) olive oil–packed tuna, drained, oil reserved	2
	Nonstick cooking spray	

1. In a medium bowl, coarsely mash beans with a fork. Stir in $^1/_4$ cup (60 mL) panko, rosemary, garlic powder, pepper and 3 tbsp (45 mL) reserved tuna oil until blended (reserve extra oil for another use or discard). Gently stir in tuna. Form into eight $^3/_4$-inch (2 cm) thick patties.

2. Spread the remaining panko in a shallow dish.

3. Dredge patties in panko, gently pressing to adhere. As they are dredged, place 3 to 4 patties in air fryer basket, leaving space in between (refrigerate the remaining patties). Spray with cooking spray.

4. Air-fry for 12 to 16 minutes or until golden brown. Serve immediately.

5. Repeat steps 3 and 4 with the remaining patties and panko. Discard any excess panko.

Thai Tuna Burgers

MAKES 2 SERVINGS

Visually, these burgers speak softly, but the flavor has such depth, you would expect an extensive ingredient list. The power ingredients are Thai curry paste — made from an array of herbs and spices — as well as the zest and juice of fresh limes.

Variations

Gluten-Free Thai Tuna Burgers: Replace the panko with an equal amount of gluten-free bread crumbs or crushed gluten-free crackers or corn flakes cereal.

Thai Salmon Burgers: Use an equal amount of canned salmon in place of the tuna.

For added flavor, add $\frac{1}{2}$ cup (125 mL) packed fresh cilantro or basil, chopped, along with the tuna in step 2.

• Preheat air fryer to 360°F (180°C)

2	medium limes	2
$\frac{1}{4}$ cup	mayonnaise	60 mL
1 tbsp	Thai red or green curry paste	15 mL
2	cans (each 6 oz/170 g) water-packed tuna, drained	2
1 cup	panko (Japanese bread crumbs), divided	250 mL
	Nonstick cooking spray	

Suggested Accompaniments

Hamburger buns, split

Large lettuce leaves (for wraps)

Sliced tomatoes

1. Finely grate enough lime zest to measure $1\frac{1}{2}$ tsp (7 mL). Juice the limes and measure 1 tbsp (15 mL) lime juice.

2. In a medium bowl, whisk together lime zest, lime juice, mayonnaise and curry paste until well blended. Gently stir in tuna and $\frac{1}{2}$ cup (125 mL) panko. Form into two 1-inch (2.5 cm) thick patties.

3. Spread the remaining panko in a shallow dish. Dredge patties in panko, gently pressing to adhere. Place patties in air fryer basket, leaving space in between. Spray with cooking spray. Discard any excess panko.

4. Air-fry patties for 13 to 17 minutes or until golden brown. Serve immediately with any of the suggested accompaniments, as desired.

Island Seafood Grill

No need to light the barbecue: this seafood mélange achieves its great flavor being "grilled" with the high heat of your air fryer.

TIPS

Large shrimp typically have a count of 35 to 45 per pound (500 g).

I recommend using unrefined virgin coconut oil for this recipe. It has a mild coconut fragrance; refined coconut oil has no fragrance.

An equal amount of butter can be used in place of the coconut oil.

• Preheat air fryer to 390°F (200°C)

3	medium limes	3
1	large skinless Pacific halibut fillet (about 8 oz/250 g)	1
8 oz	large shrimp, peeled and deveined, tails on	250 g
1½ tbsp	virgin coconut oil, melted	22 mL
2½ tsp	salt-free jerk seasoning	12 mL
½ tsp	salt	2 mL
	Chopped fresh cilantro (optional)	

1. Grate enough lime zest from two of the limes to measure 2 tsp (10 mL); juice one or two limes and measure 1 tbsp (15 mL) juice (reserve the remaining juice for another use). Cut the remaining lime into 4 wedges.

2. Cut the halibut into 1¼-inch (3 cm) pieces. In a large bowl, gently toss together halibut, shrimp, coconut oil, lime zest, lime juice, jerk seasoning and salt.

3. Place seafood in air fryer basket, spacing evenly. Air-fry for 6 to 9 minutes or until shrimp are pink, firm and opaque and fish flakes easily when tested with a fork. Serve with lime wedges and sprinkled with cilantro (if using).

Variation

Sea bass, cod or any other firm white fish fillets may be used in place of the halibut.

Garlic and Herb Fried Calamari

MAKES 4 SERVINGS

Calamari is well worth making at home, especially when no hot oil is involved. Its firm texture and delicate flavor contrast beautifully with the garlic-and-herb coating, which air-fries to perfect crispiness — without a hint of greasiness.

TIP

Freshly squeezed lemon juice has the best flavor, but an equal amount of bottled lemon juice can be used in its place.

- Preheat air fryer to 390°F (200°C)

1½ lbs	cleaned squid	750 g
1½ tbsp	freshly squeezed lemon juice	22 mL
¼ tsp	salt	1 mL
⅛ tsp	freshly ground black pepper	0.5 mL
1⅓ cups	finely crushed corn flakes cereal	325 mL
2½ tsp	dried Italian seasoning	12 mL
2 tsp	garlic powder	10 mL
	Nonstick cooking spray	
	Lemon wedges (optional)	

1. Separate the squids' tentacles from their bodies (if it has not already been done). Slice the bodies into ½-inch (1 cm) rings and cut the tentacles in half if they are large. Rinse squid in a colander and drain. Pat dry with paper towels.

2. In a large bowl, combine squid, lemon juice, salt and pepper.

3. In a shallow dish, combine crushed cereal, Italian seasoning and garlic powder.

4. Working with 1 piece at a time, lightly spray squid with cooking spray, then dredge in crushed cereal mixture, pressing gently to adhere. As they are dredged, place 6 to 8 pieces in air fryer basket, leaving space in between (refrigerate the remaining squid). Spray with cooking spray.

Air fryers become very hot, especially when heated to maximum temperature. Use oven pads or mitts when touching the appliance and when opening and closing the basket.

5. Air-fry for 3 minutes. Open basket and, using tongs or a spatula, carefully turn pieces over. Air-fry for 3 to 5 minutes or until golden brown. Serve immediately with lemon wedges, if desired.

6. Repeat steps 4 and 5 with the remaining squid and crushed cereal mixture. Discard any excess crushed cereal mixture.

Variations

Island Spice Fried Calamari: Replace the lemon juice with an equal amount of freshly squeezed lime juice and replace the garlic powder with an equal amount of jerk seasoning. Serve with lime wedges instead of lemon wedges, if desired.

You can substitute an equal amount of panko (Japanese bread crumbs) for the crushed cereal.

Chopped Clam Fritters

A lighter take on a classic New England recipe, these fritters seal the clams in a batter with fresh chives and Old Bay seasoning to delicious effect.

TIPS

Choose a pancake mix that calls for the addition of eggs and milk, rather than a "complete" pancake mix that calls for only the addition of water or milk.

For gluten-free clam fritters, make sure to use a gluten-free pancake mix.

• Preheat air fryer to 380°F (190°C)

1 cup	pancake mix (see tip)	250 mL
1¼ tsp	Old Bay or other seafood seasoning	6 mL
1	large egg	1
2	cans (each 6.5 oz/184 g) chopped clams, drained, liquid reserved	2
1½ tbsp	minced fresh chives	22 mL
	Nonstick cooking spray	

1. In a medium bowl, stir together pancake mix, Old Bay seasoning, egg and 2 tbsp (30 mL) reserved clam juice until well blended (reserve the remaining clam juice for another use or discard). Gently stir in clams and chives until well combined. Form into eight ½-inch (1 cm) thick patties.

2. Place half the patties in air fryer basket, spacing them evenly (refrigerate the remaining patties). Spray with cooking spray. Air-fry for 8 to 12 minutes or until golden brown. Serve immediately. Repeat with the remaining patties.

Oyster Dressing Dinner

This Thanksgiving-inspired, homey, oyster-packed dish — hearty enough for a main course — will have you wondering how something so delicious could be so easy to make.

Variation

Use ⅓ cup (75 mL) chopped celery in place of the water chestnuts.

- Preheat air fryer to 360°F (180°C)
- 6-inch (15 cm) round metal cake pan, sprayed with nonstick cooking spray

1	can (8 oz/225 g) whole oysters, drained, liquid reserved	1
½	package (6 oz/170 g) dry herb or chicken stuffing mix	½
½ cup	drained canned sliced water chestnuts, chopped	125 mL
¼ cup	finely chopped green onions	60 mL
2 tbsp	butter, melted	30 mL
⅛ tsp	freshly cracked black pepper	0.5 mL
	Nonstick cooking spray	

1. Pour the reserved oyster liquid into a glass measuring cup. Add enough water to measure ¾ cup (175 mL).

2. In a medium bowl, combine stuffing mix, oysters, water chestnuts, green onions, oyster liquid mixture, butter and pepper until blended. Transfer to prepared baking dish and spray with cooking spray.

3. Place dish in air fryer basket. Air-fry for 20 to 25 minutes or until liquid is absorbed and dressing is golden brown.

Smoked Paprika and Lemon Fried Oysters

MAKES 2 SERVINGS

The zing of smoky paprika coupled with the bright flavor of lemon (both the zest and juice) highlight the briny sea flavor of pantry-friendly canned oysters.

TIPS

For best results, do not use fat-free mayonnaise. It is made mostly of water and gums, a combination that does not work well in this recipe.

Smoked paprika is also labeled and sold as "pimentón."

Regular paprika or chili powder can be used in place of the smoked paprika.

- Preheat air fryer to 390°F (200°C)

2	medium lemons	2
½ cup	mayonnaise	125 mL
	Salt and freshly cracked black pepper	
2	cans (each 8 oz/225 g) whole oysters, drained and patted dry	2
½ cup	dry bread crumbs with Italian seasoning	125 mL
1 tsp	smoked paprika	5 mL
	Nonstick cooking spray	

1. Grate enough lemon zest to measure 2 tsp (10 mL). Juice the lemons and measure 2 tbsp (30 mL) juice.

2. In a small bowl, whisk together mayonnaise, lemon zest and lemon juice. Season to taste with salt and pepper. Transfer 2 tbsp (30 mL) mayonnaise mixture to a medium bowl and add oysters, gently tossing to coat. Refrigerate the remaining mayonnaise mixture.

3. In a medium bowl, whisk together bread crumbs and paprika.

4. Add half the oysters to the bread crumb mixture, gently tossing to coat (refrigerate the remaining oysters).

Air fryers become very hot, especially when heated to maximum temperature. Use oven pads or mitts when touching the appliance and when opening and closing the basket.

5. Transfer the coated oysters to air fryer basket, leaving space in between. Spray with cooking spray. Air-fry for 7 to 10 minutes or until golden brown. Serve immediately with the remaining lemon mayonnaise.

6. Repeat steps 4 and 5 with the remaining oysters and bread crumb mixture. Discard any excess bread crumb mixture.

Variation

Gluten-Free Smoked Paprika and Lemon Fried Oysters: Replace the bread crumbs with an equal amount of gluten-free bread crumbs or crushed gluten-free crackers or corn flakes cereal, and add $1/8$ tsp (0.5 mL) dried Italian seasoning.

New England Fried Scallops

These corn flakes–crusted scallops are simplicity itself, which many staunch New Englanders argue is the best approach to seafood in all circumstances.

TIP

An equal amount of panko (Japanese bread crumbs) can be used in place of the corn flakes cereal.

Variation

Gluten-Free Fried Scallops: Replace the all-purpose flour with a gluten-free all-purpose flour blend and be sure to use certified gluten-free corn flakes cereal.

• Preheat air fryer to 390°F (200°C)

¾ cup	all-purpose flour	175 mL
1 tbsp	Old Bay or other seafood seasoning	15 mL
1¼ cups	crushed corn flakes cereal	300 mL
2	large eggs, lightly beaten	2
⅛ tsp	salt	0.5 mL
⅛ tsp	freshly cracked black pepper	0.5 mL
1 lb	large sea scallops, side muscles removed	500 g
	Nonstick cooking spray	
	Lemon wedges (optional)	

1. Place flour and Old Bay seasoning in a large sealable plastic bag; seal bag and shake to combine.
2. Spread crushed cereal in a shallow dish.
3. In a shallow bowl, whisk together eggs, salt and pepper.
4. Add 8 scallops to flour mixture in bag (keep the remaining scallops in the refrigerator). Seal and toss until coated. Working with 1 scallop at a time, remove from flour, shaking off excess. Dip in egg mixture, shaking off excess, then dredge in crushed cereal, pressing gently to adhere. As they are dredged, place scallops in air fryer basket, leaving space in between. Spray with cooking spray.
5. Air-fry for 4 to 7 minutes or until golden brown. Serve immediately with lemon wedges, if desired.
6. Repeat steps 4 and 5 with the remaining scallops, flour mixture, egg mixture and crushed cereal. Discard any excess flour mixture, egg mixture and crushed cereal.

Crunchy Fried Shrimp Scampi

This crispy-crunchy, all-in-one homage to shrimp scampi makes a great appetizer or main course.

TIP

Large shrimp typically have a count of 35 to 45 per pound (500 g).

Variations

Gluten-Free Shrimp Scampi: Replace the panko with crushed gluten-free corn flakes cereal.

Crispy Creole Shrimp: Omit the chives and black pepper. Add 1 tbsp (15 mL) Creole or Cajun seasoning to the butter mixture in step 2.

Crispy Curried Shrimp: Omit the chives. Replace the lemon zest and juice with lime zest and juice. Add $1\frac{1}{2}$ tsp (7 mL) curry powder to the butter mixture in step 2.

• Preheat air fryer to 390°F (200°C)

1	large lemon	1
3 tbsp	butter, melted	45 mL
$\frac{1}{4}$ tsp	salt	1 mL
$\frac{1}{4}$ tsp	freshly cracked black pepper	1 mL
1 lb	large shrimp, peeled and deveined, tails on	500 g
1 cup	panko (Japanese bread crumbs)	250 mL
1 tbsp	minced fresh chives	15 mL
	Nonstick cooking spray	

1. Grate enough lemon zest to measure 2 tsp (10 mL). Cut lemon in half and squeeze enough juice to measure 1 tbsp (15 mL).

2. In a medium bowl, combine lemon zest, lemon juice, butter, salt and pepper. Add shrimp, tossing to coat.

3. In a shallow dish, combine panko and chives.

4. Working with 1 shrimp at a time, dredge in panko mixture, pressing gently to adhere. As they are dredged, place shrimp in air fryer basket, spacing them evenly (about half the shrimp will fit; refrigerate the remaining shrimp). Spray generously with cooking spray.

5. Air-fry for 5 to 8 minutes or until golden brown. Serve immediately.

6. Repeat steps 4 and 5 with the remaining shrimp and panko mixture. Discard any excess panko mixture.

Fried Shrimp Cakes with Wasabi Mayonnaise

MAKES 4 SERVINGS

Take a quick trip to Japan with these crispy shrimp cakes with boldly flavored wasabi mayonnaise alongside.

TIPS

For best results, do not use fat-free mayonnaise. It is made mostly of water and gums, a combination that does not work well in this recipe.

Wasabi powder can be used in place of wasabi paste. Mix 1 tsp (5 mL) wasabi powder with 2 tsp (10 mL) water before adding it to the mayonnaise in step 6.

- Preheat air fryer to 380°F (190°C)
- Food processor

1 lb	shrimp, peeled and deveined	500 g
2/3 cup	mayonnaise, divided	150 mL
1/2 tsp	salt	2 mL
1/4 tsp	freshly ground black pepper	1 mL
2/3 cup	finely chopped red bell pepper	150 mL
2 cups	panko (Japanese bread crumbs), divided	500 mL
	Nonstick cooking spray	
1 tbsp	wasabi paste	15 mL

1. In food processor, pulse shrimp, using on/off pulses, until coarsely chopped.

2. Transfer shrimp to a large bowl and add 3 tbsp (45 mL) mayonnaise, salt and pepper, stirring until well blended. Stir in red pepper and half the panko until blended.

3. Divide shrimp mixture into 12 equal portions; shape each portion into a 2½-inch (6 cm) diameter patty.

4. Spread the remaining panko in a shallow dish.

5. Working with 1 patty at a time, dredge both sides in panko, pressing gently to adhere. As they are dredged, place 3 patties in air fryer basket, leaving space in between (refrigerate the remaining patties). Spray with cooking spray.

Air fryers become very hot, especially when heated to maximum temperature. Use oven pads or mitts when touching the appliance and when opening and closing the basket.

6. Air-fry for 8 to 12 minutes or until patties are browned, firm to the touch and opaque inside.

7. Meanwhile, in a small bowl, whisk together wasabi paste and the remaining mayonnaise. Serve cooked shrimp patties immediately with wasabi mayonnaise.

8. Repeat steps 5 and 6 three times with the remaining patties and panko and serve immediately with wasabi mayonnaise. Discard any excess panko.

Variation

Gluten-Free Shrimp Cakes: Replace the panko with an equal amount of crushed gluten-free corn flakes cereal.

Chicken and Turkey

Pretzel-Coated Chicken Tenders

If there is a way to build on the appeal of fried chicken tenders, it's by giving them a favorite snack twist, flavoring them with honey mustard and covering each piece with a crispy pretzel coating.

TIP

In place of the chicken tenders, you can use 1 lb (500 g) boneless skinless chicken breasts, cut into thick fingers.

Variation

Gluten-Free Pretzel-Coated Chicken Tenders: Replace the all-purpose flour with a gluten-free all-purpose flour blend, and replace the pretzels with gluten-free pretzels.

- Preheat air fryer to 390°F (200°C)

½ cup	all-purpose flour	125 mL
½ tsp	salt	2 mL
¼ tsp	freshly ground black pepper	1 mL
1 lb	chicken tenders, patted dry	500 g
1½ cups	finely crushed pretzels	375 mL
2	large eggs	2
3 tbsp	honey mustard	45 mL
	Nonstick cooking spray	

1. Place flour, salt and pepper in a large sealable plastic bag; seal bag and shake to combine. Add chicken, seal and toss until coated.

2. Spread crushed pretzels in a shallow dish.

3. In a medium bowl, whisk together eggs and mustard.

4. Working with 1 chicken tender at a time, remove from flour mixture, shaking off excess. Dip in egg mixture, shaking off excess, then dredge in crushed pretzels, pressing gently to adhere. As they are dredged, arrange half the tenders in air fryer basket, leaving space in between (refrigerate the remaining tenders). Spray with cooking spray.

5. Air-fry for 8 to 12 minutes or until crust is golden brown and chicken is no longer pink inside. Serve immediately.

6. Repeat steps 4 and 5 with the remaining tenders, egg mixture and crushed pretzels. Discard any excess flour mixture, egg mixture and crushed pretzels.

Peanut Lime Chicken Tenders

A favorite combination in Caribbean and Southeast Asian cuisines, peanut and lime create an exotic yet familiar coating for these otherwise classic chicken tenders.

Variation

Gluten-Free Peanut Lime Chicken Tenders: Replace the panko with an equal amount of gluten-free bread crumbs or crushed gluten-free crackers or corn flakes cereal.

• Preheat air fryer to 360°F (180°C)

½ cup	salted roasted peanuts, chopped	125 mL
½ cup	panko (Japanese bread crumbs)	125 mL
2 tsp	finely grated lime zest	10 mL
⅛ tsp	freshly ground black pepper	0.5 mL
1	large egg	1
¼ tsp	salt	1 mL
1 lb	chicken tenders, patted dry	500 g
	Nonstick cooking spray	

1. In a shallow dish, stir together peanuts, panko, lime zest and pepper.

2. In another shallow dish, whisk together egg and salt.

3. Working with 1 chicken tender at a time, dip in egg mixture, shaking off excess, then dredge in panko mixture, pressing gently to adhere. As they are dredged, arrange half the tenders in air fryer basket, spacing them evenly (refrigerate the remaining tenders). Spray with cooking spray.

4. Air-fry for 11 to 15 minutes or until crust is golden brown and chicken is no longer pink inside.

5. Repeat steps 3 and 4 with the remaining tenders, egg mixture and panko mixture. Discard any excess egg and panko mixtures.

Bacon Cheddar Chicken "Fries"

MAKES 2 SERVINGS

This whimsical entrée has all the qualities you want in fried chicken and loaded French fries, all in one. It might be best to make a double batch.

Variations

Gluten-Free Bacon Cheddar Chicken "Fries": Replace the bread crumbs with an equal amount of gluten-free bread crumbs or crushed gluten-free crackers or corn flakes cereal.

Double Cheese Chicken "Fries": Replace the bacon with an equal amount of freshly grated Parmesan cheese.

- Preheat air fryer to 360°F (180°C)
- Food processor

¾ cup	shredded sharp (old) Cheddar cheese	175 mL
½ cup	plain dry bread crumbs	125 mL
2 tbsp	cooked crumbled bacon	30 mL
8 oz	boneless skinless chicken breasts, cut into ¾-inch (2 cm) strips	250 g
⅔ cup	ranch dressing, divided	150 mL
	Nonstick cooking spray	

1. In food processor, process cheese, bread crumbs and bacon until finely chopped. Spread in a shallow dish.

2. In a medium bowl, toss together chicken and 1½ tbsp (22 mL) ranch dressing.

3. Working with 1 chicken strip at a time, dredge in cheese mixture, pressing gently to adhere. As they are dredged, place half the chicken pieces in air fryer basket, spacing them evenly (refrigerate the remaining chicken strips). Spray with cooking spray.

4. Air-fry for 10 to 14 minutes or until crust is golden brown and chicken is no longer pink inside. Serve immediately with the remaining ranch dressing.

5. Repeat steps 3 and 4 with the remaining chicken strips and cheese mixture. Discard any excess cheese mixture.

Chicken Spiedini with Salsa Verde

Chicken spiedini can be made many ways, but it always has some combination of lemon, capers and olive oil to create the signature flavor. It's a breeze to make for weeknight suppers, but it's also guaranteed to wow guests.

TIP

If using wooden or bamboo skewers, soak them in a shallow dish of warm water for at least 30 minutes before threading with chicken.

- Preheat air fryer to 390°F (200°C)
- Blender or food processor
- Four 6-inch (15 cm) metal skewers or soaked wooden skewers

1	large lemon	1
1 cup	packed fresh flat-leaf (Italian) parsley leaves	250 mL
2 tbsp	drained capers	30 mL
3 tbsp	water	45 mL
1 tbsp	extra virgin olive oil	15 mL
	Salt and freshly cracked black pepper	
12 oz	boneless skinless chicken breasts, cut into 1-inch (2.5 cm) cubes	375 g
	Nonstick cooking spray	

1. Finely grate enough lemon zest to measure 2 tsp (10 mL). Cut lemon in half and squeeze enough juice to measure 2 tbsp (30 mL).

2. In blender, combine parsley, capers, lemon zest, lemon juice, water and oil; purée until smooth. Season to taste with salt and pepper.

3. Thread chicken onto skewers. Spray with cooking spray and sprinkle with $\frac{1}{4}$ tsp (1 mL) salt and $\frac{1}{8}$ tsp (0.5 mL) pepper. Place skewers in air fryer basket, spacing them evenly.

4. Air-fry for 6 to 9 minutes or until chicken is no longer pink inside. Serve with salsa verde.

Chicken Shawarma

Shawarma is quintessential Mediterranean street food, seasoned with herbs and spices, grilled and served plain or with flatbread. Similar to other grilled meats, such as Turkish döner kebabs and Greek gyros, shawarma is distinct in its combination of sweet and savory spices, including turmeric, cinnamon, cumin and cloves. I've simplified the long list of traditional spices by using curry powder and pumpkin pie spice, along with cumin, to create the signature shawarma flavors.

TIP

If using wooden or bamboo skewers, soak them in a shallow dish of warm water for at least 30 minutes before threading with chicken.

- Four 6-inch (15 cm) metal skewers or soaked wooden skewers

1 tsp	ground cumin	5 mL
¾ tsp	curry powder	3 mL
½ tsp	pumpkin pie spice	2 mL
½ tsp	salt	2 mL
⅛ tsp	freshly cracked black pepper	0.5 mL
1 tbsp	olive oil	15 mL
12 oz	boneless skinless chicken breasts, cut into thin strips	375 g

Suggested Accompaniments

Plain yogurt (regular or Greek)

Pita bread

Lemon wedges

Chopped romaine lettuce

Sliced or chopped tomato

1. In a large bowl, whisk together cumin, curry powder, pumpkin pie spice, salt, pepper and oil. Add chicken and toss to coat. Let stand for 20 minutes.

2. Meanwhile, preheat air fryer to 390°F (200°C).

3. Thread chicken onto skewers. Place skewers in air fryer basket, spacing them evenly.

4. Air-fry for 6 to 9 minutes or until chicken is no longer pink inside. Serve with any of the suggested accompaniments, as desired.

Lemon Honey Chicken Thighs

Citrusy and slightly sweet, these chicken thighs have the crispy skin you crave. Leaving the skin on also keeps the chicken moist and succulent.

TIP

Air fryers become very hot, especially when heated to maximum temperature. Use oven pads or mitts when touching the appliance and when opening and closing the basket.

- Preheat air fryer to 370°F (180°C)

4	small bone-in skin-on chicken thighs (about 1 lb/ 500 total), patted dry	4
	Nonstick cooking spray	
	Salt and freshly cracked black pepper	
1½ tbsp	liquid honey	22 mL
1 tsp	finely grated lemon zest	5 mL
2 tsp	freshly squeezed lemon juice	10 mL
½ tsp	garlic powder	2 mL

1. Spray chicken thighs with cooking spray and season with salt and pepper.
2. Place chicken thighs, skin side up, in air fryer basket, spacing them evenly. Air-fry for 22 minutes.
3. Meanwhile, in a small cup or bowl, combine honey, lemon zest, lemon juice and garlic powder.
4. Open basket and brush chicken with honey glaze. Air-fry for 3 to 7 minutes or until an instant-read thermometer inserted in the thickest part of a thigh registers 165°F (74°C).

Variation

Molasses Lime Chicken Thighs: Use dark (cooking) molasses in place of the honey, and use lime zest and lime juice in place of the lemon zest and lemon juice.

Jerk Chicken Thighs

Fried chicken thighs head to the Caribbean without the heaviness of deep-frying. Spice lovers, take note: ready-to-use jerk seasoning adds multifaceted flavor and a hit of heat in one fell swoop.

TIPS

An equal amount of granulated sugar can be used in place of the brown sugar.

If the jerk seasoning has salt added, increase the total amount to 2¼ tsp (11 mL) and omit the ¼ tsp (1 mL) salt.

• Preheat air fryer to 370°F (185°C)

1 tbsp	packed brown sugar	15 mL
2 tsp	salt-free jerk seasoning	10 mL
1 tsp	finely grated lime zest	5 mL
¼ tsp	salt	1 mL
1 tbsp	olive oil or vegetable oil	15 mL
4	small bone-in skin-on chicken thighs (about 1 lb/ 500 total), patted dry	4

1. In a medium bowl, combine brown sugar, jerk seasoning, lime zest, salt and oil. Add chicken. Using your fingers, rub mixture all over to coat.

2. Place chicken thighs, skin side up, in air fryer basket, spacing them evenly. Air-fry for 25 to 30 minutes or until an instant-read thermometer inserted in the thickest part of a thigh registers 165°F (74°C).

Variations

Indian-Spiced Chicken Thighs: Replace the jerk seasoning with an equal amount of curry powder or garam masala.

Thai-Spiced Chicken Thighs: Replace the jerk seasoning with an equal amount of Thai curry paste (red, green or yellow).

Sesame Chicken Teriyaki Skewers

No need to head to a restaurant for great Japanese food so long as you have an air fryer and two of my favorite go-to ingredients — teriyaki glaze and toasted sesame oil. Just as enticing as the flavor: the preparation is a breeze.

TIPS

If using wooden or bamboo skewers, soak them in a shallow dish of warm water for at least 30 minutes before threading with chicken.

Teriyaki glaze or basting sauce is thicker than regular teriyaki sauce. Look for it in the Asian foods section of the supermarket or where barbecue sauces are shelved.

To toast sesame seeds, place up to 1 tbsp (15 mL) seeds in a 6-inch (15 cm) round metal cake pan. Place pan in air fryer basket and air-fry at 360°F (180°C) for 30 to 60 seconds or until seeds are golden brown and fragrant. Let cool completely before using.

- Preheat air fryer to 390°F (200°C)
- Four 6-inch (15 cm) metal skewers or soaked wooden skewers

12 oz	boneless skinless chicken thighs, trimmed and cut into 1-inch (2.5 cm) pieces	375 g
2 tbsp	teriyaki glaze or basting sauce	30 mL
1 tsp	toasted (dark) sesame oil	5 mL
1	red bell pepper, cut into 1-inch (2.5 cm) pieces	1
	Nonstick cooking spray	
1 tbsp	toasted sesame seeds (see tip)	15 mL

1. In a medium bowl, combine chicken, teriyaki glaze and sesame oil until coated. Let stand for 5 minutes.

2. Remove chicken from marinade; discard any excess marinade. Alternately thread chicken and red pepper onto skewers and spray with cooking spray.

3. Place skewers in air fryer basket, spacing them evenly. Air-fry for 7 to 11 minutes or until juices run clear when chicken is pierced. Serve sprinkled with sesame seeds.

Potato Flake Fried Chicken

The secret is out: potato flakes, most often used to make instant mashed potatoes, are one of the best coatings for creating light, crispy air-fried foods. Here, the flakes are combined with Parmesan cheese and a hint of garlic for swoon-worthy, weeknight-friendly fried chicken.

TIP

You can use all drumsticks or all thighs in place of a combination.

• Preheat air fryer to 380°F (190°C)

½ cup	instant potato flakes	125 mL
¼ cup	freshly grated Parmesan cheese	60 mL
¼ tsp	garlic powder	1 mL
¼ tsp	salt	1 mL
⅛ tsp	freshly cracked black pepper	0.5 mL
1	large egg	1
1 tbsp	water	15 mL
1 lb	chicken drumsticks and thighs (2 of each), patted dry	500 g
	Nonstick cooking spray	

1. In a shallow dish, combine potato flakes, cheese, garlic powder, salt and pepper.

2. In another shallow dish, whisk together egg and water.

3. Working with 1 piece of chicken at a time, dip in egg mixture, shaking off excess, then dredge in potato flake mixture, pressing gently to adhere. As they are dredged, place pieces in air fryer basket, leaving space in between. Spray with cooking spray.

TIP

Air fryers become very hot, especially when heated to maximum temperature. Use oven pads or mitts when touching the appliance and when opening and closing the basket.

4. Air-fry for 20 minutes. Open basket and, using tongs or a spatula, carefully turn chicken over. Spray with cooking spray. Air-fry for 8 to 12 minutes or until coating is golden brown and an instant-read thermometer inserted in the thickest part of chicken registers 165°F (74°C). Serve immediately. Discard any excess egg mixture and potato flake mixture.

Variations

Herbed Fried Chicken: Add 1 tsp (5 mL) dried Italian seasoning to the potato flake mixture.

If you prefer, omit the Parmesan cheese and increase the total amount of potato flakes to ¾ cup (175 mL).

You can use 2 bone-in chicken breasts (totaling no more than 1 lb/500 g) in place of the thighs and drumsticks.

Spicy, Smoky Chicken Drumsticks

Chicken drumsticks are a frugal, foolproof option for weeknight dinners, but that doesn't mean they have to be ho-hum. Giving them some serious "wow" is as simple as a quick, spicy-smoky-tangy marinade followed by a light and crispy coating of panko. Dinner is served (with style)!

TIP

Greek yogurt is not recommended for this recipe because it is too thick to make a marinade for coating the chicken. If Greek yogurt is all you have on hand, use ¼ cup (60 mL) Greek yogurt whisked with ¼ cup (60 mL) milk.

4	chicken drumsticks (about 1 lb/500 g total), skin removed	4
½ cup	plain yogurt (not Greek-style)	125 mL
2 tbsp	liquid honey	30 mL
2 tsp	hot smoked paprika	10 mL
½ tsp	salt	2 mL
¼ tsp	freshly ground black pepper	1 mL
¾ cup	panko (Japanese bread crumbs)	175 mL
	Nonstick cooking spray	

1. In a medium sealable plastic bag, combine drumsticks, yogurt, honey, paprika, salt and pepper. Seal bag and refrigerate for 30 to 60 minutes, turning once.

2. Preheat air fryer to 390°F (200°C).

3. Spread panko in a shallow dish.

4. Remove drumsticks from bag and discard marinade. Working with 1 drumstick at a time, dredge in panko until coated, pressing to adhere. As they are dredged, place drumsticks in air fryer basket, spacing them evenly. Spray with cooking spray. Discard any excess panko.

TIPS

An equal amount of buttermilk can be used in place of the yogurt.

An equal amount of brown sugar or pure maple syrup can be used in place of the honey.

Air fryers become very hot, especially when heated to maximum temperature. Use oven pads or mitts when touching the appliance and when opening and closing the basket.

5. Air-fry for 10 minutes. Open basket and, using tongs, turn drumsticks over. Air-fry for 10 minutes.

6. Reduce air fryer temperature to 300°F (150°C) and air-fry for 5 to 10 minutes or until an instant-read thermometer inserted in the thickest part of a drumstick registers 165°F (74°C).

Variations

Gluten-Free Spicy, Smoky Drumsticks: Replace the panko with an equal amount of crushed gluten-free corn flakes cereal.

For less spicy chicken, use an equal amount of sweet smoked paprika in place of the hot smoked paprika.

If hot smoked paprika is not available, replace it with a combination of $1\frac{1}{2}$ tsp (7 mL) chili powder and $\frac{3}{4}$ tsp (3 mL) ground cumin.

General Tso's Chicken and Broccoli

Forget phone calls and ordering apps. Chinese takeout is faster and easier than ever with your air fryer and a minimalist list of ingredients.

TIPS

Look for General Tso's sauce in the Asian foods section of the supermarket.

To toast sesame seeds, place up to 1 tbsp (15 mL) seeds in a 6-inch (15 cm) round metal cake pan. Place pan in air fryer basket and air-fry at 360°F (180°C) for 30 to 60 seconds or until seeds are golden brown and fragrant. Let cool completely before using.

• Preheat air fryer to 390°F (200°C)

2 cups	frozen breaded popcorn chicken pieces	500 mL
1½ cups	small broccoli florets	375 mL
	Nonstick cooking spray	
½ cup	General Tso's sauce	125 mL
2 tsp	toasted sesame seeds (optional)	10 mL

1. Place popcorn chicken in a single layer in air fryer basket. Arrange broccoli in spaces around chicken. Spray with cooking spray.

2. Air-fry for 15 to 20 minutes, shaking basket twice, until chicken is browned and crisp and broccoli is tender when pierced.

3. Meanwhile, in a small microwave-safe cup, heat General Tso's sauce on High for 15 to 30 seconds or until hot but not boiling.

4. Transfer chicken and broccoli to a medium bowl. Add sauce and toss to coat. Sprinkle with sesame seeds, if desired. Serve immediately.

Crispy Mini Chicken Burritos

The ingredients for these petite Tex-Mex bundles are simple and familiar, but they add up to a dinner — or lunch, or snack — hearty, satisfying and irresistible. Salsa verde, made of roasted tomatillos, onions, garlic, cilantro and chiles, brings bold, nuanced flavors in one convenient step.

TIPS

The flour tortillas are easier to roll into burritos when they are not chilled.

For gluten-free burritos, use gluten-free flour tortillas.

- Preheat air fryer to 390°F (200°C)

²⁄₃ cup	shredded or chopped cooked chicken	150 mL
½ cup	shredded pepper Jack cheese	125 mL
2 tbsp	finely chopped green onions	30 mL
2 tbsp	salsa verde	30 mL
4	6-inch (15 cm) flour tortillas	4
	Nonstick cooking spray	

1. In a medium bowl, combine chicken, cheese, green onions and salsa until blended.

2. Place tortillas on work surface and spoon one-quarter of the filling down the center of each tortilla. Fold in opposite sides of each tortilla, then roll up into burritos. Arrange burritos, seam side down, in air fryer basket, spacing them evenly. Spray burritos with cooking spray.

3. Air-fry for 9 to 13 minutes or until golden brown and edges appear crispy. Transfer burritos to a plate and let cool for 5 minutes before serving.

Variations

An equal amount of tomato salsa can be used in place of the salsa verde.

An equal amount of shredded Monterey Jack or Cheddar cheese can be used in place of the pepper Jack.

An equal amount of shredded or chopped cooked pork can be used in place of the chicken.

Chicken Enchilada Meatballs

White chicken enchiladas are a Tex-Mex favorite, and this meatball rendition is destined to become one, too. Serve with seasoned black beans and salad on the side, and dinner is done!

TIP

Air fryers become very hot, especially when heated to maximum temperature. Use oven pads or mitts when touching the appliance and when opening and closing the basket.

- Preheat air fryer to 390°F (200°C)

12 oz	ground chicken	375 g
¾ cup	chopped pepper Jack cheese	175 mL
¼ cup	finely crushed tortilla chips	60 mL
¾ cup	salsa verde, divided	175 mL
1¼ tsp	ground cumin	6 mL

1. In a medium bowl, using your hands, combine chicken, cheese, tortilla chips, ¼ cup (60 mL) salsa verde and cumin until blended (be careful not to overmix or compact mixture). Form into 12 meatballs, each about 1¼ inches (3 cm) in diameter.

2. Arrange meatballs in air fryer basket, spacing them evenly. Air-fry for 6 to 10 minutes or until meatballs are browned outside and no longer pink inside. Serve with the remaining salsa.

Variations

An equal amount of lean ground turkey or lean ground pork can be used in place of the chicken.

For milder meatballs, use an equal amount of Monterey Jack cheese in place of the pepper Jack.

Caesar Chicken Wings

Why limit the distinctive, delicious flavors of Caesar dressing to lettuce? It makes a zesty coating for chicken wings, too. The signature Caesar flavor is further amped up with a garlicky Parmesan crust that is absolutely addictive.

TIP

An equal amount of panko (Japanese bread crumbs) can be used in place of the crushed crackers.

Variations

Gluten-Free Caesar Chicken Wings: Replace the crackers with an equal amount of crushed gluten-free crackers or corn flakes cereal.

Parmesan Ranch Chicken Wings: Replace the Caesar salad dressing with an equal amount of ranch dressing and omit the garlic powder.

• Preheat air fryer to 360°F (180°C)

½ cup	finely crushed buttery crackers (such as Ritz; about 12 crackers)	125 mL
¼ cup	freshly grated Parmesan cheese	60 mL
½ tsp	garlic powder	2 mL
⅛ tsp	freshly cracked black pepper	0.5 mL
6	chicken wings, tips removed and wings cut into drumettes and flats	6
2 tbsp	Caesar salad dressing (vinaigrette or creamy style)	30 mL
	Nonstick cooking spray	

1. In a shallow dish, combine crushed crackers, cheese, garlic powder and pepper.

2. In a medium bowl, toss together chicken wings and salad dressing. Working with 1 chicken wing at a time, dredge in cracker mixture, pressing gently to adhere. As they are dredged, place chicken wings in a single layer in air fryer basket, spacing them evenly. Spray with cooking spray. Discard any excess cracker mixture.

3. Air-fry for 8 minutes. Open basket and, using tongs or a spatula, turn chicken wings over. Air-fry for 8 minutes; turn pieces over again. Air-fry for 8 to 12 minutes or until coating is browned and crisp and juices run clear when chicken is pierced. Serve immediately.

Mahogany Chicken Wings

Buffalo wings, meet your new rival. Sweet, salty, tangy and spicy, these mahogany wings combine simplicity with deep, distinct flavors.

TIPS

An equal amount of spicy brown mustard can be used in place of the Dijon mustard.

For a milder sauce, reduce or omit the hot pepper sauce.

• Preheat air fryer to 360°F (180°C)

6	chicken wings, tips removed and wings cut into drumettes and flats	6
3 tbsp	dark (cooking) molasses	45 mL
2 tbsp	soy sauce	30 mL
2 tsp	Dijon mustard	10 mL
1 tsp	hot pepper sauce (such as Tabasco)	5 mL

1. Place chicken wings in a single layer (with some overlap) in air fryer basket. Air-fry for 24 to 28 minutes, shaking basket twice, until skin is browned and crisp and juices run clear when chicken is pierced.

2. Meanwhile, in a small microwave-safe cup, whisk together molasses, soy sauce, mustard and hot sauce. Heat on High for 15 to 20 seconds or until hot but not boiling.

3. Transfer wings to a bowl. Add sauce and toss to coat. Serve immediately.

Sage-Rubbed Turkey Breast

The air fryer cooks turkey breast perfectly — you'll want to make it year-round.

TIPS

An equal amount of olive oil can be used in place of the butter.

Air fryers become very hot, especially when heated to maximum temperature. Use oven pads or mitts when touching the appliance and when opening and closing the basket.

- Preheat air fryer to 360°F (180°C)

1	bone-in skin-on turkey breast (about 2 lbs/1 kg), patted dry	1
1 tbsp	butter, softened	15 mL
1 tsp	dried rubbed sage	5 mL
	Salt and freshly cracked black pepper	

1. Gently loosen skin from turkey breast (but do not remove it). Rub butter and sage under skin and over breast. Season generously, under skin and over breast, with salt and pepper. Transfer turkey breast, skin side up, to air fryer basket.

2. Air-fry for 20 minutes. Open basket and, using tongs, turn breast on its side. Air-fry for 10 minutes. Open basket and, using tongs, turn breast onto its other side. Air-fry for 10 to 15 minutes or until turkey skin is crisp and golden brown and an instant-read thermometer inserted in the thickest part of the breast registers 165°F (74°C).

3. Remove turkey from air fryer basket, cover loosely with foil and let rest for 10 minutes. Carve turkey and serve.

Variation

Replace the sage with an equal amount of dried thyme or poultry seasoning, or with 2 tsp (10 mL) chopped fresh rosemary.

Crispy Horseradish Parmesan Turkey Cutlets

MAKES 2 SERVINGS

Homey and old-fashioned goes sophisticated in this trim rendition of fried turkey cutlets, thanks to the additions of spicy horseradish and the umami nuances of Parmesan cheese.

Variations

Gluten-Free Crispy Horseradish Parmesan Turkey Cutlets: Replace the panko with gluten-free bread crumbs or crushed gluten-free crackers or corn flakes cereal.

Chicken or pork cutlets can be used in place of the turkey cutlets.

• Preheat air fryer to 360°F (180°C)

⅔ cup	panko (Japanese bread crumbs)	150 mL
2 tbsp	freshly grated Parmesan cheese	30 mL
⅛ tsp	salt	0.5 mL
⅛ tsp	freshly ground black pepper	0.5 mL
3 tbsp	buttermilk	45 mL
1 tbsp	prepared horseradish	15 mL
2	turkey breast cutlets (each about 6 oz/175 g)	2
	Nonstick cooking spray	

1. In a shallow dish, stir together panko, Parmesan cheese, salt and pepper.

2. In another shallow dish, whisk together buttermilk and horseradish.

3. Working with 1 cutlet at a time, dip in buttermilk mixture, shaking off excess, then dredge in panko mixture until coated, pressing gently to adhere. As they are dredged, spray both sides of cutlets with cooking spray and place in air fryer basket, spacing them evenly. Discard any excess buttermilk mixture and panko mixture.

4. Air-fry for 6 to 9 minutes or until crust is golden brown and turkey is no longer pink inside.

Cuban Sandwich Sliders

MAKES 2 SERVINGS

Mini turkey burgers are given the Cuban sandwich treatment — ham, Swiss cheese and dill pickles — making these simple patties come alive with flavor.

TIP

Air fryers become very hot, especially when heated to maximum temperature. Use oven pads or mitts when touching the appliance and when opening and closing the basket.

• Preheat air fryer to 390°F (200°C)

12 oz	lean ground turkey	375 g
1/8 tsp	salt	0.5 mL
1/8 tsp	freshly cracked black pepper	0.5 mL
2	slices deli Swiss cheese, quartered	2
2	slices deli ham, quartered	2
4	slider buns, split	4
4	dill pickle slices	4

1. In a medium bowl, combine turkey, salt and pepper until blended (be careful not to overmix or compact mixture). Form into 4 small patties, each about $1/2$ inch (1 cm) thick.

2. Arrange patties in air fryer basket, spacing them evenly. Air-fry for 7 to 10 minutes or until an instant-read thermometer inserted horizontally into the center of a patty registers 165°F (74°C).

3. Place a cheese piece and a ham piece on bottom halves of buns. Transfer patties to bottom halves and top each with a pickle slice and another cheese piece and ham piece. Cover with top halves of buns, pressing down gently.

Variation

An equal amount of ground chicken breast or lean ground pork can be used in place of the turkey.

Turkey and Dressing Burgers

Give thanks for turkey and dressing any time of the year with this burger interpretation of the favorite combination. If you need a suggestion for a side, you cannot go wrong with sweet potato chips or sweet potato fries.

TIP

You can use 2 tbsp (30 mL) finely chopped shallots or yellow onion in place of the green onions.

• Preheat air fryer to 360°F (180°C)

1	package (6 oz/175 g) dry chicken stuffing mix, divided	1
¼ cup	hot water	60 mL
⅛ tsp	freshly ground black pepper	0.5 mL
12 oz	lean ground turkey	375 g
3 tbsp	finely chopped green onions	45 mL
2 tbsp	freshly grated Parmesan cheese	30 mL
	Nonstick cooking spray	
2	hamburger buns or soft sandwich rolls, split	2

Suggested Toppings

Cranberry sauce

Thinly sliced Swiss cheese

Spinach leaves

1. In a large bowl, combine half the stuffing mix, hot water and pepper, stirring until well blended. Add turkey, green onions and cheese, gently combining until blended. Form into two ¾-inch (2 cm) thick patties.

2. Place the remaining stuffing mix in a large sealable bag. Seal bag, pressing out air. Using a rolling pin or a can, crush stuffing into fine crumbs. Spread crumbs in a shallow dish.

TIP

Air fryers become very hot, especially when heated to maximum temperature. Use oven pads or mitts when touching the appliance and when opening and closing the basket.

3. Working with 1 patty at a time, dredge patty in stuffing crumbs, pressing gently to adhere. As they are dredged, place patties in air fryer basket, spacing them evenly. Spray patties with cooking spray. Discard any excess stuffing crumbs.

4. Air-fry for 8 minutes. Open basket and, using a spatula, carefully turn patties over. Air-fry for 7 to 10 minutes or until coating is crisp and an instant-read thermometer inserted horizontally into the center of a patty registers 165°F (74°C).

5. Transfer patties to bottom halves of buns and layer with any of the suggested toppings, as desired. Cover with top halves of buns, pressing down gently.

Rosemary Garlic Turkey Meatballs

MAKES 2 SERVINGS

Super-easy to make and loaded with flavor, these protein-packed meatballs are great plain, doused in marinara sauce or piled onto a sub roll for a lunchtime sandwich.

TIP

You can use ¾ tsp (3 mL) dried rosemary, crumbled, in place of the fresh rosemary.

- Preheat air fryer to 390°F (200°C)

12 oz	lean ground turkey	375 g
1	large egg	1
3 tbsp	dry bread crumbs with Italian seasoning	45 mL
1¼ tsp	minced fresh rosemary	6 mL
1 tsp	garlic powder	5 mL
⅛ tsp	salt	0.5 mL
⅛ tsp	freshly cracked black pepper	0.5 mL

1. In a medium bowl, combine turkey, egg, bread crumbs, rosemary, garlic powder, salt and pepper until blended (be careful not to overmix or compact mixture). Form into 12 meatballs, each about 1¼ inches (3 cm) in diameter.

2. Arrange meatballs in air fryer basket, spacing them evenly. Air-fry for 6 to 10 minutes or until meatballs are browned and no longer pink inside.

Variations

Gluten-Free Rosemary Garlic Turkey Meatballs: Replace the bread crumbs with gluten-free bread crumbs or crushed gluten-free crackers or corn flakes cereal.

An equal amount of ground chicken breast or lean ground pork can be used in place of the turkey.

Maple-Glazed Game Hen

Cooking game hens can be tricky; their small size makes it challenging to cook thicker areas of the bird to the proper temperature without drying out the wings and legs. The problem is solved with the air fryer, which cooks the hens perfectly and evenly with no worries and almost no effort.

TIPS

To split a game hen in half, use a butcher's knife to cut down each side of the backbone; remove the backbone, then cut in half through the breast.

Air fryers become very hot, especially when heated to maximum temperature. Use oven pads or mitts when touching the appliance and when opening and closing the basket.

- Preheat air fryer to 390°F (200°C)

1	Cornish game hen (about 2 lbs/1 kg), split in half, patted dry	1
	Nonstick cooking spray	
	Salt and freshly cracked black pepper	
2 tbsp	pure maple syrup	30 mL
½ tsp	apple cider vinegar	2 mL
½ tsp	soy sauce	2 mL

1. Spray both sides of game hen halves with cooking spray and season generously on both sides with salt and pepper. Place game hen halves, skin side down, in air fryer basket, leaving space in between.

2. Air-fry for 8 minutes. Open basket and, using tongs, turn game hen halves over. Air-fry for 8 minutes.

3. Meanwhile, in a small bowl, combine maple syrup, vinegar and soy sauce until blended.

4. Open basket and generously brush skin side of game hen halves with maple glaze. Air-fry for 3 to 6 minutes or until skin is crisp and golden brown and an instant-read thermometer inserted in the thickest part of the thigh registers 165°F (74°C).

5. Transfer game hen halves to a cutting board, cover loosely with foil and let rest for 10 minutes.

Variation

An equal amount of liquid honey or dark (cooking) molasses can be used in place of the maple syrup.

Pork, Beef and Lamb

Brown Sugar Balsamic Pork Tenderloin

The sweet, acidic pungency of balsamic vinegar, together with the sharp tang of Dijon mustard, is mellowed by the smooth molasses flavor of brown sugar, making simple pork tenderloin something special.

TIP

An equal amount of Dijon or spicy brown mustard can be used in place of the whole-grain mustard.

- Preheat air fryer to 380°F (190°C)

2 tbsp	packed dark brown sugar	30 mL
1 tbsp	balsamic vinegar	15 mL
2 tsp	whole-grain Dijon mustard	10 mL
¼ tsp	salt	1 mL
⅛ tsp	freshly cracked black pepper	0.5 mL
1 lb	pork tenderloin, trimmed, halved crosswise	500 g
	Nonstick cooking spray	

1. In a small cup or bowl, combine brown sugar, vinegar, mustard, salt and pepper.
2. Brush pork all over with half the vinegar mixture. Place pork halves in air fryer basket, spacing them evenly. Spray with cooking spray.
3. Air-fry for 10 minutes. Open basket and, using tongs, turn pork halves over. Brush with the remaining vinegar mixture. Air-fry for 5 to 8 minutes or until an instant-read thermometer inserted in the thickest part of the tenderloin registers 145°F (63°C) for medium-rare.
4. Transfer tenderloin to a cutting board, tent with foil and let rest for 10 minutes. Slice tenderloin across the grain.

Variation

Replace the mustard with 1½ tsp (7 mL) minced garlic.

Stuffing-Crusted Pork Tenderloin

Stuffing mix is great with poultry, but it also shines as a flavorful crumb crust for pork tenderloin, especially when paired with an apple jelly coating.

TIP

Air fryers become very hot, especially when heated to maximum temperature. Use oven pads or mitts when touching the appliance and when opening and closing the basket.

• Preheat air fryer to 380°F (190°C)

1	package (6 oz/175 g) dry chicken-flavored stuffing mix	1
2½ tbsp	apple jelly, melted	37 mL
1 tsp	apple cider vinegar	5 mL
1 lb	pork tenderloin, trimmed, halved crosswise	500 g
	Nonstick cooking spray	

1. Place the stuffing mix in a large sealable bag. Seal bag, pressing out air. Using a rolling pin or a can, crush stuffing into fine crumbs.

2. In a small cup or bowl, combine melted jelly and vinegar.

3. Brush pork all over with jelly mixture and press stuffing mixture all over to coat. Place pork halves in air fryer basket, spacing them evenly. Spray with cooking spray.

4. Air-fry for 10 minutes. Open basket and, using tongs, turn pork halves over. Air-fry for 5 to 8 minutes or until an instant-read thermometer inserted in the thickest part of the tenderloin registers 145°F (63°C) for medium-rare.

5. Transfer tenderloin to a cutting board and tent with foil. Let rest for 10 minutes. Slice tenderloin across the grain.

Variations

Replace the apple jelly with an equal amount of liquid honey or pure maple syrup.

Other flavors of stuffing mix, such as garlic or sage, can be used in place of the chicken-flavored stuffing mix.

Herb-Crusted Pork Tenderloin

MAKES 2 TO 3 SERVINGS

In this impressive pork recipe, the bright, fresh flavor of parsley works in harmony with the robust flavor of Dijon mustard and the light crunch of panko.

TIP

Panko crumbs are larger than regular bread crumbs and have a light texture that becomes especially crunchy with air-frying.

- Preheat air fryer to 380°F (190°C)

²⁄₃ cup	panko (Japanese bread crumbs)	150 mL
½ cup	packed fresh parsley leaves, chopped	125 mL
¼ tsp	salt	1 mL
¼ tsp	freshly cracked black pepper	1 mL
1 lb	pork tenderloin, trimmed, halved crosswise	500 g
2 tbsp	Dijon mustard	30 mL
	Nonstick cooking spray	

1. In a small bowl, combine panko, parsley, salt and pepper.

2. Brush pork all over with mustard and press crumb mixture all over to coat. Place pork halves in air fryer basket, spacing them evenly. Spray with cooking spray.

3. Air-fry for 10 minutes. Open basket and, using tongs, turn pork halves over. Air-fry for 5 to 8 minutes or until an instant-read thermometer inserted in the thickest part of the tenderloin registers 145°F (63°C) for medium-rare.

4. Transfer tenderloin to a cutting board and tent with foil. Let rest for 10 minutes. Slice tenderloin across the grain.

TIP

Air fryers become very hot, especially when heated to maximum temperature. Use oven pads or mitts when touching the appliance and when opening and closing the basket.

Variations

Gluten-Free Herb-Crusted Pork Tenderloin: Replace the panko with an equal amount of gluten-free bread crumbs or crushed gluten-free crackers or corn flakes cereal.

Replace the parsley with an equal amount of fresh basil or 2 tsp (10 mL) chopped fresh rosemary.

Replace the Dijon mustard with an equal amount of prepared horseradish or spicy brown mustard.

Gingersnap-Crusted Pork Tenderloin

MAKES 2 TO 3 SERVINGS

This pork tenderloin dish gets sweet-and-spicy verve from a maple-mustard coating and a peppery gingersnap crust.

TIPS

Replace the whole-grain mustard with an equal amount of Dijon mustard or spicy brown mustard.

For a gluten-free crust, make sure to use gluten-free gingersnap cookies.

- Preheat air fryer to 380°F (190°C)

2 tbsp	pure maple syrup	30 mL
1 tbsp	whole-grain Dijon mustard	15 mL
¼ tsp	salt	1 mL
¾ cup	finely crushed gingersnap cookies	175 mL
¼ tsp	freshly cracked black pepper	1 mL
1 lb	pork tenderloin, trimmed, halved crosswise	500 g
	Nonstick cooking spray	

1. In a small bowl, combine maple syrup, mustard and salt.
2. In a medium bowl, combine gingersnaps and pepper.
3. Brush pork all over with maple syrup mixture and press gingersnap mixture all over to coat. Place pork halves in air fryer basket, spacing them evenly. Spray with cooking spray.
4. Air-fry for 10 minutes. Open basket and, using tongs, turn pork halves over. Air-fry for 5 to 8 minutes or until an instant-read thermometer inserted in the thickest part of the tenderloin registers 145°F (63°C) for medium-rare.
5. Transfer tenderloin to a cutting board and tent with foil. Let rest for 10 minutes. Slice tenderloin across the grain.

Glazed Pork Chops with Molasses and Dijon

Simple and fast, these glazed pork chops are great for busy weeknights. An almost-instant glaze of molasses and mustard infuses the chops with delectable flavor.

TIPS

An equal amount of spicy brown or whole-grain mustard can be used in place of the Dijon mustard.

Air fryers become very hot, especially when heated to maximum temperature. Use oven pads or mitts when touching the appliance and when opening and closing the basket.

- Preheat air fryer to 390°F (200°C)

2 tbsp	dark (cooking) molasses	30 mL
2 tbsp	Dijon mustard	30 mL
1/8 tsp	salt	0.5 mL
1/8 tsp	freshly cracked black pepper	0.5 mL
2	bone-in pork loin chops, about 1 inch (2.5 cm) thick, trimmed	2

1. In a small cup or bowl, combine molasses, mustard, salt and pepper.

2. Place pork chops in air fryer basket, spacing them evenly. Spoon half the molasses mixture onto chops, spreading to cover.

3. Air-fry for 6 minutes. Open basket and, using tongs, turn chops over. Spoon and spread the remaining molasses mixture over chops. Air-fry for 4 to 7 minutes or until an instant-read thermometer inserted in the thickest part of the pork, without touching the bone, registers 145°F (63°C) for medium-rare.

4. Transfer pork chops to a platter, tent with foil and let rest for 5 minutes before serving.

Variation

Replace the molasses with an equal amount of liquid honey or pure maple syrup.

Crispy Lemon Pepper Pork Chops

A bright and peppery citrus mayonnaise keeps these pork chops moist and juicy while simultaneously delivering a punch of flavor. A crunchy panko coating adds crisp contrast.

TIPS

For best results, do not use fat-free mayonnaise. It is made mostly of water and gums, a combination that does not work well in this recipe.

Although freshly grated Parmesan has the best flavor, an equal amount of pre-grated Parmesan cheese can be used in its place.

- Preheat air fryer to 390°F (200°C)

⅓ cup	panko (Japanese bread crumbs)	75 mL
¼ cup	freshly grated Parmesan cheese	60 mL
1	lemon	1
2 tbsp	mayonnaise	30 mL
¼ tsp	salt	1 mL
¼ tsp	freshly cracked black pepper	1 mL
2	bone-in pork loin chops, about 1-inch (2.5 cm) thick, trimmed	2

1. In a shallow dish, combine panko and cheese.
2. Finely grate enough lemon zest to measure 1 tsp (5 mL). Cut lemon in half and squeeze enough juice to measure 1 tbsp (15 mL).
3. In a small cup or bowl, stir together mayonnaise, lemon zest, lemon juice, salt and pepper.
4. Generously spread both sides of pork chops with mayonnaise mixture, then press into panko mixture to coat. Place pork chops in air fryer basket, spacing them evenly. Discard excess mayonnaise mixture and panko mixture.

Air fryers become very hot, especially when heated to maximum temperature. Use oven pads or mitts when touching the appliance and when opening and closing the basket.

5. Air-fry for 10 to 13 minutes or until an instant-read thermometer inserted in the thickest part of the pork, without touching the bone, registers 145°F (63°C) for medium-rare.

6. Transfer pork chops to a platter, tent with foil and let rest for 5 minutes before serving.

Variations

Spicy Fried Pork Chops: Omit the lemon zest. Replace 1 tsp (5 mL) of the lemon juice with 1 tsp (5 mL) hot pepper sauce (such as Tabasco).

Horseradish Fried Pork Chops: Omit the lemon zest. Replace the lemon juice with an equal amount of prepared horseradish.

Mustard Fried Pork Chops: Omit the lemon zest. Replace the lemon juice with an equal amount of Dijon or spicy brown mustard.

Gluten-Free Lemon Parmesan Pork Chops: Replace the panko with an equal amount of gluten-free bread crumbs or crushed gluten-free crackers or corn flakes cereal.

Spicy Lion's Head Meatballs

A streamlined version of a Chinese classic, this recipe is just right when you crave takeout.

TIP

Air fryers become very hot, especially when heated to maximum temperature. Use oven pads or mitts when touching the appliance and when opening and closing the basket.

- Preheat air fryer to 390°F (200°C)

3 tbsp	dry bread crumbs	45 mL
4 tbsp	water, divided	60 mL
5 tbsp	hoisin sauce, divided	75 mL
¼ tsp	salt	1 mL
¼ tsp	freshly ground black pepper	1 mL
8 oz	lean ground pork	250 g
½ cup	finely chopped drained canned water chestnuts	125 mL
5 tbsp	finely chopped green onions, divided	75 mL

1. In a medium bowl, using a fork, combine bread crumbs, 3 tbsp (45 mL) water, 2 tbsp (30 mL) hoisin sauce, salt and pepper. Let stand for 5 minutes.

2. Add pork, water chestnuts and 4 tbsp (60 mL) green onions to the crumb mixture, gently stirring with a fork to combine. Shape into 8 meatballs.

3. Arrange meatballs in air fryer basket, spacing them evenly. Air-fry for 8 to 11 minutes or until meatballs are firm to the touch and no longer pink inside.

4. Meanwhile, in a small microwave-safe cup, microwave the remaining hoisin sauce and water on High for 10 to 15 seconds or until heated through.

5. Drizzle sauce over meatballs and sprinkle with the remaining green onions.

Kielbasa, Potatoes and Sauerkraut

Smoky kielbasa and tangy sauerkraut turn diced hash browns into a complete, Oktoberfest-inspired supper in minutes.

TIP

Other varieties of fully cooked smoked sausage can be used in place of the kielbasa.

- Preheat air fryer to 390°F (200°C)
- 6-inch (15 cm) round metal baking pan, sprayed with nonstick cooking spray

1⅓ cups	frozen diced hash brown potatoes with peppers and onions	325 mL
8 oz	kielbasa sausage, diced	250 g
	Salt and freshly cracked black pepper	
	Nonstick cooking spray	
¾ cup	drained sauerkraut	175 mL
¼ tsp	caraway seeds (optional)	1 mL
1 tbsp	minced fresh chives (optional)	15 mL

1. In prepared pan, stir together potatoes and kielbasa. Season with salt and pepper and spray with cooking spray.

2. Place pan in air fryer basket. Air-fry for 8 to 10 minutes or until potatoes and kielbasa are beginning to brown.

3. Open basket and add sauerkraut to pan, stirring gently to combine. Sprinkle with caraway seeds (if using). Air-fry for 4 to 6 minutes or until sauerkraut is warmed through and potatoes are golden brown. Sprinkle with chives, if desired.

Steakhouse New York Strip and Fried Mushrooms

In the air fryer, New York strip loin cooks to a rich brown on the outside and becomes juicy and tender on the inside, thanks to the even heat of the air fryer chamber. Tender mushrooms, which cook alongside, are the ideal accompaniment.

TIPS

If your steak seasoning does not contain salt, rub steak with $\frac{1}{4}$ tsp (1 mL) salt in addition to the steak seasoning.

Air fryers become very hot, especially when heated to maximum temperature. Use oven pads or mitts when touching the appliance and when opening and closing the basket.

- Preheat air fryer to 390°F (200°C)

1 lb	boneless beef strip loin (New York) steak, trimmed	500 g
1½ tsp	steak seasoning	7 mL
	Nonstick cooking spray	
8 oz	sliced mushrooms	250 g
	Salt and freshly cracked black pepper	
	Minced fresh chives (optional)	

1. Rub steak all over with steak seasoning. Spray both sides with cooking spray and place on one side of air fryer basket. Add mushrooms to other side of basket. Spray mushrooms with cooking spray and season with salt and pepper.

2. Air-fry for 4 minutes. Open basket and, using tongs, turn over steak and stir mushrooms. Air-fry for 2 to 5 minutes for medium-rare to medium, or to desired doneness.

3. Transfer steaks to a platter, tent with foil and let rest for 10 minutes. Serve sprinkled with chives, if desired.

Steak Piperade

Aromatic without being overly spicy, this rendition of a Basque region favorite has a touch of the exotic but will please traditionalist steak lovers, too.

TIP

An equal amount of regular paprika or chili powder can be used in place of the smoked paprika.

• **Preheat air fryer to 360°F (180°C)**

1 lb	boneless beef strip loin (New York) steak, trimmed	500 g
2	small bell peppers (preferably 1 red and 1 orange), sliced	2
1	small onion, halved lengthwise and sliced	1
1 tbsp	olive oil	15 mL
1½ tsp	smoked paprika	7 mL
¾ tsp	salt	3 mL
⅛ tsp	freshly cracked black pepper	0.5 mL

1. Slice steak across the grain into ½-inch (1 cm) thick strips.

2. In a large bowl, toss together steak, bell peppers, onion, oil, paprika, salt and pepper. Spread in an even layer in air fryer basket.

3. Air-fry for 12 to 16 minutes, shaking basket twice, until vegetables are tender-crisp and beef is cooked through.

Bacon-Wrapped Filets Mignons

Cooking steak to perfection has never been easier. These bacon-wrapped filets are ideal when you want to go all out without the fuss.

TIP

Thick-cut bacon is not recommended for this recipe because it does not become crisp in the time required to cook the steak.

- Preheat air fryer to 390°F (200°C)
- 2 small metal skewers or toothpicks

2	slices bacon (not thick-cut)	2
2	filets mignons (each about 8 oz/250 g)	2
	Salt and freshly cracked black pepper	

1. Wrap one bacon slice around the outside circumference of each steak, securing the ends with a skewer. Season all over with salt and pepper. Place steaks in air fryer basket, spacing them evenly.

2. Air-fry for 9 minutes. Open basket and, using tongs, turn steaks over. Air-fry for 2 to 5 minutes for medium-rare to medium, or to desired doneness.

3. Transfer steaks to a platter, tent with foil and let rest for 10 minutes. Remove skewers from steaks before serving.

Variation

Sprinkle one side of each bacon strip with minced fresh rosemary or thyme before wrapping around steaks (with the herbs against the steak).

London Broil

A quick marinade, followed by a short spell in the air fryer, is all it takes to make perfect London broil.

TIP

Air fryers become very hot, especially when heated to maximum temperature. Use oven pads or mitts when touching the appliance and when opening and closing the basket.

1½ lbs	boneless beef top round or flank steak (about ¾ inch/ 2 cm thick)	750 g
	Salt and freshly cracked black pepper	
½ cup	steak sauce (such as A1 or HP Sauce)	125 mL
1 tbsp	olive oil	15 mL

1. Season steak all over with salt and pepper. Place in a large sealable plastic bag. Add steak sauce and oil. Seal bag, pressing out air. Gently turn and squeeze bag to coat steak on all sides. Refrigerate for at least 30 minutes or for up to 4 hours.

2. Meanwhile, preheat air fryer to 390°F (200°C).

3. Remove steak from marinade, shaking off and discarding excess marinade, and transfer to air fryer basket. Air-fry for 12 minutes. Open basket and, using tongs, turn steak over. Air-fry for 4 to 8 minutes for medium-rare to medium, or to desired doneness.

4. Transfer steak to a cutting board, tent with foil and let rest for 10 minutes. Cut steak across the grain into ¼-inch (0.5 cm) slices.

Carne Asada Tacos

Here, readily available chipotle-spiced taco seasoning steers steak in a south-of-the-border direction in seconds.

TIPS

To warm the tortillas, completely enclose them in foil. Place in the preheated air fryer before cooking the steak and air-fry for 5 minutes. Remove from air fryer but keep wrapped in foil until ready to use.

Regular taco seasoning can be used in place of the chipotle taco seasoning.

You can use 1 small Hass avocado, diced, in place of the guacamole.

• Preheat air fryer to 390°F (200°C)

1 lb	beef flank steak, trimmed, patted dry and halved crosswise	500 g
	Nonstick cooking spray	
1 tbsp	chipotle taco seasoning mix	15 mL
4 to 6	6-inch (15 cm) corn or flour tortillas, warmed (see tip)	4 to 6
½ cup	guacamole	125 mL
½ cup	pico de gallo or salsa	125 mL

1. Spray steak pieces all over with cooking spray. Sprinkle with taco seasoning, rubbing all over steak.

2. Place steak pieces in air fryer basket, spacing them evenly. Air-fry for 9 to 14 minutes for medium-rare to medium, or to desired doneness.

3. Transfer steak pieces to a cutting board and tent with foil. Let rest for 10 minutes. Cut steak across the grain into ¼-inch (0.5 cm) slices. Serve in tortillas topped with guacamole and pico de gallo.

Chipotle Cheddar Barbecue Burgers

Barbecue sauce does wonders for meat and chicken. Here, it works magic on burgers in two ways: mixed into the ground beef (adding both flavor and juiciness) and brushed onto the burgers for a punchy glaze. Add some easy air-frying, and you've got big, bold, straight-from-the-grill flavor.

Variations

Substitute ground turkey or lean ground pork for the beef.

If chipotle barbecue sauce is not available, use any variety of spicy barbecue sauce in its place.

- Preheat air fryer to 390°F (200°C)

12 oz	extra-lean ground beef	375 g
⅛ tsp	salt	0.5 mL
⅛ tsp	freshly ground black pepper	0.5 mL
5 tbsp	chipotle barbecue sauce, divided	75 mL
½ cup	shredded extra-sharp (extra-old) Cheddar cheese	125 mL
¼ cup	finely chopped green onions	60 mL
2	hamburger buns, split and toasted	2

Suggested Toppings

Lettuce leaves

Tomato slices

Sliced avocado

1. In a large bowl, gently combine beef, salt, pepper and 2 tbsp (30 mL) barbecue sauce. Gently stir in cheese and green onions. Form into two ¾-inch (2 cm) thick patties.

2. Place patties in air fryer basket, spacing them evenly. Air-fry for 6 minutes. Open basket and brush with half the remaining barbecue sauce. Using a spatula, carefully turn patties over. Brush with the remaining barbecue sauce. Air-fry for 4 to 7 minutes or until an instant-read thermometer inserted horizontally into the center of a patty registers 165°F (74°C).

3. Transfer patties to bottom halves of buns and top with any of the suggested toppings, as desired. Cover with top halves of buns, pressing down gently.

Streamlined Swedish Meatballs

Although untraditional in preparation, this minimalist version of Swedish meatballs is still packed with familiar — and undeniable — comfort-food flavor. And you don't have to feel confined to beef. This recipe will also turn ground turkey or pork into something worth raving about.

Variations

Gluten-Free Streamlined Swedish Meatballs: Replace the bread crumbs with an equal amount of gluten-free bread crumbs or crushed gluten-free crackers. Check the label of the alfredo sauce to ensure that it is gluten-free.

Lean ground turkey or pork can be used in place of the beef.

- Preheat air fryer to 360°F (180°C)

8 oz	lean ground beef	250 g
¼ cup	grated onion	60 mL
3 tbsp	dry bread crumbs	45 mL
½ cup	alfredo sauce, divided	125 mL
¼ tsp	ground allspice	1 mL
¼ tsp	salt	1 mL
⅛ tsp	freshly cracked black pepper	0.5 mL

Suggested Garnishes

Lingonberry jam

Chopped fresh parsley

1. In a medium bowl, combine beef, onion, bread crumbs, 1½ tbsp (22 mL) alfredo sauce, allspice, salt and pepper (be careful not to overmix). Form into 1½-inch (4 cm) meatballs.

2. Arrange meatballs in air fryer basket, spacing them evenly. Air-fry for 9 to 13 minutes or until meatballs are browned and no longer pink inside.

3. Meanwhile, place the remaining alfredo sauce in a small microwave-safe cup or bowl. Microwave on High for 20 to 30 seconds or until heated through.

4. Divide meatballs between serving plates and spoon sauce over top. Serve with the suggested garnishes, as desired.

Baja Fish Tacos (page 182)

Chicken Shawarma (page 202)

Cuban Sandwich Sliders (page 217)

Herb-Crusted Pork Tenderloin (page 226)

Bacon-Wrapped Filets Mignons (page 236)

Cheese and Garlic Monkey Bread (page 249)

Pecan Pie Roll-Ups (page 269)

Graham Cracker Toffee
(Chocolate Chip and Coconut variations, page 276)

Bacon Mesquite Mini Meatloaves

Don't say I didn't warn you! Your mouth will be watering as these bacon-packed meatloaves sizzle in the air fryer. But no need to fear: the recipe is so easy, you can whip it together whenever the craving strikes.

TIPS

For convenience, you can use packaged fully cooked bacon pieces or strips.

Air fryers become very hot, especially when heated to maximum temperature. Use oven pads or mitts when touching the appliance and when opening and closing the basket.

• Preheat air fryer to 360°F (180°C)

12 oz	lean ground beef	375 g
1/3 cup	finely chopped cooked bacon	75 mL
1/4 cup	grated onion	60 mL
1 tsp	mesquite seasoning	5 mL
2 tbsp	steak sauce (such as A1 or HP Sauce)	30 ml

1. In a medium bowl, combine beef, bacon, onion and mesquite seasoning (be careful not to overmix). Form into 2 small loaves, each about 4 1/2 by 2 1/2 inches (11 by 6 cm).

2. Place meatloaves in air fryer basket, spacing them evenly. Air-fry for 10 minutes. Open basket and brush each meatloaf with steak sauce. Air-fry for 6 to 9 minutes or until an instant-read thermometer inserted in the center of the meatloaves registers 165°F (74°C).

3. Transfer meatloaves to a plate and tent with foil. Let rest for 5 minutes.

Variation

Substitute ground turkey or lean ground pork for the beef.

Greek Lamb and Feta Mini Meatloaves

MAKES 2 SERVINGS

Feta, herbs and the citrus zing of fresh lemon zest come together in this simple lamb recipe, a nod to the warm and sunny flavors of Greece.

TIP

Hot air and steam will release from the air fryer throughout the cooking cycle. If your face is in close proximity to the appliance during the cooking cycle or when you are opening the basket, you risk being scalded by the release of accumulated steam.

• Preheat air fryer to 360°F (180°C)

12 oz	ground lamb	375 g
$\frac{1}{3}$ cup	crumbled feta cheese	75 mL
$\frac{1}{4}$ cup	finely chopped green onions	60 mL
2 tsp	finely grated lemon zest	10 mL
1 tsp	dried oregano	5 mL
$\frac{1}{4}$ tsp	salt	1 mL
$\frac{1}{8}$ tsp	freshly cracked black pepper	0.5 mL

1. In a medium bowl, combine lamb, feta, green onions, lemon zest, oregano, salt and pepper until blended (be careful not to overmix). Form into 2 small loaves, each about $4\frac{1}{2}$ by $2\frac{1}{2}$ inches (11 by 6 cm).

2. Place meatloaves in air fryer basket, spacing them evenly. Air-fry for 16 to 19 minutes or until an instant-read thermometer inserted in the center of the meatloaves registers 165°F (74°C).

3. Transfer meatloaves to a plate and tent with foil. Let rest for 5 minutes.

Variations

Substitute ground turkey or lean ground beef for the lamb.

Replace the oregano with $1\frac{1}{2}$ tsp (7 mL) dried dillweed.

Middle Eastern Lamb Kefta

Fresh mint, smoky cumin and sweet spices, common ingredients in Middle Eastern cooking, give these lamb kefta — a traditional street food — authentic flavor and flair.

TIP

Air fryers become very hot, especially when heated to maximum temperature. Use oven pads or mitts when touching the appliance and when opening and closing the basket.

• Preheat air fryer to 390°F (200°C)

12 oz	ground lamb	375 g
1/3 cup	packed fresh mint leaves, chopped	75 mL
1/4 cup	grated onion	60 mL
3/4 tsp	ground cumin	3 mL
1/2 tsp	pumpkin pie spice	2 mL
1/2 tsp	salt	2 mL
1/4 tsp	freshly ground black pepper	1 mL

Suggested Accompaniments

Pita bread or naan

Plain yogurt

Chopped cucumber

Chopped tomatoes

1. In a medium bowl, gently combine lamb, mint, onion, cumin, pumpkin pie spice, salt and pepper. Shape into 4 patties, each about 2 inches (5 cm) in diameter.

2. Place patties in air fryer basket, spacing them evenly. Air-fry for 5 to 9 minutes or until an instant-read thermometer inserted horizontally in the center of a patty registers 165°F (74°C). Serve with any of the suggested accompaniments, as desired.

Variations

An equal amount of lean ground beef or ground turkey can be used in place of the ground lamb.

An equal amount of cilantro or parsley can be used in place of the mint.

Breads and Muffins

Irish Soda Bread

MAKES 4 SERVINGS

MAKES 4 SERVINGS

Delicious, fast and fuss-free (no kneading required and only 5 minutes assembly time), this is definitely the bread you need to make for supper tonight — why wait for Saint Paddy's Day?

TIPS

If you do not have self-rising flour, use the following ratio to make your own. For every 1 cup (250 mL) all-purpose flour, whisk in $1\frac{1}{2}$ tsp (7 mL) baking powder and $\frac{1}{2}$ tsp (2 mL) salt.

If you don't have buttermilk, mix $\frac{1}{2}$ cup (125 mL) milk (dairy or plain nondairy) with $1\frac{1}{2}$ tsp (7 mL) lemon juice or white vinegar. Let stand for at least 15 minutes before using, to allow the milk to curdle.

An equal amount of vegetable oil or olive oil can be used in place of the butter.

- Preheat air fryer to 390°F (200°C)
- 6-inch (15 cm) round metal cake pan, sprayed with nonstick cooking spray

¾ cup	self-rising flour (see tip)	175 mL
1 tbsp	granulated sugar	15 mL
⅛ tsp	baking soda	0.5 mL
½ cup	buttermilk	125 mL
3 tbsp	butter, melted	45 mL

1. In a medium bowl, whisk together flour, sugar and baking soda.
2. In a measuring cup or small bowl, whisk buttermilk and butter until blended.
3. Add the buttermilk mixture to the flour mixture and stir until just blended.
4. Spread batter evenly in prepared pan. Using a serrated knife, cut a deep X across the top of the batter.
5. Place pan in air fryer basket. Air-fry for 13 to 17 minutes or until top is golden and a tester inserted in the center of the bread comes out clean. Transfer bread to a wire rack and let cool completely.

Variations

Caraway Currant Soda Bread: Gently fold in $\frac{1}{4}$ cup (60 mL) currants and $\frac{1}{2}$ tsp (2 mL) caraway seeds at the end of step 3.

Herbed Soda Bread: Add $1\frac{1}{4}$ tsp (6 mL) dried Italian seasoning in step 1.

Vegan Soda Bread: Use vegetable oil, melted vegan margarine (stick variety, not tub or spread) or melted coconut oil in place of the butter. Use buttermilk substitute made from nondairy milk (see tip, page 246) in place of the buttermilk.

Beer Bread

The simple addition of beer to quick bread yields a lusty, yeasty loaf that tastes like it took exponentially more time to prepare. Delicious warm, it also can be cooled and sliced thin for delectable sandwiches.

TIPS

If you do not have self-rising flour, use the following ratio to make your own. For every 1 cup (250 mL) all-purpose flour, whisk in $1\frac{1}{2}$ tsp (7 mL) baking powder and $\frac{1}{2}$ tsp (2 mL) salt.

Do not open and measure the beer until ready to use, to avoid losing much of the carbonation.

An equal amount of vegetable oil or olive oil can be used in place of the butter.

STORAGE TIP

Store the cooled bread, wrapped in foil or plastic wrap, in the refrigerator for up to 2 days.

- Preheat air fryer to 390°F (200°C)
- 6-inch (15 cm) round metal cake pan, sprayed with nonstick cooking spray

1 cup	self-rising flour (see tip)	250 mL
1 tbsp	granulated sugar	15 mL
$\frac{1}{2}$ cup	beer	125 mL
2 tbsp	butter, melted	30 mL

1. In a medium bowl, whisk together flour and sugar. Stir in beer and butter until just blended.

2. Spread batter evenly in prepared pan.

3. Place pan in air fryer basket. Air-fry for 11 to 15 minutes or until top is golden and a tester inserted in the center of the bread comes out clean. Transfer bread to a wire rack and let cool completely.

Variations

Herbed Beer Bread: Add 1 tsp (5 mL) dried Italian seasoning along with the sugar in step 1.

Swiss Beer Bread: Add $\frac{1}{3}$ cup (75 mL) shredded Swiss cheese and $\frac{1}{8}$ tsp (0.5 mL) caraway seeds to the batter at the end of step 1.

Whole Wheat Beer Bread: Use white whole wheat flour or whole wheat flour, $1\frac{1}{2}$ tsp (7 mL) baking powder and $\frac{1}{2}$ tsp (2 mL) salt in place of the self-rising flour, and use packed dark brown sugar in place of the granulated sugar. If desired, use dark beer or stout for the beer.

Cheese and Garlic Monkey Bread

Savory monkey bread? Absolutely! A combination of butter, garlic and two kinds of cheese launches this easy pull-apart bread into a new stratosphere of deliciousness.

Variation

Herb and Cheese Monkey Bread: Replace the garlic powder with $\frac{1}{2}$ tsp (2 mL) dried Italian seasoning. Replace the Cheddar cheese with shredded Italian cheese blend.

- Preheat air fryer to 360°F (180°C)
- 6-inch (15 cm) round metal cake pan, sprayed with nonstick cooking spray

2 tbsp	butter, melted	30 mL
$\frac{1}{4}$ tsp	garlic powder	1 mL
$\frac{1}{3}$ cup	freshly grated Parmesan cheese	75 mL
1	small can (6 oz/175 g) refrigerated dinner biscuits	1
$\frac{1}{2}$ cup	shredded sharp (old) Cheddar cheese	125 mL

1. In a small shallow dish, stir together butter and garlic powder.

2. Spread Parmesan cheese in another shallow dish.

3. Remove dough from packaging and separate into biscuits. Cut each biscuit into quarters.

4. Dip each dough piece in butter mixture and then in Parmesan, pressing gently to adhere. Arrange dough pieces in prepared pan, overlapping if needed. Drizzle any remaining butter mixture over dough and sprinkle with Cheddar cheese and any remaining Parmesan cheese.

5. Place pan in air fryer basket. Air-fry for 18 to 23 minutes or until golden brown. Transfer pan to a wire rack and let cool for at least 10 minutes. Run knife around edge of pan to loosen. Serve immediately.

Double Corn Bread

The popularity of corn bread extends far beyond the American Southwest. It's nothing short of a North American staple, beloved as an accompaniment to soups, salads, holiday meals and so much more. Make this double-corn version any time you please — it requires only minutes to assemble and air-fry.

TIP

An equal amount of vegetable oil or olive oil can be used in place of the butter.

STORAGE TIP

Store the cooled bread, wrapped in foil or plastic wrap, in the refrigerator for up to 3 days. Alternatively, wrap it in plastic wrap, then foil, completely enclosing bread, and freeze for up to 3 months. Let thaw at room temperature for 4 to 6 hours before serving.

- Preheat air fryer to 390°F (200°C)
- 6-inch (15 cm) round metal cake pan, sprayed with nonstick cooking spray

⅓ cup	self-rising flour (see tip, page 251)	75 mL
⅓ cup	yellow cornmeal	75 mL
⅛ tsp	salt	0.5 mL
1	large egg	1
⅓ cup	canned creamed corn	75 mL
1 tbsp	butter, melted	15 mL

1. In a medium bowl, whisk together flour, cornmeal and salt.
2. In a small bowl, whisk egg. Stir in creamed corn and butter until blended. Add egg mixture to the flour mixture and stir until just blended.
3. Spread batter evenly in prepared pan.
4. Place pan in air fryer basket. Air-fry for 11 to 15 minutes or until top is golden and a tester inserted in the center of the bread comes out clean. Transfer bread to a wire rack and let cool for 5 minutes. Serve warm or let cool completely.

Variations

Green Onion Cornbread: Add ¼ cup (60 mL) finely chopped green onions to the batter at the end of step 2.

Green Chile Cornbread: Reduce the creamed corn to ¼ cup (60 mL). Add ¼ cup (60 mL) canned diced green chiles to the batter at the end of step 2.

Pumpkin Spice Bread

MAKES 4 SERVINGS

Easy enough to make in the morning before work or school, hearty enough to eat for a quick breakfast or snack, this spiced pumpkin bread is anytime, anywhere comfort food.

TIP

If you do not have self-rising flour, use the following ratio to make your own. For every 1 cup (250 mL) all-purpose flour, whisk in 1½ tsp (7 mL) baking powder and ½ tsp (2 mL) salt.

STORAGE TIP

Store the cooled bread, wrapped in foil or plastic wrap, in the refrigerator for up to 1 week. Alternatively, wrap it in plastic wrap, then foil, completely enclosing bread, and freeze for up to 3 months. Let thaw at room temperature for 4 to 6 hours before serving.

- Preheat air fryer to 360°F (180°C)
- 6-inch (15 cm) round metal cake pan, sprayed with nonstick cooking spray

1 cup	self-rising flour (see tip)	250 mL
½ cup	granulated sugar	125 mL
1¼ tsp	pumpkin pie spice	6 mL
2	large eggs	2
⅔ cup	pumpkin purée (not pie filling)	150 mL

1. In a medium bowl, whisk together flour, sugar and pumpkin pie spice.
2. In a small bowl, whisk eggs and pumpkin purée until blended.
3. Add egg mixture to the flour mixture and stir until just blended.
4. Spread batter evenly in prepared pan.
5. Place pan in air fryer basket. Air-fry for 22 to 26 minutes or until top is golden and a tester inserted in the center of the bread comes out clean. Transfer bread to a wire rack and let cool completely.

Variations

Pumpkin Cranberry Spice Bread: Add ⅓ cup (75 mL) dried cranberries to the batter at the end of step 3.

Chocolate Chip Pumpkin Spice Bread: Add ⅓ cup (75 mL) miniature semisweet chocolate chips to the batter at the end of step 3.

Old-Fashioned Drop Biscuits

Ready-made biscuits are fine in a pinch, but nothing beats homemade. The biscuits rise to airy heights in the air fryer, making them a heavenly option for breakfast, lunch or dinner.

STORAGE TIP

Store the cooled biscuits, wrapped in foil or plastic wrap, in the refrigerator for up to 5 days. Alternatively, wrap them in plastic wrap, then foil, completely enclosing biscuits, and freeze for up to 3 months. Let thaw at room temperature for 2 to 3 hours before serving.

- Preheat air fryer to 390°F (200°C)

¾ cup	all-purpose flour	175 mL
1 tsp	baking powder	5 mL
¼ tsp	salt	1 mL
¼ cup	cold butter, cut into small pieces	60 mL
6 tbsp	milk	90 mL

1. In a medium bowl, whisk together flour, baking powder and salt.
2. Using a pastry blender, your fingertips or two knives, cut in butter until mixture resembles fresh bread crumbs. Add milk and stir until just blended.
3. Drop dough in 4 mounds (each about ¼ cup/ 60 mL) into air fryer basket, spacing them 2 inches (5 cm) apart.
4. Air-fry for 8 to 11 minutes or until tops are golden brown and a tester inserted in the center of a biscuit comes out clean. Transfer biscuits to a wire rack and let cool for 10 minutes. Serve warm or let cool completely.

Variation

Vegan Drop Biscuits: Use cold vegan margarine (stick variety, not tub or spread), vegan shortening or coconut oil in place of the butter. Use plain nondairy milk (such as almond, cashew, hemp or soy) in place of the milk.

Cheese Soufflé Muffins

Part muffin, part soufflé and 100% delicious, these fluffy, homey breads are always welcome — no matter what the season.

TIPS

If you do not have self-rising flour, use the following ratio to make your own. For every 1 cup (250 mL) all-purpose flour, whisk in $1\frac{1}{2}$ tsp (7 mL) baking powder and $\frac{1}{2}$ tsp (2 mL) salt.

For best results, do not use nonfat cottage cheese.

STORAGE TIP

Store the cooled muffins, wrapped in foil or plastic wrap, in the refrigerator for up to 3 days.

• Preheat air fryer to 390°F (200°C)
• 8 standard-size foil or paper muffin cup liners

$\frac{3}{4}$ cup	self-rising flour (see tip)	175 mL
$1\frac{1}{2}$ tsp	granulated sugar	7 mL
$\frac{1}{8}$ tsp	freshly ground black pepper	0.5 mL
$\frac{1}{2}$ cup	cottage cheese	125 mL
2	large eggs	2
1 cup	shredded cheese (such as Cheddar, Swiss, Gouda or pepper Jack)	250 mL

1. Place one muffin cup liner inside another. Repeat to create 4 doubled liners.
2. In a medium bowl, whisk together flour, sugar and pepper.
3. In a small bowl, mash cottage cheese with a fork until mostly smooth. Whisk in eggs until blended.
4. Add the egg mixture to the flour mixture and stir until just blended. Stir in shredded cheese.
5. Divide batter equally among the doubled liners.
6. Place filled liners in air fryer basket, spacing them evenly. Air-fry for 14 to 18 minutes or until tops are golden and a tester inserted in the center of a muffin comes out clean. Transfer muffins to a wire rack and let cool for 5 minutes. Serve warm or let cool completely.

Variation

Pesto Soufflé Muffins: Add $1\frac{1}{2}$ tbsp (22 mL) pesto at the end of step 3. Replace the shredded cheese with $\frac{1}{3}$ cup (75 mL) freshly grated Parmesan cheese.

So-Simple Supper Muffins

Light, flavorful and endlessly variable (add your favorite herbs, spices and other add-ins), these pantry-friendly supper muffins are an ideal option for making homemade bread in minutes.

TIPS

If you do not have self-rising flour, use the following ratio to make your own. For every 1 cup (250 mL) all-purpose flour, whisk in $1\frac{1}{2}$ tsp (7 mL) baking powder and $\frac{1}{2}$ tsp (2 mL) salt.

For best results, do not use reduced-fat or light mayonnaise.

- Preheat air fryer to 390°F (200°C)
- 8 standard-size foil or paper muffin cup liners

1 cup	self-rising flour (see tip)	250 mL
$2\frac{1}{2}$ tbsp	mayonnaise	37 mL
$\frac{1}{2}$ cup	milk	125 mL

1. Place one muffin cup liner inside another. Repeat to create 4 doubled liners.
2. Place flour in a medium bowl. Using a pastry blender, your fingertips or two knives, cut in mayonnaise until crumbly. Add milk and stir until just blended.
3. Divide batter equally among the doubled liners.
4. Place filled liners in air fryer basket, spacing them evenly. Air-fry for 9 to 13 minutes or until golden brown and a tester inserted in the center of a muffin comes out clean. Transfer muffins to a wire rack and let cool for 10 minutes. Serve warm or let cool completely.

Variations

Vegan Pantry Muffins: Use vegan mayonnaise in place of the mayonnaise. Use plain nondairy milk (such as almond, cashew, hemp or soy) in place of the milk.

Herb Pantry Muffins: Add ¾ tsp (3 mL) dried herbs (such as basil, dillweed or Italian seasoning), $1\frac{1}{2}$ tsp (7 mL) minced fresh rosemary, or 3 tbsp (45 mL) chopped fresh parsley, basil, dill or cilantro along with the milk in step 2.

Green Onion and Sesame Muffins: Add ⅓ cup (75 mL) finely chopped green onions at the end of step 2. Sprinkle muffin tops with 2 tsp (10 mL) sesame seeds before air-frying.

Sweet Pantry Muffins: Add ¼ cup (60 mL) granulated or packed brown sugar to the flour before cutting in the mayonnaise. If desired, add ½ tsp (2 mL) vanilla extract and ¼ tsp (1 mL) ground spices (such as cinnamon, nutmeg and/ or allspice) along with the milk in step 2.

Blender Banana Bread Muffins

Meet one of the best ways to use up the browned bananas on your counter. In fact, the browner and mushier they get, the sweeter and easier they are to mash. This no-bowl blender muffin recipe is simplicity itself, but you can gussy it up with blueberries, peanut butter or chocolate chips, as you like.

TIPS

For best results, use bananas that are extremely soft, with lots of brown spots on the peels.

If the dates are not soft and moist, soak them in hot water for 5 to 10 minutes; drain thoroughly before using.

- Preheat air fryer to 360°F (180°C)
- 10 standard-size foil or paper muffin cup liners
- Blender or food processor

2	medium very ripe bananas	2
1 cup	rolled oats (see tip, opposite)	250 mL
⅓ cup	soft pitted dates	75 mL
½ tsp	baking soda	2 mL
¼ tsp	salt	1 mL
1	large egg	1

1. Place one muffin cup liner inside another. Repeat to create 5 doubled liners.

2. In blender, combine bananas, oats, dates, baking soda, salt and egg; process until blended and smooth.

3. Divide batter equally among the doubled liners.

4. Place filled liners in air fryer basket, spacing them evenly. Air-fry for 14 to 18 minutes or until tops are golden and a tester inserted in the center of a muffin comes out clean. Transfer muffins to a wire rack and let cool completely.

TIPS

Use either quick-cooking or large-flake (old-fashioned) rolled oats.

For gluten-free muffins, be sure to use oats that are certified gluten-free.

STORAGE TIP

Store the cooled muffins, wrapped in foil or plastic wrap, in the refrigerator for up to 3 days. Alternatively, wrap them in plastic wrap, then foil, completely enclosing muffins, and freeze for up to 3 months. Let thaw at room temperature for 2 to 3 hours before serving.

Variations

Peanut Butter Banana Muffins: Decrease the dates to $1/4$ cup (60 mL) and add 2 tbsp (30 mL) creamy peanut butter in step 2.

Blueberry Banana Muffins: Dot $1/3$ cup (75 mL) blueberries on top of the batter at the end of step 3.

Chocolate Chip Banana Muffins: Dot 3 tbsp (45 mL) miniature semisweet chocolate chips on top of the batter at the end of step 3.

Flourless Chocolate Muffins

If you think chocolate muffins are indulgent fare for indulgent weekend brunches, think again. These rich-tasting muffins are chock-full of good-for-you ingredients that will power you through weekdays, workouts and so much more.

TIPS

An equal amount of creamy peanut, cashew or sunflower seed butter can be used in place of the almond butter.

If the dates are not soft and moist, soak them in hot water for 5 to 10 minutes; drain thoroughly before using.

STORAGE TIP

Store the cooled muffins, wrapped in foil or plastic wrap, in the refrigerator for up to 3 days. Alternatively, wrap them in plastic wrap, then foil, completely enclosing muffins, and freeze for up to 3 months. Let thaw at room temperature for 2 to 3 hours before serving.

- Preheat air fryer to 360°F (180°C)
- 10 standard-size foil or paper muffin cup liners
- Blender or food processor

¼ cup	unsweetened cocoa powder	60 mL
½ tsp	baking soda	2 mL
¼ tsp	salt	1 mL
2	large eggs	2
⅔ cup	almond butter	150 mL
½ cup	soft pitted dates	125 mL

1. Place one muffin cup liner inside another. Repeat to create 5 doubled liners.

2. In blender, combine cocoa powder, baking soda, salt, eggs, almond butter and dates; process until blended and smooth.

3. Divide batter equally among the doubled liners.

4. Place filled liners in air fryer basket, spacing them evenly. Air-fry for 14 to 18 minutes or until a tester inserted in the center of a muffin comes out clean. Transfer muffins to a wire rack and let cool completely.

Variation

Double Chocolate Muffins: Stir 3 to 4 tbsp (45 to 60 mL) semisweet chocolate chips into the batter at the end of step 2.

Flourless Peanut Butter Muffins

Light, fluffy and very peanut-buttery, these flourless, no-bowl muffins are great for breakfast, snacks and workout replenishers. The combination of oats, peanut butter, egg and honey is literally a recipe for energy on the go.

TIPS

Use either quick-cooking or large-flake (old-fashioned) rolled oats.

For gluten-free muffins, be sure to use oats that are certified gluten-free.

STORAGE TIP

Store the cooled muffins, wrapped in foil or plastic wrap, in the refrigerator for up to 3 days. Alternatively, wrap them in plastic wrap, then foil, completely enclosing muffins, and freeze for up to 3 months. Let thaw at room temperature for 2 to 3 hours before serving.

- Preheat air fryer to 360°F (180°C)
- 8 standard-size foil or paper muffin cup liners
- Blender or food processor

¾ cup	rolled oats (see tips)	175 mL
½ tsp	baking soda	2 mL
¼ tsp	salt	1 mL
1	large egg	1
⅓ cup	creamy peanut butter	75 mL
¼ cup	liquid honey	60 mL
1 tbsp	water	15 mL

1. Place one muffin cup liner inside another. Repeat to create 4 doubled liners.
2. In blender, combine oats, baking soda, salt, egg, peanut butter, honey and water; process until blended and smooth.
3. Divide batter equally among the doubled liners.
4. Place filled liners in air fryer basket, spacing them evenly. Air-fry for 14 to 18 minutes or until tops are golden and a tester inserted in the center of a muffin comes out clean. Transfer muffins to a wire rack and let cool completely.

Variations

Replace the peanut butter with an equal amount of creamy almond, cashew or sunflower seed butter.

Replace the honey with an equal amount of pure maple syrup or agave nectar.

Desserts

Petite Pound Cakes

So easy to prepare, and so delicious to eat, these miniature pound cakes are welcome at any occasion, including celebrations, weeknight suppers and everything in between.

STORAGE TIP

Store the cakes, loosely covered in foil or plastic wrap, at room temperature for up to 1 day or in the refrigerator for up to 5 days.

- Preheat air fryer to 330°F (165°C)
- Electric mixer
- 8 standard-size foil or paper muffin cup liners

½ cup	granulated sugar	125 mL
⅓ cup	unsalted butter	75 mL
1	large egg	1
2 tbsp	milk	30 mL
⅔ cup	all-purpose flour	150 mL

1. Place one muffin cup liner inside another. Repeat to create 4 doubled liners.

2. In a medium bowl, using an electric mixer on medium speed, beat sugar and butter until blended, light and fluffy, stopping once to scrape the bowl. Add egg and milk, mixing on low speed until just blended. Add flour, mixing on low speed until just blended.

3. Divide batter equally among the doubled liners.

4. Place filled liners in air fryer basket, spacing them evenly. Air-fry for 14 to 18 minutes or until tops are golden and a tester inserted in the center of a cake comes out clean. Transfer to a wire rack and let cool completely.

Variations

For added flavor, add ½ tsp (2 mL) vanilla extract, finely grated citrus zest (such as lemon, lime or orange) or ¼ tsp (1 mL) almond extract along with the egg in step 2.

Stir ½ tsp (2 mL) ground spice (such as cinnamon, cardamom, pumpkin pie spice or ginger) into the flour before adding it in step 2.

Chocolate Ricotta Cheesecakes

**MAKES
4 CHEESECAKES**

Easy, fast and only four ingredients, these very chocolate cheesecakes have everything going for them.

Variations

White Chocolate Ricotta Cheesecakes: Use an equal amount of white chocolate chips in place of the semisweet chocolate chips. Use vanilla wafers in place of the chocolate wafers.

You can use 8 oz (250 g) brick-style cream cheese, softened, in place of the ricotta cheese.

Vanilla wafers or crème-filled chocolate sandwich cookies can be used in place of the chocolate wafers.

- Preheat air fryer to 360°F (180°C)
- 8 standard-size foil or paper muffin cup liners

¾ cup	miniature semisweet chocolate chips, divided	175 mL
8 oz	ricotta cheese (1 cup/250 mL)	250 g
1	large egg, lightly beaten	1
4	chocolate wafers	4

1. Place one muffin cup liner inside another. Repeat to create 4 doubled liners.

2. In a medium microwave-safe bowl, microwave ½ cup (125 mL) chocolate chips on High, stopping every 30 seconds to stir, until melted and smooth (about 1 minute total).

3. Add ricotta cheese to chocolate, stirring until blended and smooth. Add egg and stir until just blended. Stir in the remaining chocolate chips.

4. Place 1 chocolate wafer, rounded side up, in each doubled liner. Divide batter equally among the liners.

5. Place filled liners in air fryer basket, spacing them evenly. Air-fry for 16 to 20 minutes or until cheesecakes are puffed and surface appears dry. Transfer to a wire rack and let cool completely. Refrigerate for at least 1 hour, until chilled, before serving.

Cheesecake Wontons

Cheesecake lovers, take note: now you can have your thrill in record time. Miniaturizing cheesecake in wonton wrappers to slash preparation and cooking time is the secret to bite-size bliss.

TIPS

While assembling the wontons, keep the stack of wrappers moist by covering them with a damp towel.

These are best eaten soon after air-frying.

• Preheat air fryer to 390°F (200°C)

1½ tbsp	granulated sugar	22 mL
¼ cup	brick-style cream cheese, softened (2 oz/60 g)	60 mL
¼ tsp	vanilla extract	1 mL
8	3½-inch (9 cm) square wonton wrappers	8
1½ tbsp	butter, melted	22 mL
	Confectioners' (icing) sugar (optional)	

1. In a small bowl or cup, stir together granulated sugar, cream cheese and vanilla until blended and smooth.

2. Place 1 wonton wrapper on work surface. Spoon 1½ tsp (7 mL) filling into the center of wrapper. Using a pastry brush or a fingertip, moisten the edges of the wrapper with water. Fold in half to form a triangle, pressing the edges to seal. Repeat with 7 more wrappers and filling.

3. Brush both sides of wontons with butter as you place them in the air fryer basket, placing them close together but not touching.

4. Air-fry for 5 to 7 minutes or until golden brown. Transfer to a plate or wire rack and, if desired, sprinkle with confectioners' sugar.

Apple Pie Taquitos

MAKES 2 TAQUITOS

Thanks to their ease of preparation and minimalist ingredient list, these not-too-sweet taquitos — think: fried, miniature apple pie roll-ups — are not just "any day" treats, but also "any hour" ones.

TIPS

Store the remaining apple pie filling in an airtight container in the refrigerator for up to 1 week.

Air fryers become very hot, especially when heated to maximum temperature. Use oven pads or mitts when touching the appliance and when opening and closing the basket.

- Preheat air fryer to 390°F (200°C)

2 tsp	granulated sugar	10 mL
½ tsp	ground cinnamon	2 mL
2	6-inch (15 cm) flour tortillas	2
¼ cup	canned apple pie filling	60 mL
	Nonstick cooking spray	

1. In a small cup, combine sugar and cinnamon.
2. Place tortillas on work surface. Spoon half the pie filling down the center of each tortilla. Roll up each tortilla, enclosing filling.
3. Place taquitos, seam side down, in air fryer basket, spacing them evenly. Spray with cooking spray and sprinkle evenly with cinnamon sugar.
4. Air-fry for 4 minutes. Open basket and, using tongs, carefully turn taquitos over. Air-fry for 3 to 4 minutes or until crispy and golden brown. Transfer to plates and let cool for 5 minutes before serving.

Variation

An equal amount of chunky applesauce (sweetened or unsweetened) can be used in place of the pie filling.

Fruit Pie Poppers

MAKES 12 POPPERS

Fruit pie is always in style, and, with this pint-sized poppers recipe, it is always a breeze to make, too.

TIP

You can use homemade or thawed frozen pie pastry dough in place of the packaged crust. Use enough dough for a 9-inch (23 cm) single-crust pie, rolled out to a 10-inch (25 cm) circle.

- Preheat air fryer to 390°F (200°C)
- 24 miniature foil or paper muffin cup liners

1	refrigerated rolled pie crust (from a 15-oz/425 g package)	1
¼ cup	fruit jam or preserves (such as cherry, apricot or peach)	60 mL
⅓ cup	confectioners' (icing) sugar	75 mL
1½ tsp	milk	7 mL

1. Place one muffin cup liner inside another. Repeat to create 12 doubled liners.

2. On work surface, unroll pie crust. Cut into 12 square pieces (some pieces will be slightly irregular). Spoon 1 tsp (5 mL) jam into center of each crust piece. Lift edges of crust to enclose filling, pinching edges firmly to seal and create a little bundle. Place each popper in a doubled liner.

3. Place filled liners in air fryer basket, spacing them evenly. Air-fry for 11 to 16 minutes or until crust is golden brown. Transfer to a wire rack to cool. Remove poppers from liners.

4. In a small cup, whisk together confectioners' sugar and milk until smooth. Drizzle icing over poppers. Serve warm or at room temperature.

Variations

Chocolate Pie Poppers: Use an equal amount of chocolate chips (such as semisweet, milk or white) in place of the jam.

An equal amount of lemon curd or canned pie filling can be used in place of the jam.

For added flavor, add a drop of vanilla, almond or lemon extract to the icing.

Banoffee Hand Pies

You can thank the British for conjuring banoffee pie, a decadent combination of bananas and toffee. Here, I've reimagined the indulgence in handheld form, to irresistible effect.

TIP

The pies are best eaten soon after they are made.

• Preheat air fryer to 360°F (180°C)

2 tbsp	packed brown sugar	30 mL
2 tbsp	butter, melted	30 mL
1	large firm-ripe banana, chopped	1
1	chocolate-covered English toffee candy bar (such as Skor; 1.4 oz/40 g), chopped	1
1	small can (6 oz/175 g) refrigerated large dinner biscuits	1
	Nonstick cooking spray	

1. In a small bowl, stir together brown sugar and butter. Gently stir in banana and chopped candy bar.

2. Remove dough from packaging and separate into biscuits. Using your fingertips or a rolling pin, press or roll each biscuit into a 4-inch (10 cm) circle.

3. Place 2 tbsp (30 mL) banana mixture slightly off-center on each dough circle. Fold biscuits over filling and press edges together with a fork to seal. Prick the top of each hand pie three times with a fork. Spray pies with cooking spray.

4. Place pies in air fryer basket, spacing them 2 inches (5 cm) apart. Air-fry for 10 to 14 minutes or until puffed and golden brown. Transfer to a wire rack and let cool for at least 10 minutes before serving. Serve warm or at room temperature.

No-Crust Pumpkin Pies

I tweaked my favorite pumpkin pie recipe to make it quick, convenient and easy enough to make any time. Mission accomplished!

TIPS

To get the cleanest break, crack eggs against the counter, not on the edge of the bowl.

Room temperature eggs will whisk more easily than cold eggs.

- Preheat air fryer to 330°F (165°C)
- Two ¾-cup (175 mL) custard cups or ramekins, sprayed with nonstick cooking spray

1	large egg	1
½ cup	sweetened condensed milk	125 mL
⅓ cup	pumpkin purée (not pie filling)	75 mL
⅓ cup	milk	75 mL
½ tsp	pumpkin pie spice	2 mL
⅛ tsp	salt	0.5 mL

1. In a medium bowl, whisk together egg and condensed milk until well blended. Whisk in pumpkin purée, milk, pumpkin pie spice and salt until blended.

2. Place prepared custard cups in air fryer basket, spacing them evenly. Carefully pour pumpkin mixture into cups, dividing evenly. Close air fryer basket, being careful not to spill.

3. Air-fry for 30 to 35 minutes or until custards are set and jiggle only slightly when nudged. Transfer to a wire rack and let cool completely. Refrigerate for at least 4 hours, until chilled, before serving.

Variation

An equal amount of ground cinnamon can be used in place of the pumpkin pie spice.

Pecan Pie Roll-Ups

The familiar flavors of pecans, brown sugar and pie crust — these roll-ups taste like bite-sized pecan pies — will make any day Thanksgiving.

TIPS

You can use homemade or thawed frozen pie pastry dough in place of the packaged crust. Use enough dough for a 9-inch (23 cm) single-crust pie, rolled out to a 10-inch (25 cm) circle.

For increased flavor, toast the pecans before adding them to the recipe. Place pecan halves directly in air fryer basket and air-fry at 360°F (180°C) for 4 to 6 minutes or until golden brown and fragrant. Let cool before chopping.

- Preheat air fryer to 330°F (165°C)
- 6-inch (15 cm) round metal cake pan, sprayed with nonstick cooking spray

5 tbsp	packed brown sugar, divided	75 mL
3 oz	brick-style cream cheese, softened	90 g
1	large egg	1
1 tbsp	water	15 mL
1	refrigerated rolled pie crust (from a 15-oz/425 g package)	1
½ cup	pecan halves, finely chopped	125 mL

1. In a small bowl, stir together 3 tbsp (45 mL) brown sugar and cream cheese until blended and smooth.

2. In another small bowl, whisk together egg and water.

3. On work surface, unroll pie crust. Spread with cream cheese mixture to within ¼ inch (0.5 cm) of edge. Sprinkle with pecans.

4. Cut crust into 16 equal wedges. Starting at a wide end, roll up each wedge toward the point.

5. Place 5 to 6 roll-ups in prepared pan, spacing them evenly (refrigerate the remaining roll-ups). Lightly brush with egg wash and sprinkle with some of the remaining brown sugar.

6. Place pan in air fryer basket. Air-fry for 24 to 28 minutes or until golden brown. Transfer to a wire rack and let cool completely.

7. Repeat steps 5 and 6 with the remaining roll-ups, egg wash and brown sugar. Discard any excess egg wash.

Scottish Shortbread

Nothing beats freshly baked cookies, especially tender, buttery shortbread. And thanks to your air fryer, you get the pleasure of filling your home with their warm, sweet scent without turning on the oven.

STORAGE TIP

Store the shortbread in a tin at room temperature for up to 1 week.

- Preheat air fryer to 330°F (165°C)
- 6-inch (15 cm) round metal cake pan, sprayed with nonstick cooking spray

7 tbsp	granulated sugar, divided	105 mL
6 tbsp	butter, softened	90 mL
½ tsp	vanilla extract	2 mL
1 cup	all-purpose flour	250 mL

1. Sprinkle 1½ tsp (7 mL) sugar into prepared pan, tilting pan to coat bottom and sides.

2. In a medium bowl, vigorously stir together 6 tbsp (90 mL) sugar, butter and vanilla until blended, light and fluffy. Add flour, stirring until just blended.

3. Evenly press dough into prepared pan. Sprinkle with the remaining sugar.

4. Place pan in air fryer basket. Air-fry for 12 to 16 minutes or until golden brown. Transfer to a wire rack and let cool completely.

5. Invert shortbread onto a cutting board and cut into 8 wedges.

Variations

Add ¼ cup (60 mL) miniature semisweet chocolate chips or chopped dried fruit (such as apricots, cherries or cranberries) along with the flour in step 2.

Stir ½ tsp (2 mL) ground spice (such as cinnamon, cardamom, pumpkin pie spice or ginger) into the flour before adding it in step 2.

Peanut Butter Cookies

Peanut butter cookies without flour? Yes! The cookies have crispy edges, tender centers and a deeply peanut butter flavor. And since they have only three ingredients, you will almost always have the fixings on hand.

TIPS

Either regular or natural peanut butter can be used with equal success.

Either smooth or crunchy peanut butter can be used.

STORAGE TIP

Store the cookies in a tin at room temperature for up to 1 week.

- Preheat air fryer to 330°F (165°C)
- 6-inch (15 cm) round metal cake pan, sprayed with nonstick cooking spray

1 cup	granulated sugar	250 mL
1	large egg	1
1 cup	peanut butter, softened	250 mL

1. In a medium bowl, stir together sugar, egg and peanut butter until well blended and smooth.

2. Spoon half the dough into prepared pan, pressing it out with your fingertips or a spoon until evenly distributed.

3. Place pan in air fryer basket. Air-fry for 11 to 14 minutes or until golden brown and set at the edges (center may look slightly underdone). Transfer to a wire rack and let cool for 15 minutes. Remove cookie to a cutting board and cut into 8 equal wedges.

4. Respray pan and repeat steps 2 and 3 with the remaining dough.

Variations

Chocolate Chip Peanut Butter Cookies: Add $1/3$ cup (75 mL) miniature semisweet chocolate chips at the end of step 1.

An equal amount of almond, cashew or sunflower seed butter can be used in place of the peanut butter.

Cookie Dough Bombs

Part cookie dough, part donut, and 100% irresistible, these treats are best served any time you like!

Variation

If desired, microwave 3 to 4 tbsp (45 to 60 mL) semisweet chocolate chips in a microwave-safe bowl on High, stopping every 30 seconds to stir, until melted and smooth (about 1 minute total). Drizzle over cooled bombs.

- 6-inch (15 cm) round metal cake pan

1/3 cup	packed brown sugar	75 mL
1/4 cup	butter, softened	60 mL
1/2 cup	all-purpose flour	125 mL
1/4 cup	semisweet chocolate chips	60 mL
1	small can (6 oz/175 g) refrigerated large dinner biscuits	1
	Nonstick cooking spray	

1. In a medium bowl, stir together brown sugar and butter until well blended. Stir in flour and chocolate chips until completely blended. Shape dough into 10 balls of equal size. Place balls in cake pan, spacing them evenly. Place pan in freezer for at least 1 hour or until firm.

2. Preheat air fryer to 360°F (180°C).

3. Remove dough from packaging and separate into biscuits. Cut each biscuit in half horizontally. Using your fingertips or a rolling pin, press or roll each biscuit half into a 3-inch (7.5 cm) circle.

4. Remove frozen balls from cake pan; wipe pan clean and spray with cooking spray.

5. Place one cookie dough ball in the center of each biscuit half. Lift edges of biscuit to enclose cookie dough, pinching edges firmly to seal and create a little bundle. Place bundles, seam side down, in prepared pan, spacing them evenly. Spray with cooking spray.

6. Place pan in air fryer basket. Air-fry for 13 to 17 minutes or until puffed and golden brown. Transfer pan to a wire rack and let cool for at least 10 minutes. Serve warm or at room temperature.

Double Chocolate Brownie Bites

Chocolate brownies are iconic treats, and this double-chocolate version has just the right balance of intense chocolate flavor and sweetness.

TIP

An equal amount of regular-size chocolate chips can be used in place of the miniature chocolate chips. Coarsely chop the reserved 3 tbsp (45 mL) chocolate chips before adding them to the batter in step 3.

- Preheat air fryer to 360°F (180°C)
- 24 miniature foil or paper muffin cup liners
- 6-inch (15 cm) round metal cake pan, sprayed with nonstick cooking spray

1 cup	miniature semisweet chocolate chips, divided	250 mL
¼ cup	butter, cut into small pieces	60 mL
⅓ cup	granulated sugar	75 mL
1	large egg, lightly beaten	1
½ cup	all-purpose flour	125 mL

1. Place one muffin cup liner inside another. Repeat to create 12 doubled liners.

2. Reserve 3 tbsp (45 mL) chocolate chips. In a medium microwave-safe bowl, combine the remaining chocolate chips and butter. Microwave on High, stopping every 30 seconds to stir, until melted and smooth (about 1 minute total).

3. Stir sugar into chocolate mixture until just blended. Add egg, stirring until just blended. Stir in flour until just blended. Stir in the reserved chocolate chips.

4. Divide batter equally among the doubled liners.

5. Place half the filled liners in air fryer basket, spacing them evenly. Air-fry for 8 to 11 minutes or until tops are just set. Transfer to a wire rack and let cool for at least 30 minutes. Repeat with the remaining filled liners.

Cinnamon Raisin Bread Pudding

MAKES 2 SERVINGS

Bread pudding is pure comfort food, and this recipe is no exception. Feel free to eat it for breakfast as well as dessert — it is essentially the same as French toast.

TIP

An equal amount of milk can be used in place of the cream.

- 6-inch (15 cm) round metal cake pan, sprayed with nonstick cooking spray

3	slices cinnamon raisin bread, torn into small pieces	3
1	large egg	1
2½ tbsp	packed brown sugar	37 mL
⅛ tsp	salt	0.5 mL
½ cup	light (5%) cream	125 mL
1 tsp	vanilla extract	5 mL

1. Place bread pieces in prepared cake pan.

2. In a small bowl, whisk egg until blended. Whisk in brown sugar, salt, cream and vanilla until blended. Pour evenly over bread in pan. Place a piece of parchment or waxed paper over pan and press down to help bread absorb liquid. Let stand for 15 minutes.

3. Meanwhile, preheat air fryer to 330°F (165°C).

4. Remove parchment and place pan in air fryer basket. Air-fry for 13 to 16 minutes or until bubbling and golden brown. Transfer to a wire rack and let cool for at least 10 minutes. Serve warm or let cool completely.

Variations

Vanilla Bread Pudding: Replace the cinnamon raisin bread with an equal amount of sturdy white sandwich bread slices. Replace the brown sugar with an equal amount of granulated sugar.

Chocolate Chip Bread Pudding: Replace the cinnamon raisin bread with an equal amount of sturdy white sandwich bread slices. Add 3 tbsp (45 mL) miniature semisweet chocolate chips to the bread pieces in step 1.

Dulce de Leche Custards

Dulce de leche custards are the Central and South American answer to French pots de crème. It's a great make-ahead dessert because the custards need to chill for several hours before serving.

TIPS

Look for cans or jars of dulce de leche in the international or Latin foods section of the supermarket.

Note that some brands of caramel ice cream topping are labeled "dulce de leche." These are not the same as canned or jarred dulce de leche, which is a thick, rich milk product.

- Preheat air fryer to 330°F (160°C)
- Two ¾-cup (175 mL) custard cups or ramekins, sprayed with nonstick cooking spray

1	large egg	1
½ cup	dulce de leche	125 mL
⅔ cup	milk	150 mL
Pinch	salt	pinch
	Additional dulce de leche	

1. In a medium bowl, whisk together egg and dulce de leche until well blended. Whisk in milk and salt until blended.

2. Place prepared custard cups in air fryer basket, spacing them evenly. Carefully pour egg mixture into cups, dividing evenly. Close air fryer basket, being careful not to spill.

3. Air-fry for 30 to 35 minutes or until custards are set and jiggle only slightly when nudged. Transfer to a wire rack and let cool completely. Refrigerate for at least 4 hours, until chilled, before serving drizzled with additional dulce de leche.

Variation

Vanilla Custard: Replace the dulce de leche with an equal amount of sweetened condensed milk. Add ½ tsp (2 mL) vanilla extract along with the milk in step 1.

Graham Cracker Toffee

In a word, this toffee is fabulous. It boasts an easy assembly, inexpensive ingredients and the most decadent, buttery toffee flavor that will please everyone, every time.

TIP

Hot air and steam will release from the air fryer throughout the cooking cycle. If your face is in close proximity to the appliance during the cooking cycle or when you are opening the basket, you risk being scalded by the release of accumulated steam.

- Preheat air fryer to 330°F (165°C)
- 6-inch (15 cm) round metal cake pan, sprayed with nonstick cooking spray

4	graham cracker squares (or 2 sheets, halved)	4
2 tbsp	packed brown sugar	30 mL
2 tbsp	butter	30 mL

1. Arrange graham crackers, touching side by side, in prepared pan, breaking as needed to fit.
2. In a small saucepan, combine brown sugar and butter. Bring to a boil over medium-high heat, stirring constantly to dissolve sugar. Boil, stirring constantly, for 2 minutes. Immediately pour over graham crackers, spreading with a spoon or spatula to cover.
3. Place pan in air fryer basket. Air-fry for 6 to 9 minutes or until bubbling and golden brown. Transfer to a wire rack and let cool completely. Break toffee into pieces.

Variations

Saltine Toffee: Use 8 to 10 saltine crackers in place of the graham crackers.

Chocolate Chip Toffee: Sprinkle toffee with 1 to 2 tbsp (15 to 30 mL) miniature semisweet chocolate chips immediately after air-frying.

Pecan Toffee: Sprinkle with 2 tbsp (30 mL) chopped pecans at the end of step 2.

Coconut Toffee: Sprinkle with 2 tbsp (30 mL) sweetened or unsweetened flaked coconut at the end of step 2.

S'mores Dip

No camping trip required: milk chocolate chips, marshmallows and the heat of your air fryer, plus graham crackers for dipping, equal campfire s'mores, year-round.

TIP

An equal amount of semisweet or bittersweet (dark) chocolate chips can be used in place of the milk chocolate chips. (Avoid using white chocolate chips, as they can scorch.)

- Preheat air fryer to 330°F (165°C)
- 6-inch (15 cm) round metal cake pan, sprayed with nonstick cooking spray

1 cup	milk chocolate chips	250 mL
1½ cups	miniature marshmallows	375 mL
	Graham crackers	

1. Spread chocolate chips on bottom of prepared pan. Arrange marshmallows evenly over chocolate chips. Place pan in air fryer basket.

2. Air-fry for 5 to 8 minutes or until chocolate is melted and marshmallows are golden brown. Serve warm with graham crackers for dipping.

Variations

Peanut Butter S'mores Dip: Dollop 9 tsp (45 mL) peanut butter (smooth or chunky) by the teaspoonful (5 mL) over the chocolate chips before topping with marshmallows.

Raspberry S'mores Dip: Use semisweet chocolate chips in place of the milk chocolate chips. Dollop 6 tsp (30 mL) raspberry jam or preserves by the teaspoonful (5 mL) over the chocolate chips before topping with marshmallows.

INDEX

Library and Archives Canada Cataloguing in Publication

Saulsbury, Camilla V., author
    5-ingredient air fryer recipes : 200 delicious & easy meal ideas including gluten-free & vegan /
Camilla V. Saulsbury.

Includes index.
ISBN 978-0-7788-0590-8 (softcover)

    1. Hot air frying. 2. Quick and easy cooking. 3. Cookbooks. I. Title. II. Title: Five-ingredient air fryer recipes
air fryer recipes.

TX689.S288 2018   641.7   C2017-906023-6

5-INGREDIENT

AIR FRYER

RECIPES